Best of Enemies

Britain and Germany:
100 Years of Truth and Lies

Richard Milton

ICON BOOKS

Published in the UK in 2007 by
Icon Books Ltd, The Old Dairy,
Brook Road, Thriplow,
Cambridge SG8 7RG
email: info@iconbooks.co.uk
www.iconbooks.co.uk

Sold in the UK, Europe, South Africa and Asia
by Faber & Faber Ltd, 3 Queen Square,
London WC1N 3AU
or their agents

Distributed in the UK, Europe, South Africa and Asia
by TBS Ltd, TBS Distribution Centre, Colchester Road,
Frating Green, Colchester CO7 7DW

This edition published in Australia in 2007
by Allen & Unwin Pty Ltd,
PO Box 8500, 83 Alexander Street,
Crows Nest, NSW 2065

Distributed in Canada by
Penguin Books Canada,
90 Eglinton Avenue East, Suite 700,
Toronto, Ontario M4P 2YE

ISBN 978-1840468-28-1

Typesetting in 11.5pt Plantin by Marie Doherty

Printed and bound in the UK by
J.H. Haynes & Co. Ltd.

*The man of knowledge must be able not only
to love his enemies but also to hate his friends.*

Friedrich Nietzsche

Richard Milton is a writer, journalist and broadcaster who also works as a PR consultant. His other books include *The Facts of Life* (1992), *Forbidden Science* (1994) and *Bad Company: Behind the Corporate Mask* (2001).

Contents

Part One: A War to End Wars, 1914–18   1
1   Cutting the Cord   3
2   A Marriage of Minds, 1840–1914   11
3   A War of Words   23
4   Atrocious Behaviour   47
5   The Sorcerer's Apprentice   71
6   Engineering of Consent   81

Part Two: The Roots of Unreason, 1919–39   91
7   The Master Race   93
8   Man and Superman   113
9   More English than the English   135
10   Influential Friends   147
11   Perfidious Albion   161
12   The Playing Fields of Eton   171
13   Mass Observations   195

Part Three: Crimes Against Humanity, 1939–45   207
14   Finest Hour   209
15   The British Way   225
16   Black Games   239
17   The Pied Piper   247
18   Business as Usual   259
19   Class Distinction   269
20   Judgement at Nuremberg   277
21   Natural Selection   293
22   Lucky Winners   303
23   This Happy Breed   313

A Postmodern Postscript   323
References   329
Bibliography   339
Special Acknowledgements   349
Index   351

Part One

A War to End Wars, 1914–18

1

Cutting the Cord

In August 1914, as the Great Powers of Europe began marching to disaster, Britain's first act of war was not to send men and guns into the field or to order the Grand Fleet into action. Rather, it was to cut the transatlantic telegraph cables between Germany and the United States, to prevent German war propaganda from reaching American newspapers.

Within hours of the declaration of war on 4 August, the steam cable vessel *Telconia,* requisitioned for government service, anchored in the North Sea under cover of darkness several miles off the German town of Emden and began to trawl for cables on the sea-bed. By dawn, her engineers had located and cut all five German cables: to France, Spain, Tenerife and two to New York.[1]

This severing of the transatlantic links signalled the beginning of a war of words that was soon to become as vicious as the slaughter of the Western Front. And, like the death and destruction of the trenches, the deep wounds caused by the propaganda war would last far beyond the armistice, creating a climate of suspicion and mistrust of

Germany that poisoned Anglo-German relations for a generation, leaving traces that still persist down to the present.

As well as signalling the start of a new kind of war, the severing of the cable link was also symbolic of the cutting of ties that had bound Britain and Germany closer than any other two nations on earth for the previous hundred years.

From our perspective today, with the propaganda from two global wars against Germany still ringing in our ears, it is difficult to appreciate the extent of the historical closeness between the two countries before 1914. It is just as difficult to appreciate the extent to which Germany willingly Anglicised its culture and habits during the 19th century, and – equally surprising – the extent to which Britain itself took on German ideas, customs and beliefs.[2]

This Anglo-German intimacy was unique in Britain's international relationships in the Victorian age. In recent times it has become customary for British politicians, following Sir Winston Churchill, to speak of having a 'special relationship' with the United States; a relationship founded on the perception that we in Britain share a common heritage, cultural background and intimate historical links with America, based on kinship and blood. But in the 19th century, it was normal for British people and German people to think of having such a 'special relationship' with each other – a relationship also based on common heritage, kinship and blood.

The conflagration of the First War obliterated both this intimate friendliness and the perception of common heritage that had existed for generations. Yet, strangely, for all its ferocity and its barbarity, the war did not bring about an irrevocable break between Britain and Germany. Instead, in the decades between the First and Second wars, Anglo-German relations underwent a curious transformation into something almost resembling a covert mutual admiration society.

This strange and corrupt form of the earlier intimacy had two main driving forces, equally perverse and historically aberrant. The first was the parallel development in Britain and Germany of closely similar thinking on social beliefs and ideas – issues such as racial superiority and eugenics, ethnic origins, national identity, and imperial aspirations.[3] The second driver was an unhealthy and self-deluding admiration among many Germans for all things English – an admiration that was especially marked in some nouveau riche leaders of German society and some members of the higher echelons of the Nazi Party, including Hess, Himmler, Goering and even Hitler himself.[4] How this national infatuation with England came about, and the kind of grotesque and disastrous consequence it gave rise to, is a key part of the story this book has to tell. Those consequences ultimately include otherwise incomprehensible actions by Adolf Hitler and the Nazi government of Germany.

The close similarity of thinking on racial and other ethnic issues in Britain and Germany arose primarily from common sources such as Charles Darwin's theory of evolution, with its emphasis on survival of the fittest, and Francis Galton's theories on eugenics and the 'purification' of the race through eugenic legislation and medical practices. These English 'scientific' ideas were taken up widely in all developed countries, but most enthusiastically in Germany. Within decades of the publication of Darwin's *On the Origin of Species*, for example, German professors of biology, such as Ernst Haeckel, were lecturing Darwin himself on the finer points of Darwinism.[5]

By the turn of the century, German ethnologists had added a whole new dimension to Darwinism – the supremacy of the Aryan race, whose chief present-day representatives they saw as themselves, the Teutons, and their English cousins. The eugenics movement, so strongly associated with Nazism, actually had an even more enthusiastic following in Britain among writers, intellectuals, leading members of the scientific and medical professions and even some Members of Parliament.[6] It is astonishing to learn, for example, that no less a figure than George Bernard Shaw expressed the view that 'Extermination must be put on a scientific basis if it is ever to be carried out humanely and apologetically as well as thoroughly ... if we desire a certain type of civilisation and culture, we must exterminate the sort of people who do not fit into it.' Shaw thought extermination a desirable thing because 'the majority of men at present in Europe have no business to be alive'. D.H. Lawrence agreed that 'The mass of mankind, is soulless. ... Most people are dead, and scurrying and talking in the sleep of death.' Indeed, Lawrence went even further than Shaw when he called for 'three cheers for the inventors of poison gas'.[7] These views were shared by other leading intellectuals, in Britain and in the United States, Sweden, Australia and other countries, where they inspired legislation to sterilise compulsorily people considered 'unfit'.[8]

The growing convergence of ideas and ideals on nationalism and race in Britain and Germany was brought to an abrupt end by the storm of metal and blood that tore through Europe from 1914 to 1918. No less destructive was the torrent of lies and smears that was unleashed by both sides in clandestine PR campaigns whose full extent is only today being realised. In the years immediately before 1914, for example, the secret German Information Bureau spent billions of pounds at today's prices laying the foundations of a global propaganda network that even included secretly purchasing cinemas in neutral countries where German newsreels could be shown.[9]

The equivalent secret British organisation, hastily set up under Lloyd George in 1914, clandestinely enlisted the active support of virtually every great British writer then alive, including Conan Doyle, Arnold Bennett, John Buchan, John Masefield, G.K. Chesterton, Thomas Hardy, Rudyard Kipling, H.G. Wells and many others, whose pens were dipped in the poison of lies and half-truths and then directed against Germany, with some extraordinary results.[10] The range and extent of these covertly-inspired propaganda works is truly astounding, and includes a number of famous books and stories whose content has until now puzzled literary critics and reviewers.[11]

British intelligence did not stop at mobilising the literary big guns for its propaganda campaigns, but covertly scraped the barrel for German atrocity stories which it recycled for consumption by the international community, dressed up in the guise of an independent judicial review published under the name of Britain's respected former ambassador to Washington, James Bryce.[12]

As well as the legacy of bitterness and illusion left by this war of words, the propaganda war also had a completely unforeseen outcome for the post-war era. In the United States, one of the most gifted exponents of this new brand of warfare was Sigmund Freud's nephew, Edward Bernays, who went on to found Madison Avenue and the PR industry. The techniques used by Bernays against Germany in 1914–18 he later developed to sell consumer goods to the American and British public in a process he called *The Engineering of Consent*. He also used the same techniques to get Calvin Coolidge elected President of the United States in 1924. But Bernays' 'engineering' techniques were to be taken up and used to even more devastating effect by Joseph Goebbels to sell Adolf Hitler to the German people.[13]

And there were even more extraordinary outcomes of the propaganda war. For, despite the vilest of lies and deceptions, the First World War did not end the century-long German infatuation with the English. Instead, the twists and turns of the propaganda war transformed German infatuation into a new and even more dangerously delusive post-war phase in the 1930s, in which Adolf Hitler, and many of his Nazi colleagues, saw the English ruling class as fellow members of the master race – and, in some respects, almost wished to become English aristocrats themselves.[14] The greatest irony of this unhealthy passion was that the image of the Englishman which the Nazis bought into so completely – as the cool, public-school hero and representative of the Master Race, presiding over the greatest empire the world had seen – was every bit as phoney and manufactured by British propaganda as the wartime lies had been; yet it continued to be swallowed whole because of the effectiveness of Britain's propaganda machine, an infernal engine created in war, but impossible to switch off in peace.[15]

The fatal attraction of the Nazi leaders for all things English continued, past the declaration of war in September 1939, and lasted until 1940 when Hitler was finally compelled to accept that a war of conquest against the British Empire was unavoidable. It was to surface again in the Nuremberg trials of 1945, and its echoes can still be detected even today.[16]

How this transformation of Anglo-German relations came about, from the intimacy and blood ties of family relationships to a murderous mutual destruction a century later, is a surprising tale of self-delusion and deception on both sides; a tale of how truth and lies came to be used as increasingly powerful weapons of war in their own right.

But above all, it is a tale of the power of ideas to corrupt not just individuals, but entire nations, in the name of scientific and social progress.

2

A Marriage of Minds,
1840–1914

When British and German soldiers came face to face on the Western Front in September 1914, it was a confrontation that previously had been conceivable only in fantasy fiction. For a century, the two nations had taken for granted an intimacy in their relationships that was usually enjoyed only by members of the same family. It was an intimacy that started at the top and was rooted in blood.

From the day in February 1840 that England's young Queen married Albert, Duke of Saxony, the upper classes of British and German society became intimately linked in ties of friendship that continued uninterrupted, almost like matrimonial bonds, until 1914.

Aside from her marriage, Victoria already had strong family links to Germany. As a descendant of Hanoverian kings and daughter of a Princess of Saxony, she had almost pure German blood running in her veins. But her union with Albert made doubly sure that, henceforward, Great Britain was closer to Germany than any other nation in the world.

A princely husband and Christmas trees were not the only German imports that became familiar to Victorians. From 1840 onwards, a torrent of German inventions and manufactured goods flooded into the country as Britain gradually became Germany's most receptive overseas market, and German names became so familiar here that today many are regarded as being British in origin.[1]

In the 1850s, William Siemens opened the British end of the Siemens electrical engineering company, which manufactured and laid the thousands of miles of under-sea telegraph and telephone cable that made Britain the hub of a global empire and London the world financial centre.[2] Julius Reuter set up an office in the Stock Exchange, took British nationality, and founded the organisation that added news and financial information to this cable network.[3] Much of this growth was financed by the House of Rothschild, the biggest bank in the world, and equally prominent in Frankfurt and in London.[4]

Famous German brands from the period that became well known here include Nivea face cream, Osram light bulbs and Agfa. Aspirin is a German brand name, registered by Bayer in 1897. Persil washing powder, once found in every British kitchen, is not only German but dates from as far back as 1876. And when Karl Benz and Otto Daimler invented the motor car, Daimler named the vehicle after his daughter, Mercedes. BASF is the Baden Aniline and Soda Factory. AEG is the Allgemeine Elektricitäts-Gesellschaft, founded in 1884 by Emil Rathenau, whose son Walther would organise the reconstruction of the German economy so effectively in 1921.

Rowenta, founded in 1884, was renamed after its founder, Robert Weintraub, in 1909. Emil Berliner invented the 'gramophone' and 'microphone' in 1887, and in 1885

Rudolf Diesel invented the engine that bears his name and which powered the British Grand Fleet. Fluorescent lamps, the Geiger counter, radio waves and X-rays were also German discoveries.

Middle-class British homes became filled with china from Meissen and Dresden and with Leica and Voigtlander cameras, Zeiss binoculars, and Adler and Olympia typewriters, while a hundred thousand British children went to bed with teddy bears by Steiff, having put their German-made train sets or china dolls away for the night. From 1851 onwards, some of those British children would have spent the day attending a new kind of elementary school recently imported from Germany. Friedrich Froebel introduced the Kindergarten system in Germany in 1837 and, a little more than a decade later, the first Kindergarten was opened in London.

Culturally, too, Germany was riding high. German composers had been considered 'ours' since Handel's day, but in the 19th century Germans were musically unrivalled – Beethoven, Brahms, Mendelssohn, Schubert, Schuman, Haydn, Wagner, Offenbach – all found appreciative audiences in Britain, especially for the Scottish fantasies of Mendelssohn and Haydn, written following visits to the Highlands by the composers in search of musical inspiration.

This cross-cultural tide flowed both ways. For every British housewife washing with Persil, dabbing Nivea on her cheeks or taking aspirin after a hard day, there were two Hausfraus somewhere in Germany putting money into the pockets of British manufacturers by buying British-made wares. The early part of the period, from 1840 to around 1860, was the high-water mark of Britain's position as 'workshop of the world', supplying roughly half of all the manufactured imports of Germany (and of France and the United States). German breakfast tables boasted Oxford Marmalade, English Mustard and Golden Syrup, and were laid with Sheffield cutlery and Wedgwood china, while German passengers travelled on British-built trains and steamships.

One industry in which Germany was later to establish a dominant position was that of optics and optical instruments such as cameras, but German expertise in both photography and optical technology was transplanted from Britain, where optics had been developed during the 1800s. In the first decade of the 19th century, for example, an Austrian named Johan Voigtlander (whose family name later became well known in the manufacture of cameras) came to London to study lens-making. While there, Voigtlander was struck by the English fashion among upper-class gentlemen for wearing monocles. He returned home to Vienna and in 1814 began to make and sell monocles as the height of English fashion.[5] By 1850 Austrian and Prussian officers of noble birth sported a monocle, whether their eyesight was defective or not, and by 1914 it had become an essential fashion accessory for German officers of every rank. It seems odd to reflect that the classic image of the monocled Prussian officer is, at root, a fashionable imitation borrowed from the English gentleman.

It is said that the first time Britain's manufacturers realised that they had a fight on their hands for world markets was when they saw the huge number and variety of German manufactured goods at the Great Exhibition in Hyde Park in 1851. It must have been quite a shock for them. Prince Albert and the government had organised the Exhibition as a showcase for British industrial products. It was anticipated that France, because of its dominant international position, would also be prominent at the show. But what few foresaw was that one of the most conspicuous displays in the 'Foreign Nave' at Hyde Park would be the Zollverein (the customs union of German states), which sent more than 1,500 exhibitors and occupied a space almost equal to that of France. As well as fine arts including bronzes, marbles and paintings, German exhibits included manufactures from porcelain to musical instruments, small arms, cameras and clothes.[6]

It wasn't only in the sphere of industry that the British were in for a shock to their prestige in 1851. The first International Chess Tournament was organised in London that year, to coincide with the Great Exhibition, by England's world chess champion, Howard Staunton (who gave his name to the design of the modern chess set). Staunton no doubt hoped to crown this first tournament with an English win, but the title actually went to the German competitor, Adolph Anderssen. In both the mundane world of crockery and knitwear and the loftier intellectual world of chess, the seeds of rivalry were sown.[7]

As well as having a vast appetite for consumer goods, Germany was culturally insatiable too. The German middle classes read Shaw and Wells, thrilled to the cases of Sherlock Holmes, listened to Elgar and Delius, and even hummed along to *Der Mikado* (including Kaiser Wilhelm II, who was an enthusiastic Gilbert and Sullivan fan).

English fashions were quickly emulated in Germany – some with unexpected results. The fashion for outfitting children in sailor suits originated in the 1840s when Victoria dressed her eldest son, Edward, in naval costume. The fashion quickly spread throughout European royal families and eventually to children of every class. The young Wilhelm was dressed in sailor suits by his English mother and almost all German princes were decked out in naval costumes, even those of the most landlocked principalities. Looking back later on the sailor-suited holidays he spent in England with his cousins, Wilhelm wrote: 'When as a little boy I was allowed to visit Portsmouth and Plymouth … I admired the proud English ships in those two superb harbours. Then there awoke in me the wish to build ships of my own like those some day when I was grown up to possess as fine a navy as the English.'[8]

While it was easy for Germans to buy their English Tea from Fortnum & Mason or their clothes from Savile Row, some English habits and customs proved easier than others to transplant. Cricket was played in Berlin as early as 1850 by the resident English, but it was not until 1883 that Berlin Cricket Club was established and native Germans took to the field in whites. The club played against other German elevens in a Berliner League which, by 1914, numbered no fewer than fourteen teams. Lawn Tennis was introduced in England in 1887 and by the 1890s the fashion had spread to Germany. The Berlin-Wannsee Golf Club opened in 1895, followed by Hombourg in 1899 and Baden Baden in 1901. By 1905, Germans could lose their golf balls in the rough, lakes and bunkers at eight courses from Kiel to Leipzig, dressed in argyle socks and plus fours from Lillywhites or Harrods, in the best British manner.

When it came to hunting, Germans had been renowned for centuries, but in search of food rather than sport – their quarry was the angry wild boar rather than the wily fox. This was remedied by the simple expedient of shipping packs of English foxhounds to German country estates where German ladies could pursue foxes side-saddle while German gentlemen dressed in hunting pink direct from Savile Row. English riding boots, too, were particularly sought after, and the boot-makers of Jermyn Street were kept busy outfitting both sausage barons keen to follow the hounds and monocled Prussian officers keen to cut a dash on the parade ground. Fox hunting with hounds was banned by the Nazis in 1934 (on the grounds of being unsporting to the fox) and replaced by hunting following drags, yet even today there are more packs of hounds in Germany than in any other European country outside Britain, an unexpected legacy of German Anglophilia.[9]

In the early 1900s, attempts were made to emulate the British pheasant and grouse shooting enjoyed so much by King Edward. Birds were shipped off to be installed on German country estates and reared ready for the season. When the glorious day dawned, the hapless birds were simply corralled into pens and slaughtered wholesale on the ground, to the horror of the few English guns who had been invited over to share the sporting occasion.

Despite social hiccups like this, at almost any time during the second half of the 19th century, an educated middle-class English man or woman who was fluent in languages would have felt more at home touring in Germany than in France or Italy or any other European country. And, indeed, it was during this time that the tourist industry in the picturesque mountainous regions of Germany, Austria and Switzerland originated and underwent its most rapid period of growth. In 1863, Thomas Cook led his first parties of package tourists to Germany, and the first cuckoo clocks (a German, rather than Swiss invention) began to adorn British sitting room walls. By the early 1900s, young Englishmen and Englishwomen were emulating their German counterparts by taking hiking tours of the most scenic areas, complete with such innovations as rucksacks, alpenstocks and even Tyrolean hats.[10]

As well as these tours for the middle classes, contacts at high level were just as frequent throughout the century. Queen Victoria visited her husband's homeland on six occasions, even though the arduous journey took up to ten days by steamship, rail, and horse-drawn carriages. She first visited Germany in 1845, aged 26. Her final visit was in 1894 when her granddaughter, Princess Victoria Melita, married Grand Duke Ernst Ludwig of Hesse. Between these two dates, there were many other family occasions to celebrate, not least of which was the birth of her grandson Willi, later to become Emperor Wilhelm II.[11]

But, used as they were to everyday German influences, the patriotic British public in the 19th century might well have been shocked to realise that, in the privacy of their own home, Victoria and Albert spoke German almost exclusively to each other.

The Germany to which Victoria journeyed towards the end of her reign was very different from the collection of Ruritanian principalities that Albert had left several decades earlier. Nowhere was this emergence of confidence and power more apparent than in Berlin. In 1871, following German emergence as a unified state, Berlin was chosen as the capital of the new empire, and an immense victory parade was organised. Some 40,000 soldiers paraded from the Tempelhof Field via the Brandenburg Gate to the Royal Palace on Unter den Linden.

Princess Victoria, daughter of the English Queen and wife of Crown Prince Friedrich Wilhelm of Germany, had deep reservations about this new Reich born of blood and iron, but she enthusiastically expressed her admiration for the victory parade, declaring it 'the greatest fête Berlin, and I may say Germany, has ever seen'.[12]

The new capital grew rapidly, from a population of 865,000 in 1871, to 1 million in 1877 and 2 million by 1905.[13] The city also quickly began to acquire its requisite quota of neo-classical buildings both for government offices and the new institutions that were essential for an imperial city – museums, art galleries, concert halls and universities.

The modern lecture theatres and laboratories were populated with a new generation of home-grown German professors, who strove not only to put German scholarship on the map but also to find a distinctively German academic voice. The subjects they concentrated on reflected German preoccupations of the age but they also borrowed heavily from British scholarship: evolutionary biology, linguistics, anthropology, eugenics, race studies and geo-politics. Germans became the most enthusiastic exponents of Charles Darwin's evolutionary theories: the survival of the fittest and mankind's descent from ape-like ancestors.

In both countries it became increasingly fashionable throughout the 19th century to explain English and German national success in terms of Nordic or Teutonic racial superiority. Why else were the Germans and the Anglo-Saxons dominating the world, if not because of their innate natural superiority? And what else could explain this excellence but racial supremacy?

As the 19th century closed and the new century began, diplomatic and military relations between the two countries continued to be just as intimate. Nor did the death of Victoria in 1901 signal any immediate change in Anglo-German relations. At the personal level, King Edward was always close to his many German relations and he kept in touch with them, visiting Germany on numerous occasions. Strictly speaking, Edward was, in fact, German. He was the first monarch of the house of Saxe-Coburg-Gotha, created by the marriage of Victoria and Albert (Victoria herself being a Hanoverian monarch). It was his son, George V, who changed the family name to Windsor in 1917.

When Edward had been born in 1841, King Frederick William IV of Prussia was invited by Victoria to be his godfather. As a young man in 1866, he spent his birthday in Berlin, and he visited Germany again on many subsequent occasions, on one of which the Emperor appointed him a Field Marshal in the Prussian army, a uniform he often wore.[14] What this great national intimacy meant was that politically, diplomatically, and militarily Britain was closer to Germany than any other country in the world, and that war between the two nations was inconceivable in either country. Take, for example, the conversation Emperor Wilhelm II had with the British ambassador in Berlin, Sir Frank Lascelles, as late as December 1898. At a private dinner, Wilhelm told Lascelles that if war broke out between Britain and France (a possibility at that time) Germany would not intervene.

> His Majesty ... said that he understood that the idea was that if either of our two countries were to be attacked by two Powers at the same time, the other would come to its assistance, and that he would be prepared to act accordingly.
>
> The Emperor said that ... if ever England were in serious danger, he would certainly come to her assistance, as Europe was not conceivable without England, and he believed that under similar circumstances England would do the same by him.[15]

Of course, this was a diplomatic conversation designed to grease the wheels of Anglo-German relations and inspire mutual confidence at a time of tension. But such a conversation would have been impossible at this time between a representative of the British government and any other nation in the world – even the United States.

A few years earlier, in 1890, English newspaper journalist William Beatty-Kingston interviewed Bismarck at his estate at Friedrichsruh. Bismarck told the reporter that he was optimistic about the chances for continuing peace in Europe and that he considered war between England and Germany 'wildly improbable'.[16]

If this was merely an illusion, it was an illusion shared by many professional politicians. The German Chancellor, Theo von Bethmann-Hollweg, was an Anglophile who pursued a policy of detente with Britain and worked with British foreign secretary Sir Edward Grey to improve relations and reduce tensions during the Balkan Crises of 1912–13. So successful was their working relationship that Grey predicted in 1912 that any differences between Britain and Germany would never assume dangerous proportions 'so long as German policy was directed by Bethmann-Hollweg'. Even as late as August 1914, Anglo-German relations were described by Sir Edward Goschen, the British ambassador to Berlin, as 'more friendly and cordial than they had been in years'.[17]

Tragically, this generation of friendship and mutual respect was about to be shattered by an eighteen-year-old Bosnian Serb student, who stepped onto the running board of the limousine carrying Archduke Franz Ferdinand and his wife through the streets of Sarajevo, and emptied his revolver into its passengers.

3

A War of Words

The orders of British Prime Minister Herbert Asquith, that Germany's transatlantic telegraph must be cut, may have been carried out instantly but the action came too late. Within days of the outbreak of war, Asquith received disturbing intelligence from the United States. He was told that German agents, acting in secret before war was declared, had set up a local propaganda agency, the German Information Bureau, specifically to feed stories favourable to Germany directly to newspapers in the US and other countries. Also in secret, the German Foreign Office had set up and funded the Zentralstelle für Auslandsdienst (Central Office for Foreign Services) under the direction of Matthias Erzberger, a leader of the Catholic Centre Party and member of the Reichstag. These propaganda organisations had been created at the direct instigation of German Chancellor Theo Betthman-Hollweg.[1]

The Foreign Services Office was ostensibly concerned with collecting and studying printed works from abroad. In reality its main task was to distribute German printed material around the world – buying up promising pro-German material from publishers and encouraging or commissioning propaganda works. In time this material would include pamphlets, books, official documents, speeches and even anthologies of war poetry, fiction, and children's books. There were also a few German newspapers and magazines distributed abroad, especially *The Continental Times* which ran to 15,000 copies in 1916; the monthly *Kriegs-Chronik* (*War Chronicle*), 12,000 copies of which were printed in English, and *Der große Krieg im Bildern* (*The Great War in Pictures*), with each photograph captioned in up to six languages, including English; and the weekly *Illustrierter Kriegs-Kurier* (*Illustrated War-Courier*). The Office was especially keen on distributing photographs because visual propaganda needed no translation and pictures could touch the emotions directly. Later in the war it would also distribute films, in cinemas some of which it covertly owned.[2]

This huge, well-funded and well-organised effort caught the British completely by surprise and largely unprepared. Just how seriously the Germans had taken this venture was not to become public knowledge until 1922, when the man charged with running the US propaganda machine, George Creel, wrote an article in the magazine *Popular Radio*. According to Creel:

> Russians competent to judge assured us that the agents of Berlin spent $500,000,000 in that country alone, and their expenditures in Spain were estimated at $60,000,000. Close to $5,000,000 went to Bob Pasha for the corruption of the Paris press, and the sums spent in Mexico ran high into the millions. I knew that they owned or subsidised dailies in most of the important cities of Spain, South America, the Orient, Scandinavia, Switzerland and Holland; that their publications, issued

in every language, ran from costly brochures to the most
expensive books and albums; that they thought nothing
of paying $25,000 for a hole-in-the-wall picture house,
and that in every large city in every country their black-
mailers and bribe-givers swarmed like carrion crows.[3]

The expenditures claimed by Creel amount to billions of
dollars in today's money. By comparison, the investment of
the British government in propaganda had until then been
mere pocket money. The government simply relied on a
gentleman's agreement with Reuters news agency to relay
its announcements to the world's press. Because Britain
was plentifully equipped with more than a dozen transatlantic telephone and telegraph cables, which it permitted
Reuters and others to use at commercial rates, the arrangement worked well. But government press communiqués
were written by civil servants in the stilted language of
diplomats and bureaucrats. What was urgently needed now
to counter the German PR menace was some inspired
British spin.

Asquith turned the problem over to his young, media-
savvy Chancellor of the Exchequer, David Lloyd George.
As a man of the people, rather than the usual aloof patrician statesman, Lloyd George was one of the first politicians to understand how the media game was played, and
he shamelessly exploited the press for personal and professional advantage. More importantly, for Asquith's purposes, Lloyd George had recently scored a notable political
success, which he pulled off by manipulating the media to
get public opinion on his side. This earlier episode, in 1911,
was possibly the first time that a modern, democratically
elected government had spent public money setting up an
organisation specifically to influence public opinion.

The occasion was the passage by Parliament of the 1911 National Insurance Act, one of the most important foundation stones of the Welfare State in Britain. The Act, championed by Lloyd George and the Liberal government, gave British working-class men and women the first contributory system of insurance against illness and unemployment. The Act was highly controversial and was strongly resisted, both by Tories who saw the move as a charter for malingerers and by Britain's doctors, who felt they would be exploited by the system. To counter this, Lloyd George had set up the National Insurance Commission to oversee the introduction of the Act. But the Commission was also the first government PR machine, producing newspaper articles, pamphlets and nationwide lectures in favour of the legislation.[4]

The man that Lloyd George found to head this Commission was a fellow Liberal Member of Parliament, a young journalist named Charles Masterman. Masterman had quickly proved himself to have a natural talent for spin. Equally important, he was a highly capable administrator who quickly recruited a team of men and women and got them working so well together, manning the typewriters and the telephones, touring the country speaking, that they persuaded press and public to come down squarely in favour of the new Act.

It was to Charles Masterman that Lloyd George turned again now, in 1914, and charged with setting up a brand new government department in complete secrecy to combat the menace of the German Information Bureau. Masterman's new organisation, the British War Propaganda Bureau, was based in Wellington House, London (appropriately enough, camouflaged behind the National

Insurance Office), and was soon known – by the few who were aware of its existence – simply as 'Wellington House'.[5]

Masterman worked with his usual energy to comb out the people he had recruited three years earlier, and within weeks many of the fledgling spin doctors who had manned the typewriters and telephones of the National Insurance Commission were again seated behind desks at Wellington House racking their brains for ways to influence the foreign press, especially in the United States.

Masterman soon realised, however, that what the Bureau needed was not merely hacks to turn out routine PR puffs about how well the war was going, but some seriously thoughtful creative writing from people whose names the public already knew and trusted; material that would not merely pander to public opinion but lead it. On 2 September 1914, less than a month after Britain had declared war, Masterman invited a star-studded list of Britain's top literary talent to a meeting at Wellington House, to discuss ways in which Britain's interests could be promoted and, more importantly, to try to get the glitterati to sign up to lending their names to the war effort. Among the 25 famous names invited to attend the meeting were Arthur Conan Doyle, J.M. Barrie, Arnold Bennett, John Buchan, John Masefield, Ford Madox Ford, G.K. Chesterton, Sir Henry Newbolt, John Galsworthy, Thomas Hardy, Rudyard Kipling, G.M. Trevelyan and H.G. Wells. It was like holding a meeting with *The Oxford Companion to English Literature*.[6]

The conference was held in complete secrecy – indeed, even the existence of the War Propaganda Bureau was not made public until 1935, nearly twenty years after the war had ended. This long period of continued secrecy – comparable perhaps with the secret cracking of Enigma signals traffic at Bletchley Park in the Second World War – was a measure of the importance that the government attached to war propaganda as a clandestine weapon. It was probably also a measure of the sensitivity of the authors who attended, to the public disclosure that they had allowed their literary gifts to be harnessed to the expediencies of government policy.

As a result of the September meeting a number of authors agreed to produce books, articles and pamphlets promoting British interests and war aims. Even more important, they would pass these propaganda works off as their own inspirations and the Bureau would arrange to have them published through their normal commercial publishing houses – Hodder & Stoughton, Methuen, Oxford University Press, John Murray, Macmillan and Thomas Nelson.

One writer who was especially thrilled at being asked to participate in clandestine war work was John Buchan, author of espionage tales such as *The Thirty-nine Steps*. Even better from the Bureau's standpoint, Buchan was a trusted former senior civil servant and he was a director of his own publishing house, Thomas Nelson. Through his work with the Bureau, Buchan was later to go one better than even his fictional hero Richard Hannay by becoming a real-life spy when the Army appointed him to the Intelligence Corps. Buchan would finish the war as director of the Ministry of Information.

One immediate outcome of this meeting was that full-page advertisements appeared in the New York newspapers, signed by all the big literary names, deploring Germany and its uncivilised conduct and appealing for American support. Though ostensibly a spontaneous expression of patriotism by the writers, the ads were, of course, a concoction written and paid for by Wellington House.

A week after his meeting with the literary stars, on 11 September, Masterman held a second meeting, this time with editors from leading newspapers that included *The Pall Mall Gazette* and *The Standard*. One result of this meeting was the formation of the Neutral Press Committee under the direction of G.H. Mair, formerly the assistant editor of the *Daily Chronicle*. Mair's job was to arrange the 'exchange of news services between British and foreign newspapers; the promotion of the sale of British newspapers abroad ... the dissemination of news articles among friendly foreign newspapers and journals; and the transmission of news abroad by cables and wireless.' The references to wireless meant the Marconi radio transmitters at Poldhu in Cornwall and Caernavon in Wales, both powerful enough to reach the east coast of the United States with their wireless telegraph broadcasts.

The meeting with the press resolved:

> That it is essential that all the unnecessary obstacles to the speedy and unfettered transmission of news should be done away with and that all matter which has appeared or has been authorized to appear in English newspapers should be put upon the telegraph wires and cables without further censorship or delay in London.[7]

Despite this promising agreement to play ball, Wellington House remained nervous of trusting the press and at first it concentrated mainly on producing pamphlets, whose real origin was concealed by the simple expedient of charging a small sum for them. After all, no one would have the gall to *charge* for government propaganda.

Regardless of this sophistication, the Bureau's first major foray into print was a beginner's blunder that for some time sullied Wellington House's reputation and was to have serious long-term consequences for Anglo-German relations. In May 1915, the Bureau published the pamphlet *Report on the Alleged German Outrages*. The *Report* was intended to be an independent and objective official review of the atrocity stories emanating from Belgium about the bayoneting of babies, raping of nuns and cutting off of children's hands and feet. It was promoted internationally as a full and fair judicial investigation by a government-appointed committee under the chairmanship of Viscount Bryce, former British ambassador to the United States and a distinguished historian. Because of the secret involvement of Masterman's organisation the report was, in fact, little more than a piece of black propaganda which repeated as true virtually every story told to it, in almost all cases without any corroboration. It also accepted that acts such as the cutting off of hands and gang rape of young women occurred routinely.[8] (The truth or otherwise of these atrocity reports is an issue examined in the next chapter.)

Although losing some credibility over this first effort, at least in circles of those in the know, Wellington House soon lived up to Lloyd George's expectations. It produced a list of over 1,100 pamphlets and a string of books from its star authors. The list included *To Arms!* by Arthur Conan Doyle, *The Barbarism in Berlin* by G.K. Chesterton, Rudyard Kipling's *The New Army*, Hilaire Belloc's *The Two Maps of Europe*, and two titles from Arnold Bennett: *Liberty, A Statement of the British Case* and *War Scenes on the Western Front*. Gilbert Parker produced *Is England Apathetic?* And John Masefield wrote both *Gallipoli* and the *Old Front Line*, while John Galsworthy wrote *A Sheaf* and *Another Sheaf*.

H.G. Wells produced several books including *The Research Magnificent* and *Mr Britling Sees It Through*. But his greatest contribution was to coin in 1914 the book title that became the most memorable slogan of the conflict and one that turned the squalid slaughter of the Western Front into an honourable aim: *The War That Will End War*.[9]

John Buchan responded with two flag-waving works, *The Battle of Jutland* and *The Battle of the Somme*. But he also came through with the one really big fictional success in response to Masterman's request. As spy-mania gripped Britain in 1915, Buchan scored his biggest hit with his espionage adventure *The Thirty-nine Steps*. Fortuitous timing and fast, clever plotting made the story, and its hero, Richard Hannay, a huge hit with the public. So great was its success that in 1916 Buchan followed it up with a sequel, *Greenmantle*, another tale of espionage and international intrigue, starring Hannay. By now, though, feelings against Germany had reached fever-pitch, so Buchan was able to find plenty of opportunities to slip into his text some devastating black propaganda – including some rather clumsy homophobia. First he created a caricature German officer, Colonel von Stumm, with the obligatory bullet head and monocle, and arrogant bullying manner. Having set up the character, Buchan then creates a scene in which we learn that the vile von Stumm is secretly nothing less than an effeminate homosexual, who drenches himself in cheap perfume and attempts to seduce our hero, British secret agent Richard Hannay.

> It was the room of a man who had a passion for frippery, who had a perverted taste for soft delicate things. It was the complement to his bluff brutality. I began to see the queer other side to my host, that evil side which gossip had spoken of as not unknown in the German army.[10]

Hannay soon shows this German pansy how decent English chaps respond to that sort of beastly behaviour by punching him on the nose and escaping. Clearly, the German army is not, after all, the most highly-trained and highly-disciplined body of men in the world, but merely a bunch of sissies who like nothing better than dressing in women's knickers. At another point in the story Hannay, in disguise, is travelling through wartime Germany and just happens to meet the Kaiser, to whom he is introduced. It is plain from the gaunt, haggard expression on the Kaiser's face that he is a beaten man and that Germany is already finished, though it is only early 1916. Hannay tells us:

> The last I saw of him was a figure moving like a sleep-walker, with no spring in his step, amid his tall suite. I felt that I was looking on at a far bigger tragedy than any I had seen in action. Here was one that had loosed Hell, and the furies of Hell had got hold of him … I would not have been in his shoes for the throne of the Universe …[11]

It wasn't only in works billed as fiction that Buchan allowed his patriotism to get the better of his judgement. In his *Illustrated History of the War*, Buchan told his readers in 1915 that the Germans were on the verge of defeat, with an estimated loss of over 1,300,000 soldiers compared to a loss of only 100,000 British lives.

Arthur Conan Doyle responded to Masterman's plea by bringing the world's most famous detective out of retirement to turn his formidable deductive powers to trapping Von Bork – Germany's most dangerous spy in England – a feat which Sherlock Holmes manages with his customary efficiency.

Though authors like Buchan and Doyle played along willingly with the government's propaganda policy, some of their publishers were not happy with the arrangement. In his post-war memoirs, J.M. Dent disclosed that 'I cannot say my heart leapt up as I thought of my country's stand for righteousness'. Stanley Unwin confessed in *The Truth About a Publisher*: 'So great was the war-time prejudice on the subject that many booksellers refused to stock or handle [propaganda works].'[12] Though the press was in on the deception, the public and most members of the government remained in the dark and accepted the ever-growing torrent of pro-British, anti-German literature as the spontaneous expression of a wronged people.

These efforts taking place in London were mirrored in every detail in Berlin. German writers, journalists and artists were pressed into the service of the state and generated works extolling German courage, self-sacrifice and military prowess, while bewailing English perfidy, cowardice and military failure.

The powerful propaganda machines that Britain and Germany thus constructed each had three main strategic targets. First, they aimed to demoralise the enemy's armed forces and civil populations by damaging press reporting and by dropping leaflets from the air, although, as described later, Britain devised more ingenious methods later in the war.

Second, they were aimed at their own civilian populations for a whole range of purposes, which multiplied as the war dragged on. These included spurring young men to enlist and fight, gaining the moral support of civilians for the war, encouraging greater industrial and agricultural production, and persuading people to buy war bonds to finance the war.

Thirdly, they were aimed at gaining the support of neutral countries. In this respect, both Britain and Germany had the same primary propaganda target – the United States. If Germany could persuade the US to remain neutral, there was a good chance she could force Britain and France to their knees and hence to some form of negotiated peace. If Britain could persuade the US to come in on the Allied side, there was a strong probability that Germany could be decisively beaten militarily. This issue proved to be profoundly important to the outcome of the war. Given that the Western Front remained locked in stalemate for four years because the opposing forces were evenly matched, then, whether they realised it or not, those responsible for running the propaganda war would ultimately be responsible for deciding the outcome of the conflict itself.

For the next four years, the staff at Wellington House acted as a sieve through which all press statements and all news for foreign consumption was passed and censored. With few exceptions, there was little attempt to falsify news, but censorship relied on selection and presentation of items favourable to the Allies. Bad news for the Allies was played down or buried on the back pages, while any German success was belittled. It is only fair to add that, in doing so, newspaper editors were merely carrying on business as usual – giving their readers news they wanted to hear.

In 1915, Masterman appointed five reporters to become official war correspondents with the British Army. The five had to submit all their reports to the censor, C.E. Montague, a former leader writer for the *Manchester Guardian*. One of the five, Philip Gibbs, a journalist with the Northcliffe press, had managed to get himself posted to the Western Front as early as 1914, but the War Office decided it would manage all reporting of the war through censorship and ordered Gibbs back to England. To his credit, Gibbs refused to leave and was arrested and sent home.

Ironically, as Gibbs wrote after the war, the War Office's fears were groundless – no official censor was necessary.[13]

> We identified ourselves absolutely with the Armies in the field. We wiped out of our minds all thought of personal scoops and all temptation to write one word which would make the task of officers and men more difficult or dangerous. There was no need of censorship of our despatches. We were our own censors.

Masterman imposed a number of rules on his contributors for war propaganda purposes, rules that were followed not only by his tame authors and correspondents but also by the British press. There were to be no photographs published of the war except those taken by two official photographers he appointed and sent to France. In particular there were to be no pictures of dead soldiers published to upset British wives and mothers.

Masterman correctly foresaw that allowing unrestricted photography of the war would be very dangerous to civilian morale (it was television pictures of the Vietnam war, five decades later, that turned American public opinion against US involvement in the war). As a result, the prohibition of cameras was enforced very seriously, and officers and men on the Western Front were periodically reminded of this in bulletins such as this one:

> As the intention of General Routine Order No.1137 appears in some cases to be misunderstood, it is notified

that no Officer or soldier (or other person subject to Military law) is permitted to be in possession of a camera.

Technically speaking, owning and using a camera in a theatre of war was punishable by drastic penalties up to and including death by firing squad. In practice the regulation must have been widely ignored, because London's Imperial War Museum today has in its collection several million photos taken by serving men. But though many pictures were taken, only those approved by the Bureau ever found their way into print – a minute proportion of those taken.

Anyone who has seen uncensored photographs from the Western Front that were never published can be in no doubt that Masterman's decision was a correct one. Many of the scenes photographed by soldiers are utterly sickening and, even in a book such as this, which seeks to peer behind the censor's veil, I don't feel comfortable about describing their contents. For anyone who wishes to satisfy their morbid curiosity, there is a small privately-owned war museum at the site of 'Hill 60', three miles south-east of Ypres, where hundreds of contemporary monochrome slides can be viewed in ancient brass-and-mahogany coin-in-the-slot machines in a macabre peep show. I still vividly recall visiting the museum some twenty years ago with three friends, all, like me, fascinated by the First War and eager to learn more. I also recall that, after leaving, none of us spoke, as there really wasn't anything we could say about what we had seen.

Though considered essential for morale, a blanket ban on pictures was paradoxically also damaging to the propaganda effort, because visual material had a far more powerful effect than words alone, especially for the tabloid-reading general public. In 1916, Masterman experimented by recruiting a talented artist, Muirhead Bone, and sending him to France with his sketch book – pencil and charcoal could be censored in a way that the camera could not. The 150 or so drawings of British successes that Bone brought back were a hit with the public and this encouraged Masterman to expand the experiment.

In the following year, more artists were sent abroad. Famous names included William Orpen and William Rothenstein and, in all, some 90 war artists were used. But there was still censorship over what could be shown and what could not. Paul Nash complained that: 'I am not allowed to put dead men into my pictures because apparently they don't exist.'[14]

One of the most critical war artists was Charles Nevinson, whose painting *Paths of Glory*, showing two Tommies dead and impaled on the murderous barbed wire, was banned by the Bureau and not publicly exhibited until after the war was over. Returning from Flanders in 1917, deeply shocked at the carnage of the trenches, Nevinson refused to compromise with Masterman's directives and tried to show *Paths of Glory* in an exhibition in 1918. The painting was banned but Nevinson refused to take it down and instead covered it in brown paper on which he wrote 'Censored'. This led to an official rebuke from the War Office and Nevinson was not invited to paint any more official war pictures.

One of Masterman's innovations is still a bookstall favourite today. He decided to publish a part work magazine entitled the *Illustrated History of the War*. John Buchan was made editor-in-chief of the project and Buchan's publishing company, Thomas Nelson, handled the printing, publishing and distribution, although all proceeds were given to war charities. The magazine was a big hit with a public hungry for news of the war, and 24 issues were produced in all. Bound copies of the part work can still be found in second-hand bookshops today, an odd but tangible legacy of the secret propaganda war.

In its routine press announcements for the next four years of war, the War Propaganda Bureau played its cards pretty much as any government department today would. After its initial blunder over German atrocity stories in 1914, the Bureau mainly kept the truth within call in case it should undermine official credibility. Masterman's spin doctors concerned themselves with countering German propaganda against Britain and making available a Briton's-eye-view of the battles that raged, while taking full advantage of real German atrocities such as the sinking of the passenger liner *Lusitania* and the execution of nurse Edith Cavell on charges of spying. If reports were over-optimistic, it was usually because the generals themselves were over-optimistic and Masterman gave them the benefit of the doubt. If military disasters such as the battle of the Somme in 1916 were played down, it was because things were black enough already without handing the enemy a propaganda victory on a plate.

By February 1917, Lloyd George had become Prime Minister, largely thanks to attacks on Asquith by the newspapers of Lord Northcliffe, owner of *The Times* and the *Daily Mail*, who believed the generals should be given a free hand to run the war. In what had become by now a perilous war situation, Lloyd George's government decided an all-out propaganda offensive was needed, and established a new Department of Information to oversee all propaganda activities. Promoted to the rank of Lieutenant Colonel, John Buchan was put in charge of the department.

Charles Masterman retained responsibility for books, pamphlets, photographs and war paintings, and T.L. Gilmour dealt with cables, wireless, newspapers, magazines and the cinema. Lloyd George detested Northcliffe (he is reported to have said: 'I would as soon go for a sunny evening stroll round Walton Heath [golf course] with a grasshopper as try and work with Northcliffe'[15]), but felt compelled to offer the newspaper magnate a Cabinet propaganda post purely as a defensive measure. Fortunately for Lloyd George, Northcliffe turned down the offer on this occasion.

In the following year, 1918, the war situation became even more critical and Whitehall decided to centralise all propaganda effort in a new headquarters, Crewe House, and to fund an all-out propaganda campaign on German morale. It also decided that propaganda had become so important that a senior government figure should take over responsibility for the campaign, and on 4 March Lord Beaverbrook, proprietor of the *Daily Express*, was made Minister of Information. Under him was Charles Masterman as Director of Publications and John Buchan as Director of Intelligence. This time, Northcliffe accepted a job and was put in charge of all propaganda directed at enemy countries. Robert Donald, editor of the *Daily Chronicle*, was appointed director of propaganda in neutral countries.

Northcliffe now assumed responsibility for distributing anti-government pamphlets, leaflets, and newspapers in the territories of the Central Powers. This meant primarily dropping leaflets by aircraft and from balloons, but also the ingeniously simple method of posting propaganda to selected addresses through the enemy mails. For this purpose they forged German and Austrian postage stamps. This technique was used again with success in the Second War.

Although he had been slow to accept an official role in government propaganda, and did not become involved until only nine months before the war ended, Northcliffe was quick to claim a lion's share of the credit after the war for having pulled the wool over the eyes of the Germans. This boasting was to have fateful consequences, for it enabled some Germans to claim that they had not been beaten militarily in a fair fight, but had been tricked into defeat by the evil genius of British black propaganda of the kind described in detail in the next chapter – thus helping lay the foundations for the 'stab in the back' theory and the post-war resurgence of German nationalism and militarism.

General Erich von Ludendorff, for example, wrote in his post-war memoirs:

> We were hypnotised by the enemy propaganda as a rabbit is by a snake. It was exceptionally clever, and conceived on a great scale. It worked by strong mass-suggestion, kept in the closest touch with the military situation, and was unscrupulous as to the means it used.
>
> ... While Entente propaganda was doing ever more harm to the German people and the army and navy, it succeeded in maintaining the determination to fight in its own countries and armies, and in working against us in neutral countries ... In the neutral countries we were subjected to a sort of moral blockade.[16]

Praise from one's enemy is praise indeed, although it was also convenient for a soldier like Ludendorff to have British propaganda as a handy excuse for losing the war militarily. Just how effective British propaganda was at influencing people's hearts and minds at home and abroad is still much debated. Take, for example, the question of recruitment for the armed forces. The image of General Kitchener, glaring down from the poster and announcing that 'Your Country Wants You!', is still one of the most memorable propaganda images of the war nearly a century later. Yet, memorable though it is, the image was ineffective – voluntary recruitment fell below the levels needed in 1915 and the government was obliged to introduce conscription the following year.

In the primary external target for much of this activity – the United States – the propaganda effort seems to have been effective in the sense that as late as 1917, when the US was on the point of entering the war, most Americans, including politicians, had little inkling of what the war was really like or what it would cost the US to enter on the Allied side. It came as a surprise to the Senate Majority Democratic Leader to learn that the US would have to send an army to Europe, especially as the US newspapers had been assuring their readers for some time that no European army would be sent.

As Thomas Fleming wrote:

Leading newspapers such as the *New York Tribune* and the *Los Angeles Times* assured their readers that no American army was needed in Europe. General Hugh Scott, chief of the army's general staff, put a memorandum in his files to this effect, a month after Congress declared war.

Everyone thought that the war was as good as won. All the virtually victorious English, French and Russians needed from the United States was large amounts of food, weapons and ammunition, paid for by American loans, and some help from the American navy to fight Germany's troublesome submarines.[17]

Fleming blames this state of ignorance on the effectiveness of the British War Propaganda Bureau, telling his readers of the cutting of the German telegraph cables and the censorship advantage this gave Britain.

American newsmen reporting the war from Berlin's side of the lines soon learned that descriptions of German battlefield prowess were cut to ribbons and often suppressed. In 1916, a troubled congressman inserted into the Congressional Record a complaint from a number of newsmen to this effect.

The censors of Wellington House, he explained:

... deluged the country with stories puffing British and French battlefield superiority. Speakers by the hundreds toured America telling the same lie.[18]

Although Britain was slower off the mark than Germany in setting up a sophisticated censorship organisation, it was the British propaganda campaign that was ultimately far more successful at hitting its targets both at home and abroad.

Like the British, German propaganda produced a good deal of visual material both for domestic consumption and for influencing nations abroad. Artistic creations ranged from elaborate poster paintings of the Kaiser dressed in shining armour like a Teutonic knight, hovered over by protecting angels, to comic postcards ridiculing Britain and the British. There seemed to be a particular German obsession with depicting Tommies sitting on chamber pots while the Grand Fleet ran all the risks and did all the fighting. But though the material was visually attractive and vaguely amusing, it was difficult to say just who these messages were aimed at and what exactly they were meant to convey.

The chief problem with German propaganda was that, although Berlin appreciated the potential importance of winning hearts and minds, in practice they simply didn't get the basic principles right. Ridiculing your enemy may be good for morale at home, but it doesn't impart any sense of war aims, nor any sense of fighting for a cause greater than merely narrow nationalism.

Not only were German propagandists confused about the messages they sent, they were also confused about how best to communicate them. Perhaps because those in authority in Germany were used to barking orders, German propaganda simply told people what conclusion they should come to. The British way was infinitely more sophisticated. Masterman knew that if you tell people what to think they will resent it, whereas if you give them inescapable facts and leave them to draw their own conclusion, they will reach it without realising that they have had their mind made up for them by someone else. The trick was to present people with facts in such an authoritative and reasonable manner that they neither questioned them nor felt it necessary to look for fresh facts elsewhere.

Compare the thinking behind a German postcard of Tommy Atkins sitting on a chamber pot, with the sophistication of the famous British poster in which a child of the post-war future asks her father: 'What did you do in the war, Daddy?' Where the first merely arouses an embarrassed titter, the second has the power to cut one to the heart.

British propaganda, for home and overseas consumption, was more sophisticated than Germany's in another important respect. Masterman and his team took care to seize the moral high ground from the outset and to inject a moralising tone into most items, even ordinary humorous postcards and posters. While German postcards ridiculed the British soldier, depicting him for example with bandages and a bloody nose received from the German army, the equivalent English postcards also contained a message. The Kaiser might be ridiculed as a fly that must be swatted by soldiers from many nations, but he is at the same time depicted as an international menace that the civilised nations have come together to eradicate. Such a postcard doesn't just say that the Kaiser is ridiculous and a pest; it also says that Germany is isolated and in the wrong. Similarly, the subject matter chosen for official British posters often showed that its authors were not only manipulating feelings against Germany and for the Allies but also adopting a moral position, as in the poster illustrating the treaty guaranteeing Belgian neutrality, which the German Chancellor contemptuously brushed aside as a 'scrap of paper'.

But if the honours for propaganda effectiveness were divided unevenly during the four years of war, the final PR conflict was an unmitigated disaster for Germany. The final nail in Germany's PR coffin was the Versailles Peace Treaty of 1919 where the Allies insisted on pinning war guilt exclusively on Germany.

The extent to which this final PR victory was deliberate policy on the part of the victors is not easy to say. Britain, France, Belgium and Italy all wished to see someone compelled to make financial restitution for the death and destruction that four years of war had brought to their homes and their economies. To the people and leaders of these nations it was plain that it was the defeated Germans who were responsible and should be made to pay. The French especially had a score to settle, as Germany had compelled them to pay reparations after defeating them in

1870. But in order to make this extraction of reparations legal, it was first necessary to make Germany accept the entire guilt for the war, and this was demanded in the draft Treaty handed to the German delegation at the Peace Conference.

The German delegation initially resisted this demand. They pointed out that the individuals who had represented the war party, including the Kaiser and his generals, were gone and had been replaced by a new, democratically elected government assembly consisting of individuals who had fought for peace – that a whole nation could not be found guilty for the crimes of the few. They pointed out that the atrocities attributed to them in Allied propaganda were largely false.[19] And they had the audacity to point out that England and France were merely protecting their own financial and imperial interests by waging war with Germany and were now intent on carving up German overseas possessions in order to extend their commercial interests still further.

Despite the best efforts of President Woodrow Wilson, who sought to exonerate Germany and institute collective security through a League of Nations, Germany was strong-armed into pleading guilty and Article 231 was written into the Treaty of Versailles, placing on record that it was Germany and the other Central Powers who were solely responsible for the outbreak of the First World War.

Whether intentional or not, this single act legitimised all the Allied propaganda victories of the previous four years. There would have been little point in Germany publicly protesting: Yes, it's true we did start the war in which 20 million people died – but we didn't rape nuns or bayonet babies.

At Versailles, Germany lost what turned out to be the most crucial battle of the war: the battle for its reputation. But it was a battle that had been decided by the actions of British intelligence long before, almost as soon as the war had started.

4

Atrocious Behaviour

From the moment that the First World War began in August 1914, and the German army marched into Belgium and France, Germany was accused of committing war atrocities. The stories were so widespread, and such a valuable and unexpected propaganda gift for the Allies, that the British War Propaganda Bureau lost no time in 'substantiating' them by means of an official report and then publicising them as widely as possible, especially in neutral America.

There was no one in Britain, and few in the United States, who had not heard or read of German soldiers running wild like beasts through the towns and villages of Belgium and France, killing women and children indiscriminately, raping nuns, cutting off children's hands and feet, and bayoneting babies in their prams.

Few people at the time stopped to reflect that the German army of 1914 was one of the most disciplined military instruments the world had ever seen; an instrument that was totally obedient to its officers and which carried out every order to the letter. If anyone did question how a

47

force of this kind could carry out such bestial acts, the only reply possible was that they must be obeying orders.

The most puzzling aspect of the German atrocity stories is that decades of investigation have produced little in the way of credible evidence for the kind of tales spread by British propaganda. So how on earth did these tales get started in the first place?

On at least two well-attested occasions, at Dinant and Louvain in Belgium, German troops claimed to have been fired on by snipers and retaliated savagely by killing civilians and burning their houses. But these incidents – savage though they were – could not justify British claims that the German army had embarked on a planned strategy of atrocities. To understand how British propaganda was able to depict the atrocity stories as deliberate German policy, you have to look more closely at the factual elements from which the propaganda myths were fabricated. These elements included PR blunders such as Germany's violation of Belgian neutrality and the deliberate taking of hostages in French villages to counter guerrilla warfare, but they also included purely technical developments connected with artillery warfare. Finally, and most importantly, the raw urban myths that resulted from these circumstances were processed into permanent historical fact by one of the most sophisticated and ruthless PR machines ever assembled. How these elements came together to create the image of the Barbaric Hun is one of the most extraordinary legacies of 1914. Germany's first propaganda gift to the allies was its invasion of Belgium despite an international treaty guaranteeing Belgian neutrality, signed by England, France, Russia, Austria and Germany in 1839. In reality, its invasion was caused not by Machiavellian intent but simply by railway timetables. German mobilisation plans called for the transport of no fewer than 2.5 million men to the battle front. To accomplish this, the army commandeered the entire German rail network and its 11,000 trains. Putting so many trains onto the network at once would create bottlenecks at busy rail junctions, especially the main junction at Aachen on the German–Belgian border – trains and men would be backed up for miles, bringing the rail network to a standstill and creating chaos. Simply to keep the network running, it was necessary for trains that reached Aachen junction to keep on moving forward, through Belgian territory, to their destinations.[1]

Thus, as A.J.P. Taylor pointed out, for reasons no more important than railway timetables, the German plan necessarily involved the violation of Belgian neutrality. The plan's originator, Count von Schlieffen, must have been fully aware of the implications of his strategy for international diplomacy, but he was a soldier, not a diplomat, and his aim was not to protect Germany's reputation but to win a war against France and Russia without having to fight on two fronts simultaneously.

There is still intense debate about whether the Kaiser and his military advisers really understood the point that mobilisation of the army must make war inevitable. It is certainly true that after he had issued orders for mobilisation in August 1914, the Kaiser later tried to rescind this directive and ordered General von Moltke, Chief of the General Staff, to recall some troop trains, but it was too late – troops had already crossed the border into Belgium. In an emotional interview with the British ambassador, Sir Edward Goschen, on the fateful day of 4 August, the German Chancellor, Bethmann-Hollweg, pleaded with him to understand that violating Belgian neutrality was a matter of life and death to Germany and an act that could not be undone. It is, however, also true that in the same interview, Bethmann-Hollweg dismissed the treaty guaranteeing Belgian neutrality as nothing more than 'a scrap of paper', thus losing all hope of Germany regaining the slightest trace of PR respectability.[2]

The second logistical problem encountered by the German army would lead to even more vocal and bitter international recriminations. By a curious irony, the German actions were based largely on a British precedent.

As its massive column marched through France, the German army took hostages in each village it passed through. Its reason for this policy was its experience in the Franco-Prussian war of 1870 when French guerrilla fighters in civilian dress fired off a few rounds from makeshift positions in a farmhouse or cottage, before melting away and rejoining the local population. This sniping caused panic and loss of morale among the normally disciplined Prussian troops out of all proportion to the actual casualties sustained.[3]

To prevent this happening again, in August 1914, when the German army marched into France, detachments of troops went ahead into every town and village on the invasion route armed with pre-printed posters. These posters, meticulously researched in the previous years by German spies, named the town's prominent citizens – mayor, priest, doctor, lawyer – who were arrested and taken into custody for the duration of the army's passage. The posters informed would-be guerrillas that if German soldiers were fired on, the hostages would be executed in retaliation.

In practice, the scheme worked as the Germans intended. Caught completely by surprise by such thorough preparation, French civilians submitted tamely to invasion. Unlike 1870, there were few cases of troops being fired on and the prominent citizens held hostage were released unharmed. Militarily it was a great success. In PR terms it was the Germans' second major defeat.

When news of such cold-blooded and carefully orchestrated hostage-taking filtered through to London, the press reacted with unprecedented hostility. Soon the word 'atrocity' was appearing in headlines in Lord Northcliffe's newspapers, *The Times* and *Daily Mail*, and in other papers abroad. To Northcliffe's tabloid readers, there was something so cold and calculating about secretly knowing and planning in advance who you were going to kidnap and threaten to kill that it seemed barbaric in the extreme. Such cold-blooded blackmail was seen as the work of gangsters, not soldiers, and was clear evidence of the true nature of the beastly Hun.

In reality, the German plan was based on a British precedent. Fourteen years earlier, in South Africa, British troops under Lord Kitchener had brutally resolved the Boer War by taking hostage the wives and children of Boer commandos and incarcerating them in 'concentration camps' – a British, rather than German invention.

Conditions in the camps were overcrowded, with little or no medical facilities and poor sanitation. Wives and children of Boers who continued to fight were denied meat in their rations, and there were no fresh vegetables and no milk for children and babies. As a result, diseases became epidemic and 26,370 women and children died in the concentration camps, the vast majority of them children. The Boers eventually surrendered.[4]

This 'successful' action was the model on which the German High Command based its hostage-taking plans in 1914, but whereas Kitchener was applauded by the British press and returned home a hero, the Germans' behaviour became the focus for national hatred.

This reaction was doubly reinforced when German troops occupying the Belgian towns of Dinant and Louvain said they had been fired on by snipers and went on a rampage of killing civilians, looting and burning in reprisals. The actions at Dinant and Louvain meant that the atrocity stories filtering through to the British and American press would now multiply and spin completely out of control. An army that was capable of planning to kidnap victims in advance and shoot civilians in reprisals was capable of any act. Before long the British and French newspapers were vying with each other to print the worst German atrocity story. Women were being raped at gunpoint while their children were stood against the wall and shot. Babies were bayoneted in their cribs. Toddlers had their hands and feet cut off. Women had their breasts cut off. Nuns were raped and – in what must rank as the most bizarre tabloid invention of all time – priests used as human clappers in the bells of their own churches. Later it was even alleged by Wellington House that the Germans were boiling down the bodies of their own war dead to make soap, though just how they found the time to embark on this industrial activity while also invading France was not explained.

The Germans were stung by international accusations that they had invaded Belgium without cause and sought to rebut the charge. They counter-charged that Belgian neutrality was first violated by France and Britain. In the *Norddeutsche Allgemeine Zeitung* of 24 November 1914, Dr Münsterberg said that 'Belgium chose to put itself on the side of France, with which its sympathies have always connected it. ... Belgium was one great fortified camp [against Germany].'[5]

In fact, said the Germans, the French had beaten them to it – France had guns and troops in Belgium by 30 July and the British had landed in Ostend the same day. Dr Münsterberg complained that 'when Germany goes through Belgium, America shares the indignation of England to which it serves as a welcome pretext. But that France went into Belgium first is kept a secret in most American papers. This means playing the reporter's game with loaded dice.'[6]

It may well be that violating Belgian neutrality and taking hostages, reinforced by the outrages in Dinant and Louvain, would have been enough by themselves to fuel atrocity stories of gang rapes and baby-bayoneting in the British and US media. But when international reporters starting showing up on the edges of the battle zone they encountered sights that appeared to confirm the stories and seemed to lend truth to the refugees' tales, but which in many cases resulted from devastating developments in the field of artillery.

A.J.P. Taylor remarked that if Napoleon had come back to life in 1914 he would have found little different from the battle of Waterloo a century earlier – masses of men, marching into battle carrying rifle and pack – whereas had he returned in 1915, he would hardly have recognised the Western Front as a battlefield.[7] The factors that transformed war into the horrors of 1915 were several small but highly significant technical innovations. In Napoleon's day, cannon were inaccurate, muzzle-loading devices that fired solid iron balls, or the canisters of metal fragments invented by Henry Shrapnel, over distances of a few hundred yards. A century later, artillery pieces could be loaded rapidly through a breech-block, had rifled barrels and calibrated sights for pinpoint accuracy, and fired high-explosive shells over long distances with devastating effects on people and buildings.

Given these powerful new weapons by science, modern armies had developed new tactics. Instead of wasting men on a frontal assault, an attacking army would bring up its guns and saturate the target with shell-fire to obliterate its defences before marching in to occupy what was left.

Towns and cities had been shelled before by ordinary cannon-fire with horrifying results, the most striking example being Atlanta during the American Civil War.[8] But the consequences of concentrated firing of thousands of high-explosive shells into civilian areas had been foreseen by no one in Europe, least of all by the civil populations in Belgium and France who had no idea that they stood in the way of Schlieffen's precision timetable and were caught up in the first vast army manoeuvres of 1914.

The result was a very high level of civilian casualties and refugees streaming away from the shelling, many of them terribly wounded in the bombardment. This sight was to become commonplace later, especially during the Second World War.

So it came about that, when the German army marched through Belgium and into northern France in August 1914, its mobile artillery caused injury and death to soldiers and civilians, damage and destruction to buildings, on a far greater scale than anything that had been seen before, even in the war of 1870 – a level of destruction that astonished everyone, including the Germans.

The sight of these hundreds of refugees, some with terrible injuries, gave credence to the stories that German soldiers were routinely committing atrocities as a matter of policy.

Events in Belgium coincided with the setting up by Lloyd George of the British War Propaganda Bureau. As described earlier, one of the very first major efforts by the Bureau was the publication in May 1915 of the pamphlet entitled *Report on the Alleged German Outrages*.[9] The report was heralded as an independent and objective official review of the atrocity stories coming from Belgium, by a committee of lawyers sitting under Viscount Bryce who, until 1913, had been British ambassador to the United States and who was a well-known and respected figure there, as well as being a distinguished historian. Nominally, the committee was entirely independent and the involvement of Masterman's Propaganda Bureau was secret. In fact, Bryce was chosen because his word would carry weight with the US public and the document was published simultaneously in 30 languages, to persuade other neutrals.

The report accepted without question virtually every story told to it, in most cases without any corroboration. It also accepted that acts such as the cutting off of hands and gang rape of young women occurred routinely. In some cases, the acceptance of atrocities contrasted starkly with actual eyewitness reports. According to the report, Members of the Bryce committee

> ... were instructed not to 'lead' the witnesses, or make any suggestions to them, and also to impress upon them the necessity for care and precision in giving their evidence. They were also directed to treat the evidence critically. ... They were, in fact, to cross-examine them.[10]

The committee also insisted that it included 'in full' all statements 'tending to exculpate the German troops' and rejected any testimony from questionable witnesses. Nevertheless, the committee concluded that:

In the present war, however – and this is the gravest charge against the German army – the evidence shows that the killing of non-combatants was carried out to an extent for which no previous war between nations claiming to be civilized … furnishes any precedent.[11]

A typical example of the kind of eyewitness testimony on which the Bryce Report was based is:

One witness saw a German soldier cut a woman's breasts after he had murdered her, and saw many other dead bodies of women in the streets of Belgium. Another witness testified that she saw a drunken German soldier kill a two-year-old child: The soldier drove his bayonet with both hands into the child's stomach, lifting the child into the air on his bayonet, he and his comrades were singing. Other witnesses saw a German soldier amputate a child's hands and feet.[12]

The Bryce Report concluded that the reports were essentially all true, and that the Germans were barbarians who had put themselves beyond the pale of civilised behaviour. And, although largely discredited after the war, it was widely accepted at the time in Britain, America and elsewhere.

The Propaganda Bureau also over-egged the pudding in other ways. John Buchan introduced well-known Dutch cartoonist Louis Raemakers to the Bureau. He was commissioned to produce illustrations for the pamphlet, depicting Germans committing the alleged atrocities, which he did with his customary skill as an illustrator – without ever having set foot in Belgium or witnessed any atrocities. But his Dutch name suggested that Raemakers was himself an eye-witness, hot-foot back from the front, the sketches in his satchel stained red with blood. Raemakers' skill at depicting bestial Hun-like German soldiers in his cartoons so angered the German government that they placed a bounty of 12,000 guilders on his head.

Even before the Bryce Report was published, newspapers in England and France were full of atrocity reports. As early as 27 August 1914, a *Times* reporter told his readers:

> Nearly all the people I interrogated had stories to tell of German atrocities. Whole villages, they said, had been put to fire and sword. One man, whom I did not see, told an official of the Catholic Society that he had seen with his own eyes Germans chop off the arms of a baby which clung to its mother's skirts.[13]

By January 1915, *The Times* confirmed to its readers that its reports had not been exaggerated:

> The stories of rape are so horrible in detail that their publication would seem almost impossible were it not for the necessity of showing to the fullest extent the nature of the wild beasts fighting under the German Flag.[14]

Hardly less sensational was the account of Phyllis Campbell, who was in Paris in the early months of the war and wrote about the arrival of Belgian refugees in her 1915 book *Back to the Front*:

> In one wagon, sitting on the floor, was a naked girl of about 23. One of her suffering sisters, more fortunate than the rest in possessing an undergarment, had torn it in half and covered the front of her poor body. It was saturated with blood from her cut-off breasts. On her knees lay a little baby, dead. There were women covered with

sabre cuts, women who had been whipped, women
burned alive escaping from their blazing homes, little
boys maimed in the hands and feet, their wounds done
up in sacking or any kind of old rag. On one side of a
door sat a soldier who had lost both his legs, and he
was supporting a boy whose arms were gone. One
Highlander implored me to run away – 'Get away, lassie,'
he said, heavily. 'They're no men, they're devils!' His
dying eyes seemed to look at an awful something beyond
us.[15]

Many British people, both among civilians and in the
armed forces, read and believed the atrocity stories. The
better-educated section of the community treated them
with caution, and the few writers who had first-hand
knowledge rejected them entirely. Margaret Cole was an
English socialist and feminist who campaigned against conscription in 1914 but who later supported Britain's involvement in the Second World War. She wrote:

Conscription did not arrive until 1916, after every
expedient, including solemn promises not to introduce
conscription, had been used to man the armies with
volunteers; but right from the start any critics of the war
suffered a great deal of sporadic persecution by victims
of war hysteria. They were booed and pelted, served
with white feathers by excited young women, and subjected, particularly as the news of Mons and Charleroi
began to come through and it appeared that our army
and the French armies were not marching on Berlin but
rather running away from it, by a barrage of untrue and
idiotic 'atrocity stories' about children with their hands
cut off by the Germans, priests tied upside-down to the

clappers of their own bells, dead bodies boiled down for fat, and the like. (It was unfortunate that subsequent exposure of all stories as lies conditioned some muddled souls into rejecting any atrocity story whatsoever and so led them to deny or to discount up to the last any reports, however factual, about the doings of the Nazis.)[16]

Irving Cobb was an American reporter for the Hearst press who was in Belgium when the country was occupied by the Germans in 1914 and who sent back despatches from the front line. Cobb wrote:

> Every Belgian refugee had a tale to tell of German atrocities on non-combatants: but not once did we find an avowed eye-witness to such things. Always our informant had heard of the torturing or the maiming or the murdering, but never had he personally seen it. It had always happened in another town – never in his own town.[17]

Robert Graves recorded his experiences as a young officer on the Western Front in the First World War in his book *Goodbye to All That*:

> Propaganda reports of atrocities were, it was agreed, ridiculous. We no longer believed the highly-coloured accounts of German atrocities in Belgium. By atrocities we meant, specifically, rape, mutilation, and torture – not summary shootings of suspected spies, harbourers of spies, or disobedient local officials. If the atrocity-list had to include the accidental-on-purpose bombing or machine-gunning of civilians from the air, the Allies were now committing as many atrocities as the Germans.

French and Belgian civilians had often tried to win our sympathy by exhibiting mutilations of children – stumps of hands and feet, for instance – representing them as deliberate, fiendish atrocities when, as likely as not, they were merely the result of shell-fire. We did not believe rape to be any more common on the German side of the line than on the Allied side.

As for atrocities against soldiers – where should one draw the line? The British soldier, at first, regarded as atrocious the use of bowie-knives by German patrols. After a time, he learned to use them himself; they were cleaner killing weapons than revolvers or bombs. The Germans regarded as equally atrocious the British Mark VII rifle bullet, which was more apt to turn on striking than the German bullet. For true atrocities, meaning personal rather than military violations of the code of war, few opportunities occurred – except in the interval between the surrender of prisoners and their arrival (or non-arrival) at headquarters. Advantage was only too often taken of this opportunity. Nearly every instructor in the mess could quote specific instances of prisoners having been murdered on the way back. The common-est motives were, it seems, revenge for the death of friends or relatives, jealousy of the prisoner's trip to a comfortable prison camp in England, military enthusi-asm, fear of being suddenly overpowered by the prison-ers, or, more simply, impatience with the escorting job. In any of these cases the conductors would report on arrival at headquarters that a German shell had killed the prisoners; and no questions would be asked. We had every reason to believe that the same thing happened on the German side, where prisoners, as useless mouths to feed in a country already short of rations, would be even less welcome.[18]

The German Propaganda Bureau hit back at once in May 1915 by publishing its 'White Book' of atrocities committed against its own forces. It claimed:

> It has been established beyond doubt that Belgian civilians plundered, killed and even shockingly mutilated German wounded soldiers, in which atrocities even women and children took part. Thus the eyes were gouged out of the German wounded soldiers, their ears, noses and finger-joints were cut off, or they were emasculated or disembowelled. In other cases German soldiers were poisoned or strung up on trees; hot liquid was poured over them, or they were otherwise burned so that they died under terrible tortures.[19]

But there are no prizes for coming second in a propaganda contest, especially one fought with incredible stories as weapons. It was the Bryce Report's version that stuck (at least until after the war), and from 1914 onwards, Germans would be perceived by the newspaper-reading public in France, Britain and the US as militaristic, brutal, cowardly, bestial and mindless barbarians, incapable of any finer sentiment and scarcely worthy of a place in the international community of civilised nations.

So effective was this black propaganda that it became near-universally believed not only in target neutral countries but also in Britain itself and even by some of the people responsible for promulgating the stories in the first place. And, although Charles Masterman seems to have tried hard to keep his organisation as straight as possible for the remainder of the war, the early sins of the War

Propaganda Bureau were bound one day to catch up with him, as they eventually did in 1917 with the bizarre case of the 'corpse factory'.

The roots of this story are difficult now to discern with any clarity, but three contributory sources have been identified. In late May 1917, a Belgian newspaper carried a report claiming that a railway carriage had been discovered in Holland loaded with the bodies of dead German soldiers. It was claimed that the bodies were destined for a factory in Liège where they were to be melted down for soap, but had been sent into Holland by mistake. On 10 April, a Berlin newspaper, *Lokal Anzeiger* (Local Journal), carried a story about a factory used to convert *what appeared to be* human corpses into war commodities. A week later, *The Times* in London accused the Germans of boiling down dead bodies to make soap and the Foreign Office launched an investigation.

Masterman came under immediate pressure from the more hawkish members of the intelligence community to confirm the story with an official pamphlet, but he resisted for some time. He realised that there was very little real evidence for the story, and further research suggested that the bodies in question were not human but those of dead horses being rendered down. In Wellington House there was much debate by German language experts over the exact meaning of the word *Kadaver*, used in the German press, as to whether the word denoted a human corpse or an animal carcass.

The question of whether the story should become the subject of propaganda was put up to Foreign Secretary A.J. Balfour, who admitted that the evidence was inconclusive, but added:

While it should not be desirable that His Majesty's Government should take any responsibility as regards the story pending the receipt of further information, there does not, in view of the many atrocious actions of which the Germans have been guilty, appear to be any reason why it should not be true.

Certainly the Germans were far from blameless, but it's difficult to identify the 'many atrocious actions' spoken of by Balfour, other than the bogus atrocities of the Bryce Report. Quite simply it meant that one fabricated propaganda document was used to justify the publication of a second, equally bogus story.

As a result of Balfour's ruling, Wellington House was instructed to press ahead with pamphlets in Portuguese, Spanish, Swedish and Dutch, while further research was put in hand for a German edition. Reluctantly, Masterman went ahead with the publication in 1917 of *A Corpse-Conversion Factory*, which seemed to provide the final conclusive proof of German barbarism, brutality and lack of civilised values.

These feelings would persist throughout the 1920s and 30s and would to some extent poison Britain's perception of Germany, at least among those who had innocently accepted the unrelenting wartime propaganda campaigns. There would no longer be any kind of equivalence or parity in actions that were in reality mirror images. British tanks were ingenious defensive weapons; German tanks were barbaric instruments of Hun bestiality. British poison gas was an attempt to use science humanely to end the war; German poison gas was merely more proof of Hun frightfulness. German occupation of Alsace Lorraine was a crime against democracy; British occupation of India was an act of humanitarian charity, protecting the Indian peoples from savages like the Germans.

This relativist attitude to the truth was obvious to those in power in Germany and it rankled, not merely during the First World War but for decades afterwards. English cruelty in the Boer War had an unexpected epilogue in 1941, when Joseph Goebbels resurrected Britain's culpability as the originator of concentration camps and produced a historical propaganda film entitled *Ohm Kruger* in which arrogant, monocled English officers not only herded the wives of Boers into concentration camps but also raped them at pistol point.[20] While still a crude distortion, this picture was somewhat closer to the facts than the British and French newspaper stories about the Germans in 1914.

It was not until ten years after the end of the war that anything like the real truth about the war atrocity stories was told. In 1928, Member of Parliament Arthur Ponsonby broke ranks with his establishment colleagues and published a book uncompromisingly titled *Falsehood in Wartime*.[21]

Ponsonby was a Liberal MP who had joined with others to oppose the war and who wrote and spoke out against British involvement. In his book he was at pains to try to reassure his former government colleagues that his book was not intended to 'cast fresh blame on authorities and individuals'. Having made this disingenuous claim, Ponsonby then filled almost 200 pages with detailed examples of blatant lies and black propaganda put out chiefly by British government departments and censor-controlled newspapers from 1914 to 1918.

By careful comparison of newspapers in different countries, Ponsonby was able to track down to its source one of the most bizarre of all the early atrocity stories – the terrible fate of the priests in Antwerp. What he showed taking place was an almost comical game of Chinese whispers between the principal newspapers of England, France and Italy, all equally keen to act as patriotic government mouthpieces.

In November 1914, the German newspaper *Kölnische Zeitung* (Cologne Daily News) carried an item that read: 'When the fall of Antwerp became known, the church bells were rung.' This story referred to the ringing of church bells to celebrate a victory. But the item was picked up in France and run in *Le Matin* with a deliberate misunderstanding that puts a different slant on the story, thus: 'According to the *Kölnische Zeitung*, the clergy of Antwerp were compelled to ring the church bells when the fortress was taken.'

By the time the story was picked up in London by *The Times*, it was embellished still further: 'According to what *Le Matin* has heard from Cologne via Paris, the unfortunate Belgian priests who refused to ring the church bells when Antwerp was taken have been driven away from their places.'

And when the story was in turn picked up and run in Italy by *Corriere della Sera*, the Antwerp clergymen suffered even more harshly: 'According to what *The Times* has heard from Cologne via Paris, the unfortunate Belgian priests who refused to ring the church bells when Antwerp was taken have been sentenced to hard labour.'

But it was when the story was on its return journey on the rumour mill to *Le Matin* in France that the luckless priests paid the ultimate price of their obstinacy: 'According to information to the *Corriere della Sera* from Cologne via London, it is confirmed that the barbaric conquerors of Antwerp punished the unfortunate Belgian priests for their heroic refusal to ring the church bells by hanging them as live clappers to the bells with their heads down.'[22]

Regardless of the true facts, Britain's War Propaganda Bureau quickly turned the stories from the Bryce Report into various forms of anti-German propaganda.

A poster published by the British Empire Union warned 'Once a German always a German' and showed various drawings of uniformed, moustachioed Huns in the act of committing atrocities that by now had become familiar to all – bayoneting a baby, torching a poor home, getting drunk on champagne while eyeing up a cowering young woman preparatory to rape, executing a wounded Tommy by firing squad, and torpedoing unarmed British merchant vessels.

Perhaps the most vicious poster of all shows a German nurse standing beside a wounded British soldier, lying in his poor makeshift sick-bed, under the watchful eye of a smirking Kaiser and one of his portly, overfed generals. According to the caption, 'Wounded and a prisoner our soldier cries for water. The German "sister" pours it on the ground before his eyes. There is no woman in Britain who would do it. There is no woman in Britain who will forget it.' As advertised, the German nurse pours water onto the ground while the helpless wounded Tommy stretches out his arm begging for a drink.

Apart from the appalling crudity and mendacity of the image, it is difficult to see precisely what the authors of this poster hoped to achieve, other than to instil into British women a hatred of all Germans that would last a lifetime. Whether the intention or not, that is pretty much what this poster and those like it did achieve.

Many people will respond to an analysis of this sort by saying: 'So what? It was total war – us or them. All's fair in war. In any case, everyone knows what bastards the German soldiers were. We were only responding in kind.'

Arthur Ponsonby tells us with stark clarity why such a response is misguided; 'If [lies] were only used to deceive the enemy in the game of war it would not be worth troubling about. But, as the purpose of most of them is to fan indignation and induce the flower of the country's youth to be ready to make the supreme sacrifice, it becomes a serious matter.'[23]

Propaganda lies are lies that kill innocent people – usually the youngest and most easily influenced.

A second problem with the dismissive response to propaganda is that it ignores the damage done to public credibility. If it is acceptable for a government department to lie to the public in certain extreme circumstances, where do we draw the line? If the justification for lying is that it was done from the best of motives, to achieve the greatest good for the greatest number, then the groundwork has been laid for a permanent official culture of lying from the best of motives whenever it is nationally expedient to resort to dishonesty – or as Cabinet secretary Robert Armstrong so memorably put it in 1986, being 'economical with the truth'.

In practice, this is precisely the legacy that the First World War did leave for subsequent generations: the casual dismissal of official announcements with the words 'it's only government propaganda'.

Looking closely at Anglo-German relationships before and after the First War, it seems clear that it was the harm done by the propaganda war that proved to be the most damaging and the most persistent in the long run. To be sure, the personal agony and destruction caused by trench fighting, unrestricted submarine warfare, and aerial bombing of civilian targets created lasting physical and emotional trauma for individuals and lasting enmity between the nations. But the indelible memory of atrocity stories that had taken place only in the imaginations of British propaganda agents proved to be stronger and more persistent than any facts. This curious discovery, the power of myths over facts, was the real legacy of the First War, and it was to prove one of the most important influences on future Anglo-German relations from both the British and the German points of view.

And it wasn't only in Europe that these after-effects remained to influence future events. Propaganda was a genie that proved even more difficult to get back into the bottle in the United States.

The German Information Bureau and the secret British War Propaganda Bureau had identical targets for their activities. In a world war, they naturally projected their messages to a world audience, but the big prize, of course, was the USA. Could America be persuaded to come into the war on the Allied side? Or could she be persuaded to remain neutral permanently? This question would ultimately decide the outcome of the war. And it was a question that in turn resolved itself into a competition not between battleships or battalions but rather between the civilians concocting propaganda campaigns in Whitehall and Berlin.

In the end, the question of US involvement was decided by a spectacular propaganda own-goal by Berlin when, at the insistence of Admiral von Tirpitz and the war faction, Germany resumed unrestricted submarine warfare in 1917. The German High Command gambled that they could starve England into submission and a negotiated peace before America could react and mobilise an army in Europe. The gamble was fatally miscalculated – American ships were sunk at sea by U-boats, and outraged US public opinion demanded immediate action.

5

The Sorcerer's Apprentice

By 1917, Germany had devoted three years to relentless propaganda with a single aim: keeping America out of the war. When these efforts failed and the US finally mobilised its military forces to aid Britain and France, America itself became embroiled in this new kind of warfare, the battle for control of public opinion.

But unlike Britain and Germany, where propaganda was still a sportsmanlike pastime for gentlemen authors and Machiavellian politicians, in the United States the shaping of democratic public opinion was already an embryonic professional business system. The coming of war would transform the infant business of persuasion in America into one of the most powerful and dangerous propaganda techniques of the 20th century, and one that would be revisited upon the Allies two decades later with horrifying results.

When America entered the war on 6 April 1917, the country was still split over the issue of whether to fight. Less than a year earlier, President Woodrow Wilson had been re-elected for a second term by standing on a ticket reminding voters that he 'had kept them out of the war'. In Washington it was clear that those Americans who still doubted the wisdom of joining the war had to be won over in the interests of national unity – and there was the broken promise to be squared with the voters.

Within days of declaring war on Germany, on 13 April 1917, Wilson ordered the setting up of the Committee on Public Information – the CPI – both to sell the war to Americans and to publicise America's war aims abroad. Unlike Britain three years earlier, the US knew what to expect from the global German propaganda machine, as it had already been subjected to its full force. The CPI was therefore plentifully supplied with resources including a staff of 100, recruited from press, advertising, films, business, the arts and the academic world. At the head of the new organisation Wilson placed George Creel, a charismatic 40-year-old journalist with a reputation for gutsy investigative reporting – or tabloid muck-raking, depending on whose point of view you accept.[1]

Perhaps because of the success of some German propagandists in the US, Creel acted almost at once to gag the US press, which traditionally had enjoyed complete freedom. As a journalist, Creel had been a champion of this freedom, but as poacher turned gamekeeper he proved something of a tyrant. Warning of the threat posed by German propaganda, Creel issued 'voluntary guidelines' for the news media and helped inspire Congress to pass the Espionage Act of 1917 and the Sedition Act of 1918. The CPI itself had no legal powers to enforce the Acts, but its influence was so great that it amounted to censorship. Like journalists today who gain access to the parliamentary lobby in return for surrendering freedom to publish whatever they please, American journalists grudgingly complied with the CPI's guidelines in order to avoid being frozen out of official press briefings. Publications who refused to toe the line – such as the radical newspaper *Appeal to Reason* – were virtually killed off by being starved of information. In practice, the CPI was a virtual press censorship organisation just like its British counterpart.[2]

While acting to control what the domestic papers could print, Creel also started a steady flow of official press releases, the first of which, in June 1917, was grotesquely egotistical and over the top. The release began:

> *Official Announcement by the US Government Press Bureau Regarding Destroyers by George Creel, June 1917*
> Accompanying the first US Transport Fleet to France German submarines attacked the transports in force. They were outfought by the American escorting destroyers, and at least one submarine was destroyed.
>
> No American ship was hit, and not a life lost. The German submarines attacked twice. On both occasions the U-boats were beaten off with every appearance of loss. One boat was certainly sunk, and there is reason to believe that the accurate fire of our gunners sent others to the bottom.[3]

It was widely suspected that this heroic first action at sea was a complete invention by Creel and his department, and it led to widespread outrage to which Creel responded by toning down future releases. After this shaky start, the CPI's news division ultimately distributed more than 6,000 press releases and was the primary channel of war news for the American press. Creel, who loved to brag, claimed that in any given week more than 20,000 newspaper columns were filled with material originating in CPI press handouts.

Like Masterman in Britain, Creel managed to recruit prominent writers and academics to voice their support for the war. Famous names like John Dewey and Walter

Lippmann were among his recruits, but some academics refused to toe the party line. One of Dewey's students, Randolph Bourne, wrote with savage irony: 'The German intellectuals went to war to save their culture from barbarisation and the French went to war to save their beautiful France! ... Are not our intellectuals equally fatuous when they tell us that our war of all wars is stainless and thrillingly achieving for good?'[4]

The CPI's division of Pictorial Publicity turned out material from a studio full of advertising illustrators and artists who worked closely with people in the Advertising Division. Newspapers were full of CPI-generated adverts and striking posters were plastered on billboards across the country, urging men to join the navy and everyone to buy war bonds. There were CPI photographs of Americans in action, too, but as in Britain there was a complete ban on showing dead bodies of US soldiers. Many US audiences gained the subliminal impression during the war that no Americans were killed on the Western Front – in fact, the butcher's bill was well in excess of 100,000 dead.

The Division of Films ensured that the war was promoted in the cinema through both newsreels and feature films. Films with titles such as *The Kaiser: The Beast of Berlin*, *Wolves of Kultur* and *Pershing's Crusaders* were widely shown in American cinemas. One film, *To Hell With The Kaiser*, was so successful that Massachusetts riot police had to quell an angry mob that had been turned away from a full picture house.

Among the many experts who volunteered their services for the CPI was a Broadway press agent who, despite being only 26, had already landed some major clients, had established a growing reputation as a publicity prodigy, and who was destined to play an important role in the future of

Anglo-German relations. The young man was Edward Bernays, the Viennese-born nephew of Sigmund Freud. Bernays would prove to have an influence on the 20th century that was arguably greater than that of his famous uncle.[5]

Bernays' mother was Freud's sister, while his father's sister was Freud's wife, Martha – a double family bond. During visits to Europe, he was a member of Freud's inner circle and was privy to his early success and celebrity. Bernays had no medical training but his natural gifts and his conversations during walks with Uncle Sigmund enabled him to gain an intuitive grasp of the practical application of Freud's discovery of the unconscious mind and the systematic analysis of unconscious motivations. What Bernays did in the course of an astoundingly long and varied career (he died in 1996 aged 104 and was still working in the 1990s) was to take the psychological theories of his uncle and translate them into publicity and marketing strategies to influence the public's unconscious minds, in a process he would later call 'the engineering of consent'.

Bernays' first publicity triumph came in 1915 when he was employed by ballet impresario Serge Diaghilev to promote the American tour of the Ballets Russes and its star dancer, Nijinsky. The problem, Bernays found, was that middle-America felt dancing was decadent and saw male dancers as effeminate perverts. He equipped an army of advance men in every stop on the tour with publicity material to use with the local press, taught them how to tailor national stories for local consumption, and provided them with a question and answer sheet which asked: 'Are American men ashamed to be graceful?' The result was a hugely successful tour for Diaghilev that was quickly followed by contracts for Bernays to act as press agent to famous names like Florenz Ziegfeld and Enrico Caruso on Broadway.

In 1917, Bernays used his press contacts to get an interview with Ernest Pool, head of the Foreign Press Bureau of the CPI, and through this to get a job with the Bureau. Initially, Bernays' contribution to the war effort was straightforward press work – persuading American firms to distribute literature on American war aims to foreign contacts, and organising rallies at Carnegie Hall for freedom fighters from Poland, Slovakia and other states keen to shake off Austro-Hungarian rule. He also applied his skills as a spin doctor to war propaganda, and is credited with having written the patriotic slogan 'Make the world safe for democracy', later to become enshrined as one of President Woodrow Wilson's famous 'Fourteen Points' that he wished to make the basis of the Treaty of Versailles.[6]

It was at the end of the war that he made the greatest impact on events, although he also made a rare error when he fell foul of public opinion. Bernays was appointed as a member of the sixteen-strong CPI press team that accompanied President Wilson on his visit to Europe in 1919, following the armistice. Before the team set sail for Europe, Bernays issued a press release announcing the mission, and the *New York World* ran a story based on the release, saying that:

> The announced object of the mission is to 'interpret the work of the Peace Conference by keeping up a world wide propaganda to disseminate American accomplishments and ideals.'[7]

Using the word 'propaganda' so casually in a peacetime context was lighting a very short fuse in Washington. Republicans in Congress pounced on the press announcement as evidence that Creel and his CPI were still running a censorship regime even though hostilities were over, and were using the CPI to improve the press coverage of Wilson, a Democratic President. Creel retorted that the mission was not intended to influence American reports, merely those of overseas nations.

This backlash was part of the reassertion of American isolationism now that the war was over, and evidence of a profound desire to consign the wartime apparatus of propaganda and censorship to the past – a desire that culminated in the refusal of Congress to ratify the charter of the League of Nations.

But if Bernays made a rare error of judgement in disclosing the real nature of his mission to Paris, he more than made up for it in organising for Woodrow Wilson the kind of reception he had arranged in the past for showbiz clients like Nijinsky and Caruso. As a result, Wilson was greeted like a hero by rapturous crowds wherever he went and was soon established in the mind of the international press corps at Versailles as the most visionary world statesman present, making it possible for him to dictate much of the agenda at the Versailles peace conference and the adoption of his 'Fourteen Points' a much easier task.

This kind of approach to publicity was a novel experience for the staid British and French civil servants who accompanied their national delegations and whose contacts with the press were confined to handing out communiqués written in dull bureaucratic jargon. They saw this kind of press manipulation as mere fairground ballyhoo, yet, already, they had fundamentally mistaken what Bernays had achieved.

For what Bernays had learnt at the CPI was to avoid the kind of direct approach that had got Creel into trouble with his first efforts and that had made much German propaganda resented by American audiences. Instead, Bernays realised, it was far more effective to set up stories that the press was bound to cover because it wanted to, rather than because it was being spoon-fed with information or because its arm was being twisted. This is a fundamental principle that many government PR people still have not learned even today.

In 1919, after the peace conference, Bernays returned to ordinary commercial life, except that now he had a brand new set of business ideas to try out. He later wrote: 'It was, of course, the astounding success of propaganda during the war that opened the eyes of the intelligent few in all departments of life to the possibilities of regimenting the public mind. It was only natural, after the war ended, that intelligent persons should ask themselves whether it was not possible to apply a similar technique to the problems of peace.'[8]

Bernays not only had a new set of ideas, he also had a brand new name for them. When he opened his office in Madison Avenue in 1919, the sign on his door described him not as a Press Agent but as a Counsel in something called Public Relations – the term he himself coined to replace the already loaded word propagandist. He had little difficulty selling his counselling services to some of America's biggest corporations. His first big account, and the one for which he was remembered long afterwards, was Lucky Strike cigarettes. The manufacturers realised that they could double their market if only the taboo against women smoking could be broken down and overcome. His solution was not to approach the press directly, but instead to organise a stunt they would be bound to cover – a march of women, many of them very attractive, through the streets of New York carrying placards announcing a 'March for Freedom' and openly smoking cigarettes. He cleverly exploited the desire of women for greater liberty, and turned smoking into a symbol of that desire. Any woman who wished to assert her individuality had only to light up in public, while anyone criticising women smoking in future would be seen as against greater freedom for women. The campaign was highly successful and spread both via the press and through the various women's movements. Sales of Luckies skyrocketed as women asserted their independence by taking up smoking.

In the 1920s, Bernays continued to use Freudian psychology to design campaigns of mass public persuasion for a number of clients. He described his campaigns in these words: 'If we understand the mechanism and motives of the group mind, it is now possible to control and regiment the masses according to our will without their knowing it.' He called this scientific moulding of opinion the 'engineering of consent'.[9]

He continued to act indirectly on leading opinion-formers, rather than directly on the media. 'If you can influence the leaders, either with or without their conscious co-operation', he said, 'you automatically influence the group which they sway.'[10] He carried out campaigns for Procter & Gamble, CBS, General Electric, Dodge Motors. It was inevitable that, sooner or later, he would turn his techniques back to politics and in 1924 he was hired by Calvin Coolidge to run his publicity campaign for the Presidential election. With Bernays 'engineering consent' for him, Coolidge easily won, with 54 per cent of the popular vote.

Bernays wrote three books setting out his ideas: *Crystallizing Public Opinion*, *Propaganda* and *The*

Engineering of Consent. The first two were published in 1923 and 1928. Initially, they had little social impact other than to cause the same kind of affront to bourgeois values that Niccolò Machiavelli's *Address to the Prince* had caused five hundred years earlier. It was not long, however, before they were discovered by someone who understood their real meaning and who was capable of transforming their content into policies that would have far-reaching consequences – greater than even Bernays could ever have imagined.

6

Engineering of Consent

Like the guns of the Western Front, the war of words between Germany and Britain fell silent with the signing of the armistice in 1918, but the effects of the propaganda war did not come to such an abrupt end. The desks, the typewriters, and the telephones were returned to dull civilian tasks, and the secret records were filed away in basement registries. But the seeds planted in wartime continued to bear fruit in post-war years with consequences both unexpected and dramatic.

The first was that Edward Bernays took the lessons he had learned in 'engineering consent' and used these new techniques of manipulation for commercial and political rather than military purposes when he founded the modern PR and advertising industry in Madison Avenue. It was his application of these techniques to mass marketing that, more than any other single factor, led to the almost continual increase in consumer sales for the rest of the 20th century and to the creation of the consumer society where industrial growth is king.

It has even been seriously suggested that blame for the Wall Street Crash of 1929 belongs at least in part to the runaway success of Bernays' marketing techniques in the 1920s. It was argued that from 1919 on, east coast banks such as Lehman Brothers invested heavily in the setting up of department stores, retail and mail order businesses, confident that they could create demand for a whole range of household goods by manipulating consumer demand using Bernays' techniques. So great was the demand that they created, with consequent boosting of manufacturing production, that the banks were encouraged to advance massive credit to buyers. There was nothing to regulate the burgeoning cycle of production–buying–investment–credit which expanded, uncontrolled, into a massive credit bubble. It was this bubble that finally burst in 1929 when market confidence faltered.

Whatever the truth of this theory, no one can doubt that in the longer term, from 1920 to the 1960s (when Prime Minister Harold Macmillan was quoted by one British newspaper as claiming: 'You've never had it so good'), industrial production continued to grow on the strength of credit-driven consumer spending, and that the sales and marketing end of the funnel was greased by Bernays' brand of soft soap.

The second consequence was that Bernays' new techniques for mass manipulation so impressed a young German radical politician that he took them and adapted them to his political campaigning. The young radical was Joseph Goebbels. In this extraordinary, roundabout way, one of the most successful innovations of the First World War became an essential tool in laying the foundations for the Second.

It is a commonplace observation that Goebbels took the techniques of modern propaganda and used them very effectively to put Hitler in power and consolidate his position into that of unchallenged dictator. I have a strong suspicion that for many people this statement is likely to be interpreted to mean something along the lines of: 'Goebbels was a very clever and unscrupulous little fellow who told lots of lies and was believed. Of course, the Germans are very gullible and were used to doing as they were told. It would never work over here.'

An interpretation of this sort misunderstands fundamentally what Goebbels did, and also underestimates the magnitude of his achievement (if one can apply such a word to such a man). It would be comforting to think that much of what Goebbels accomplished rested merely on telling lies or on intuitive opportunism. It is rather more disturbing to recognise that his achievements rested on a rigorously analytical understanding of what Germans wanted to hear, and on reinterpreting political policies so that they matched these public yearnings – the same method that has been used by every British and American political party since 1945.

That Goebbels was influenced by Bernays and the techniques developed by the US Committee on Public Information from 1917–19 is attested to by Bernays himself. Though a Jew, he seems to have taken a perverse pride in the influence he had on the Nazis. In his autobiography, *Biography of an Idea*, Bernays recalls a dinner held at his home in 1933 at which he entertained Karl von Weigand, foreign correspondent of the Hearst newspaper chain. Weigand, said Bernays, had

... just returned from Germany, [and] was telling us about Goebbels and his propaganda plans to consolidate Nazi power. Goebbels had shown Weigand his propaganda library, the best Weigand had ever seen. Goebbels, said Weigand, was using my book *Crystallizing Public Opinion* as a basis for his destructive campaign against the Jews of Germany. This shocked me. ... Obviously the attack on the Jews of Germany was no emotional outburst of the Nazis, but a deliberate, planned campaign.[1]

Perhaps the most extraordinary thing about Edward Bernays' propaganda and PR techniques is that they were so innovative that they are still not widely understood even today. When he was interviewed by journalist Stuart Ewen shortly before his death in 1996, Bernays made an astonishing admission. When asked by Ewen to describe how he set about planning a specific public relations assignment, Bernays revealed that he had made no direct contact with the mass media for 50 years. A PR man who doesn't even talk to the press? What's going on?

In the early days of his new Madison Avenue agency in the early 1920s, Bernays was retained by the Beech-Nut Packaging Company of New York, a seller of pre-packaged bacon. How he turned Beech-Nut into a major nationally-known US brand illustrates very clearly the indirect techniques that he pioneered. First he conducted a survey of doctors, asking them how important they considered a hearty breakfast to be to the general health and well-being of their patients. Unsurprisingly, an overwhelming majority of medical men surveyed declared that a good breakfast was essential to healthy living.

Bernays circulated the results of the survey to 5,000 local doctors nationwide, together with a pack of material containing medical-sounding background on the nutritional value of the traditional breakfast of bacon and eggs.

Finally, he had the medical survey results indirectly leaked to the media without attribution. Before long, journalists throughout America, sensing an off-beat human interest feature, were phoning their local physicians to ask about what kind of breakfast they considered best for health. In most cases, they were told that it was hard to beat bacon and eggs. Because the stories had been 'originated' by the individual journalists in response to the survey, they carried the full weight of objective, independent reporting. Bacon sales soared and Beech-Nut's revenues climbed with them. Nobody even suspected that the question had been planted in their minds, much less that the answer had been planted even before the question.

Part of Bernays' style seems to have been a personal obsession with secrecy and behind-the-scenes influences. Perhaps this is the reason he took so readily to his Uncle Sigmund's theories of an unconscious mind – a hidden mind, influencing people in unsuspected ways to act out concealed motives of which even they themselves are not consciously aware. Bernays seems to have considered himself the unconscious mind of the entire nation.

As well as the indirect approach, Bernays also made use of the unconscious connotations carried by common words. He pointed out that in Britain, during the First War, 'evacuation hospitals' dealing with the wounded coming home from the Western Front came in for widespread press criticism because of the summary way in which they processed these casualties. 'It was assumed by the public', he said, 'that a hospital gives prolonged and conscientious attention to its patients. When the name was changed to evacuation posts, the critical reaction vanished. No one expected more than an adequate emergency treatment from an institution so named.'

But, while hyping bacon sales and changing hospital signs are interesting case histories, it is the application of his techniques to politics and politicians that is of real interest, and the process that fascinated Goebbels. In his 1928 book *Propaganda*, Bernays wrote that:

> No serious sociologist any longer believes that the voice of the people expresses any divine or specially wise and lofty idea. The voice of the people expresses the mind of the people, and that mind is made up for it by the group leaders in whom it believes and by those people who understand the manipulation of public opinion. It is composed of inherited prejudices and symbols and clichés and verbal formulas supplied to them by the leaders.[2]

Bernays pointed out that, while US businesses had grasped the importance of studying and understanding its customers in order to be able to influence them, politicians were still virgins by comparison when it came to influencing voters.

> It is, indeed incomprehensible that politicians do not make use of the elaborate business methods that the industry has built up. Because a politician knows political strategy, can develop campaign issues, can devise strong planks for platforms and envisage broad policies, it does not follow that he can be given the responsibility of selling ideas to a public as large as that of the United States. The politician understands the public. He knows what the public wants and what the public will accept. But the politician is not necessarily a general sales manager, a public relations counsel, or a man who knows how to secure mass distribution of ideas.[3]

If political leaders wish to be as successful at selling themselves and their policies as businessmen are at selling cigarettes, or bacon, then they must be prepared to undertake strategic marketing, Bernays told them.

> Big business is conducted on the principle that it must prepare its policies carefully, and that in selling an idea to the large buying public of America, it must proceed according to broad plans. The political strategist must do likewise. The entire campaign should be worked out according to broad basic plans. Platforms, planks, pledges, budgets, activities, personalities, must be as carefully studied, apportioned and used as they are when big business desires to get what it wants from the public. The first step in a political campaign is to determine the objectives and to express them exceedingly well in the current form – that is, as a platform. In devising the platform the leader should be sure that it is an honest platform. Campaign pledges and promises should not be lightly considered by the public, and they ought to carry something of the guarantee principle and money-back policy that an honourable business institution carries with the sale of its goods. The public has lost faith in campaign promotion work. It does not say that politicians are dishonourable, but it does say that campaign pledges are written on the sand. Here then is one fact of public opinion of which the party that wishes to be successful might well take cognizance.[4]

As well as Freud's theory of the unconscious, Bernays was also familiar with the contemporary ideas of Gustave le Bon and Wilfred Trotter on the dynamics of what had become called the 'group mind'. But again, Bernays' understanding of the group mind was his own secretive version. Groups, he thought, were not just crowds in the street, but suburban man and woman going about their business as individuals.

If you can influence the leaders, either with or without their conscious cooperation, you automatically influence the group that they sway. But men do not need to be actually gathered together in a public meeting or in a street riot, to be subject to the influence of mass psychology. Because man is by nature gregarious he feels himself to be a member of a herd, even when he is alone in his room with the curtains drawn. His mind retains the patterns which have been stamped on it by the group influences.

Trotter and le Bon concluded that the group mind does not *think* in the strict sense of the word. In place of thoughts it has impulses, habits and emotions. In making up its mind, its first impulse is usually to follow the example of a trusted leader. This is one of the most firmly established principles of mass psychology. It operates in establishing the rising or diminishing prestige of a summer resort, in causing a run on the bank, or a panic on the stock exchange, in creating a best seller, or a box-office success.[5]

Once can almost hear Bernays adding, under his breath, 'or the election of the President of the United States' – a feat that he had achieved only four years earlier when he helped elect Calvin Coolidge in the 1924 Presidential election.

It is interesting that Bernays recommends honesty as the best way of overcoming voter cynicism and disenchantment. It was precisely this aspect of Bernays' *Propaganda* that – contrary to the received image – Goebbels picked up on and employed with outstanding success, as described in Chapter 17. There can be no doubt that Hitler, Goebbels and other Nazi leaders told barefaced lies when it was expedient to do so. But for the carefully analysed and thought-out programmes that were the centre-pieces of events like the Nuremberg rallies, Goebbels put the truth into Hitler's mouth. This was recognised by the German people who responded with their wholehearted support.

I believe that to say, as some commentators have, that the German people were misled or fooled by Hitler is to misunderstand the genius of Nazi propaganda techniques. The Nazis went to great trouble to understand what ordinary Germans wanted – a task that was greatly simplified for them by the short-sightedly punitive Versailles Treaty, with its insistence on exclusively German war guilt, and its demands for crippling reparations. The Nazis went to even more trouble to align government policies with what they had determined the man and woman on the Düsseldorf omnibus wanted. And this was done not merely with the kind of superficiality that policies are dished out with today ('this tax break will please the single mothers'), but to such a depth that when Hitler spoke at mass rallies, he wasn't promising tax cuts, he was speaking to the heart and soul of the German people, promising them national greatness.

Bernays clearly saw how potentially powerful were the techniques for manipulating mass psychology that he originated. Equally, he recognised how perfectly suited they were to selling politics. But even he could never have foreseen the extent to which his techniques would be taken and used by the Nazis.

In the 1930s, Bernays' methods were developed into the means of making Nazi ideology the most widely accepted political doctrine among the majority of German people, giving a unity of purpose to Germans that they had lacked since 1914. Yet, although such sophisticated propaganda techniques were not employed by the government in England in peacetime, it is remarkable how the same, or closely similar, ideas were taken up in the 1920s and 30s by a significant section of the English ruling classes. Even more remarkable is the fact that the main lines of German policy pursued by the Nazis between the wars were not, as they are often perceived, essentially Germanic in origin. Rather Nazism was firmly rooted in pseudo-scientific beliefs that originated in England and were nurtured by English intellectuals and writers. How this remarkable convergence of ideas and ideals came about is a convoluted tale of pseudo-science, snobbery and sadism on a national scale.

Part Two

The Roots of Unreason, 1919–39

7

The Master Race

Anglo-German relations in the 1930s were dominated by the policies of Hitler and the Nazis to the extent that British foreign policy was devoted largely to the appeasement of Nazi Germany. Yet the German domestic and foreign policies that Britain strived so hard to appease were themselves rooted in a series of irrational and unscientific beliefs that became elevated to the status of national policy because they enjoyed the personal support of Hitler, Himmler and other leading Nazis. On one hand, those beliefs involved ideas of the superman and the triumph of his will over the mediocrity of the masses. On the other, they involved racist eugenics policies and ideas of Aryan ethnic supremacy conferring a historic destiny to rule a world empire.

To find the roots of these irrational Nazi beliefs, you have to go back, not to German thinkers, but to the beliefs and writings of prominent Englishmen of the 19th century, men such as Charles Darwin, Thomas Huxley, Francis Galton, and Houston Stewart Chamberlain. And not only were these ideas English rather than German in origin, but they were enthusiastically embraced and put into practice in the years between the wars in Britain and many of the other great powers, including the United States.

Among the most fundamental sources of Germany's long love affair with England was the question of race and blood, and German belief in deep-rooted kinship with the English people. The theoretical basis for this belief sprang from 19th-century ideas that were fostered and cross-fertilised in both countries – but for very different reasons.

A seminal event for both nations was the publication in 1859 of Charles Darwin's *On the Origin of Species* and its 1871 sequel, *The Descent of Man*.[1] In these works Darwin proposed that evolution is driven by natural selection, the survival of the fittest.

The struggle for survival, said Darwin, means that many more individuals of every species are born than can possibly survive, so only those individuals best fitted or best adapted to their environment will live to produce offspring. The less well adapted, the unfit, will merely perish and not reproduce. This iron law, Darwin believed, was an inescapable scale in which nature weighs every individual, and it was as true for humans as it was for mosquitoes or sardines.

But Darwin's idea of natural selection as the driver of human evolution also included racist assumptions as an essential component from the outset. Like many white Englishmen of the 19th century, Darwin and his principal scientific supporter, Thomas Huxley, took it for granted that whites are physically and mentally superior to other races. They envisaged the various tribes of humans on the planet as representing a spectrum of evolutionary development with the white European race at the top, Asian people somewhere in the middle, and the coarse, barbaric aborigines of Australia and Africa at the bottom of the evolutionary tree.

These stone-age people with their crude features, small brains, grunting language and primitive lifestyles, Darwin believed, were most closely related to apes and were destined to become extinct, replaced by the more advanced white race. Thomas Huxley observed that:

> No rational man, cognizant of the facts, believes that the negro is the equal, still less the superior, of the white man.[2]

In *The Descent of Man,* Darwin indicated his belief that the negro races were more closely related to the apes than white people when he wrote:

> At some future period, not very distant as measured by centuries, the civilised races of man will almost certainly exterminate and replace the savage races throughout the world. The break between man and his nearest allies will then be wider, for it will intervene between man in a more civilised state, as we may hope, even than the caucasian, and some ape as low as a baboon, instead of as now between the negro or Australian and the gorilla.[3]

Darwin also accepted and repeated a misconception common among scientists of his day that the 'savages' of Africa and Australia were unable to count higher than four or to grasp any abstract concept because their primitive languages lacked the necessary vocabulary.

> No doubt the difference in this respect [human mental powers] is enormous even if we compare the mind of one of the lowest savages, who has no words to express any number higher than four, and who uses hardly any abstract terms for common objects, or for the affections, with that of the most highly organised ape.[4]

I wonder how Darwin would have replied if told that, in 2007, the Professor of Indigenous Studies at the Australian National University would be Mick Dodson, of Aboriginal descent, who not only managed to count higher than four but has obtained degrees in Law and Jurisprudence and a Doctorate in Letters from Sydney University.

What is especially noteworthy about these views is that, at the time they were expressed, there was not the faintest trace of any scientific evidence in support of them apart from purely ideological Darwinist thinking, yet the remarks were made in a scientific context as though they were scientifically-based views, and were widely accepted as such. This in turn created what seemed like a wider scientific context into which other equally bogus racist ideas were planted and flourished later on.[5]

Darwin's ideas chimed perfectly with the racist, imperialist tenor of the mid-Victorian age in Britain and also caught the same spirit of the age in Germany, where they were enthusiastically received and taken up, and where his greatest champion was Ernst Haeckel, who promoted Darwinism as keenly in Germany as Thomas Huxley did in Britain. Haeckel was appointed Professor of Biology at Jena University in 1862, and he popularised Darwin's ideas to a succession of German audiences from the 1880s until his death in 1919. He originally trained as a medical doctor, but abandoned medicine on reading Darwin's *On the Origin of Species* in 1859 and took up the study of evolutionary biology instead. Haeckel studied the development of embryos and noticed some similarities between the embryos of animals as different as dog, rabbit, pig and sheep. From this he formulated what he called the 'biogenetic law', by which he meant that the embryo of any species repeats during its development the evolution of its entire ancestral tribe. If true, this would appear to be strong direct evidence of Darwinian evolutionary processes at work. So persuasive was the idea that Haeckel converted most Darwinists to it – including Charles Darwin himself. Haeckel wrote:

> When we see that at a certain stage the embryos of man and the ape, the dog and rabbit, the pig and sheep, though recognisable as vertebrates, cannot be distinguished from each other, the fact can only be elucidated by assuming a common parentage ... I have illustrated this significant fact by a juxtaposition of corresponding stages in the development of different vertebrates in my *Natural History of Creation.*[6]

There was, however, a problem with Haeckel's theory. The remarkable similarity between the various embryos in his illustration arose not from nature but from the fact that Haeckel had embellished his own drawings of them – editing some parts out and adding parts that didn't exist – to make them look similar. In reality, the embryos of humans, apes, dogs, rabbits, pigs and sheep are not the same but differ crucially in important details.

Haeckel was eventually charged with academic fraud by a university court at Jena. Although he admitted altering his drawings, Haeckel escaped being dismissed or even disgraced. In 1908, he defended himself in a Berlin newspaper by saying:

> To cut short this unsavoury dispute, I begin at once with my contrite confession that a small fraction of my drawings of embryos (perhaps six or eight per cent) are in a sense falsified – all those, namely, for which the present material of observation is so incomplete or insufficient

as to compel us, when we come to prepare a continuous chain of evolutionary stages, to fill up the gaps by hypotheses and to reconstruct the missing links by comparative synthesis.[7]

What is perhaps most revealing about Haeckel's frauds is that they show an otherwise honest and careful scientist becoming so convinced that Darwin's ideas are self-evidently true, despite the lack of scientific evidence supporting them, that he sees nothing wrong with helping to provide the missing evidence, for the greater good of science. Even more extraordinary is that Haeckel was able to convince Darwin himself of the validity of his 'biogenetic law', even with no real evidence to support it. Such is the power of scientific myths. This same process of self-delusion was to be frequently repeated over the coming decades and to affect otherwise rational individuals in Germany and England as the ideas of Darwin and Haeckel influenced the thinking of successive generations of scientists.

Through modern DNA techniques, we now know that 19th-century racist evolutionary ideas are without any basis in fact. Indeed, all the races of mankind are so closely related to each other genetically that we are not merely members of the same species, but members of the same sub-species. Research in genetics has revealed that there is greater genetic variation *within* ethnic groups than there is *between* ethnic groups. In other words, all humans, whether white, black, brown or yellow, are as closely related as, say, all Golden Retrievers, or all Shetland ponies. Genetically, we are all as peas in a pod.[8]

Some 30 years after Darwin shocked the Victorian world with his 'scientific' discoveries, a near relative of his shocked them all over again with equally convincing – and equally flawed – scientific thinking.

In 1889, Francis Galton dared to suggest that ability was not the result of education and nurture, but of inheritance alone – that there is an entire spectrum of genetic endowments from the highest intelligence in the land to the lowest and that, consequently, greatness was not merely the prerogative of those of royal birth but was within the reach of anyone of superior pedigree. The king's subjects might be equal, but some were more equal than others, and, said Galton, there exists a kind of natural genetic aristocracy, every bit as real as the aristocracy of the landed gentry.

Galton became convinced that character and ability are primarily inherited rather than learned, and it was this thesis that he set out to prove in his 1889 book, *Natural Inheritance*. He wrote:

> I have no patience with the hypothesis occasionally expressed, and often implied, especially in tales written to teach children to be good, that babies are born pretty much alike, and that the sole agencies in creating differences between boy and boy, and man and man, are steady application and moral effort. It is in the most unqualified manner that I object to pretensions of natural equality. The experiences of the nursery, the school, the University, and of professional careers, are a chain of proofs to the contrary.[9]

Galton based much of his thinking on his personal inherited characteristics and the pedigree of his own and other famous families, which he considered to be superior to that of the common man. He was also a grandson of Erasmus Darwin and hence cousin of Charles. Galton had seized on Darwin's book and said that he

... devoured its contents and assimilated them as fast as they were devoured, a fact which may be ascribed to an hereditary bent of mind that both its illustrious author and myself have inherited from our common grandfather, Dr Erasmus Darwin.[10]

An idea of the quality of Galton's scientific thinking can be gained from his attempts to measure intelligence in human subjects. He set up an 'Anthropometric Laboratory' at the International Health Exhibition in London in 1884. Here he charged visitors to the show three pence to learn how clever they were, but rather than administer any kind of intelligence test, Galton took a number of body measurements, including their skull size, and issued them with a score card giving them his opinion of their ability, based on physical characteristics.

Like Darwin and Huxley, Galton was a racist. Of course, it is true that many of his European contemporaries at this time were also racist in outlook in a casual, almost unthinking way, and it would be arbitrary to single out Galton for judgement by the standards of today. But the fact remains that he was responsible, as one of the leading scientific voices of his age, for promoting the unwarranted and unscientific assumption that black people are less intelligent than white people, and that white people are thus superior. Once you have taken that leap intellectually, it is only a small step further to concluding that it would be better for everyone if the government were composed of white people alone, or that the coloured people of the world are better off being governed by whites – assumptions that did indeed underlie European colonial imperialism.

Galton accepted Darwin's theory of evolution by natural selection and took it one step further. If nature produced individuals better and better adapted to life through natural selection, the struggle for survival, then how much better still to eliminate the haphazard trial-and-error methods of nature and apply artificial selection techniques to produce even better adapted species? This is, of course, precisely what the farmer or animal husbandry expert does when breeding a new strain of wheat or sheep. What Galton now proposed was applying animal husbandry techniques to breeding people.

Galton called this new 'science' eugenics, and he devoted the remainder of his life to fostering it. But eugenics had both a positive and a negative side. According to Galton and many of those who adopted his ideas, not only should genetically healthy people be encouraged to breed, because they would strengthen future generations, but genetically defective people should be discouraged from breeding because they would weaken future generations. Of course, this policy leaves open some rather important questions. What exactly is genetically desirable and what genetically defective? Who exactly was qualified to take these decisions? And, most crucial of all, what steps exactly should be taken to discourage or prevent breeding by genetically defective people? How far do you go?

Galton and the racial theorists who came after him believed that they knew the answers to these questions. The genetically most healthy individuals – those with the best pedigree and highest intelligence – were best qualified to decide who were defective and what should be done with them. The defectives should be discouraged from breeding and, if necessary, sterilised. What the world needed, Galton believed, was more people like himself: intelligent, well-bred, white people. For those people who have the misfortune not to be intelligent, physically fit and white, society should prescribe compulsory sterilisation, for the greater good of mankind as a whole. These views would be cause for concern in any educated group. Even more worrying, as described later, such views were espoused by many prominent members of the medical profession who flocked to support Galton's movement.

It took only a very small step from the views of Darwin, Huxley and Galton on white racial superiority to a further refinement – that of white-on-white racism. However, this was one step initiated not in Britain but in Germany. If the races of mankind represent a spectrum of evolutionary development, then the white race itself must also be such a spectrum of evolutionary progress. It followed that there must be a least-developed and a most highly developed stratum of humans among the white races, with, at the very top, the most highly evolved of all – a race which was to humans what Arab stallions are to horses or lions are to cats.

It was not German professors of anthropology or ethnology who supplied the missing candidate, but rather the German language scholars who had been puzzling over the origins of the ancient 'Aryan' language and had decided that its homeland was on their own doorstep in Germany and Scandinavia, in very much the same way that Galton had concluded that it was families like his own who carried the most desirable genetic inheritance.

The 'Aryan' race

At the beginning of the 19th century, Western linguists were hunting for the root tongue that they believed was ancestral to all European languages, including Greek, Latin and Anglo-Saxon. They found a major clue in the Zoroastrian scriptures, known as the *Zend Avesta*, written in the first millennium BC in a very ancient language, now identified as Avestan.

Avestan became the subject of intense interest among linguistic scholars, who realised that it was closely related to the ancient tongue of north India, Sanskrit, and hence could be a key to identifying the root language, the mother of all tongues. Studies of the Avestan and Sanskrit languages became the foundation of modern linguistics, which flourished throughout the 19th century, especially in Germany, where language scholars pursued an even more fascinating question: Who exactly were the people who spoke these early languages? Where was their homeland? For, surely, they must be the ancestors of the European people – our ancestors.

Although the quest had now become one for anthropologists or ethnologists, it was still linguistics that made the running. Both Avestan and Sanskrit have the word *Arya*, meaning 'noble person' or 'spiritual person'. Linguistics scholars thus named the speakers of the ancestral language Aryans. This term was understood to mean the ancestors of all present-day speakers of the Indo-European group of languages – roughly equivalent to 'white European'. The term excluded Jews and Arabs because their ancestral languages – Hebrew and Arabic – are not part of the Indo-European group, suggesting a different line of descent for Semitic people. In this innocent manner, the word Aryan became transformed from a purely technical name for a dead language into a racial description that was to have far-reaching consequences later.

Where, though, was the geographical origin of the Aryan-speaking people? Where was their homeland? The question was and still remains controversial.

The most widely accepted theory was that the people who spoke Aryan originated in the Asian Steppes, from which they migrated both west into Europe and south into Afghanistan, Iran, Pakistan and parts of northern India around 1800 BC. This widespread diffusion, it was thought, explained how the Indo-European languages became so widely adopted in Europe and Asia. This explanation also fitted with what was known of the people who inhabited the Steppes, who were essentially warlike nomads. The favoured model was thus one of displacement of earlier settlers by conquest.

German scholars in the 19th century, however, rejected the theory of an origin in the Russian Steppes and instead advanced their own theory. The Aryans, they said, had originated in ancient Germany and Scandinavia. They believed that the Aryans referred to in the Sanskrit Vedas were the Goths and the Vandals and other ancestral Germanic people whom they collectively called the *Volkwanderung*, or Wandering People. These were similar in character to the warlike nomads of the Steppes but had one crucial difference: they were Nordic in appearance and origin. One widely read Nazi science textbook that promoted this view was *Heredity and Racial Biology for Students* by Jakob Graf, which asserted that:

The Aryans (Nordic people) were tall, light-skinned, light-eyed, blond people. The Goths, Franks, Vandals, and Normans, too, were peoples of Nordic blood.

It was Nordic energy and boldness that were responsible for the power and prestige enjoyed by small nations such as the Netherlands and Sweden. Everywhere Nordic creative power has built up mighty empires with high-minded ideas, and to this very day Aryan languages and cultural values are spread over a large part of the world.[11]

Indeed, the 19th-century German scholars with whom these views originated went even further. Not only were the people in Germany and Scandinavia the true Aryans; so, too, were those of their tribe who had populated surrounding lands by conquest, displacing the indigenous peoples. So the Angles and Saxons and Jutes who had colonised England, driving the native Britons into the remoter corners of the British Isles, were also Aryans and hence Nordic first cousins of German blood, as were the Normans who conquered France and, later, England.

Between 1853 and 1855, French writer and diplomat Joseph Arthur de Gobineau published a four-volume work drawing together much of this thinking of the previous 50 years under the title *An Essay on the Inequality of the Human Races* – adding a unique slant of his own. Gobineau, a reactionary aristocrat who detested democracy and mass culture, put forward two ideas that were to become highly influential both in Germany and elsewhere. First, he said that the ancient Aryans were not merely a distinct tribe; they were a race that was separate from, and superior to, the rest of mankind – the master race. Gobineau also said that the rise of empires inevitably led to the mixing of races, with consequent degeneration of their societies. Because Aryans were the root race and racially pure, they were the only race capable of ruling, and fit to rule, the world. The Aryans were, he said, like Adam before the fall.

Gobineau intended his book as a timely warning to Aryans about the effects of intermixing on the purity of the race. 'We do not descend from the ape, but are headed in that direction', he said.[12]

These ideas were enthusiastically taken up in Germany and in Britain, but for rather different reasons and with rather different objectives. To the insular Germans (not yet united as a nation) Gobineau's ideas were taken to confirm Germanic racial unity, racial purity, and racial superiority. The Aryans had been ancient Germans or Nordic people. They had populated much of Europe and Asia over the past two millennia, no doubt mixing with the people they conquered, but in their northern homeland they remained racially pure – tall, blond, blue-eyed, the Teutonic Knights of legend. The fact that many Germans were short, podgy and dark-complexioned did not seem to undermine this theory in any way. Thus, to the Germans, Gobineau's ideas of a master race were seen as theoretical confirmation of the Germanic dream of world status.

In Britain, the ideas were welcomed not by an insular, inward-looking nation, aspiring to overseas power, but by the controllers of the greatest empire the world had ever seen; men who roamed the globe, pacifying and subjugating entire peoples, putting into practice on a daily basis the kind of racial mastery and superiority that the Germans could only dream about. Gobineau's ideas also found a receptive audience among those writers on English history in the late Victorian and Edwardian periods who were Anglo-Saxonists and who readily accepted that England had been colonised and developed by Germanic people, with the result that the original British inhabitants had been marginalised. T.P. Taswell-Langmead, for example, in his *English Constitutional History: From the Teutonic Conquest to the Present Time*, published in 1919, wrote:

It is not unusual to speak of the English as a mixed race formed out of the fusion of the Britons, the Anglo-

Saxons, the Danes, and the Normans; but this form of expression is apt to convey an erroneous idea of the facts. No modern European is, indeed, of pure unmingled race; yet in all some one element has maintained a clear and decided predominance. In the English people this predominant element is the Germanic or Teutonic. The Teutonic conquest of Britain was something more than a mere conquest of the country; it was in all senses a national occupation, a sustained immigration of a new race, whose numbers, during a hundred and fifty years, were continually being augmented by fresh arrivals from the fatherland ...[13]

Gobineau's ideas were influential throughout Europe, but it was an English exponent of this view of history who was later to develop the same themes with astonishing consequences for the German nation – writer Houston Stewart Chamberlain.

Chamberlain was born in England in 1855, son of a Royal Navy admiral. As a teenager he was sent on a tour of Europe in order to improve his health, which was always poor, in the company of his tutor Otto Kuntze, a Prussian who taught him to speak German and gave him an appreciation of German culture and history. Chamberlain became an ardent admirer of the operas of Richard Wagner and he wrote critical books and essays in both French and German. He met Wagner at the Bayreuth Festival in 1882 and, after the composer died, became a close friend and companion of Wagner's widow Cosima, who was fanatically anti-Semitic, like Chamberlain himself. Later still, in 1908, he married Wagner's daughter Eva and the couple moved to Bayreuth.

In 1899, Chamberlain wrote the book that made him famous, *Die Grundlagen des neunzehnten Jahrhunderts* (The Foundations of the 19th Century). In it, he took Gobineau's ideas on the Aryan or Germanic master race and raised them to new depths. In essence, he advanced the notion that Western civilisation was the work primarily of the Aryan or Germanic race in conflict with the Jewish race, who were the enemies of human progress.[14]

He also put forward the ideas that Jesus was not Jewish but Aryan, and that the dark side of Christianity, such as the Inquisition, was the result of the Jewish influence of the Old Testament, combined with the malign influence of the Catholic Church.

His book became a bestseller in many European countries, especially in Germany, which he had made his adopted homeland and where Chamberlain became an instant celebrity. He was invited to stay at the court of Kaiser Wilhelm II, where his theories were much discussed and admired. In a letter to Chamberlain, the Kaiser wrote: 'It was God who sent the German people your book and you personally to me.'[15] Chamberlain later wrote that it was the Kaiser who suggested to him that the Old Testament should be re-edited to remove all connections between Judaism and Christianity.[16]

Chamberlain seems to have become a close personal adviser of the Kaiser, and wrote numerous letters to him. In one such letter to Wilhelm he wrote:

> Germany … can achieve complete control of the world (partly by direct political means, partly by language, culture, methods), only if it succeeds in taking a new direction in time, which means the final rupture with Anglo-American ideals of government. The freedom

that Germany needs is the ... unlimited freedom of thought, of religion, of science – not the freedom to rule itself badly.[17]

Chamberlain's book also had a dramatic impact in other European countries, especially Britain. George Bernard Shaw, reviewing the book in *Fabian News*, the socialist journal, described it as 'the greatest Protestant Manifesto ever written, as far as I know'. Shaw added:

It is a masterpiece of really scientific history. It does not make confusion, it clears it away. He is a great generaliser of thought, as distinguished from the crowd of our mere specialists. It is certain to stir up thought. Whoever has not read it will be rather out of it in political and sociological discussions for some time to come.[18]

Shaw's praise is all the more surprising since Chamberlain's book was plainly opposed to any kind of international organisation that might achieve global influence, such as the Roman Catholic Church and the socialism that Shaw advocated.

Chamberlain became more and more pro-German, seeing the future of Europe resting in the hands of the Germanic people. When the First War broke out, Chamberlain accused England of betraying the Aryan race and began to write propaganda essays against the country of his birth. In 1915 the Kaiser showed his appreciation of these efforts by awarding Chamberlain the Iron Cross for services to the German Empire and, the following year, Chamberlain took German nationality.

It was after the war, in the political ferment that produced the Nazi Party with its accompanying wave of anti-Jewish hysteria, that Chamberlain's ideas came fully to fruition. Central to his writings was his idea that the Aryan race was awaiting its Messiah, an Aryan Christ, who would lead the Germanic people to its historical destiny. Chamberlain identified Hitler as this Messiah figure as early as 1923 after meeting him in Bayreuth. He wrote a notorious letter to Hitler, saying – among other things –

> You are not at all, as you have been described to me, a fanatic. In fact, I would call you the complete opposite of a fanatic. The fanatic inflames the mind, you warm the heart. The fanatic wants to overwhelm people with words, you wish to convince, only to convince them – and that is why you are successful. Indeed, I would also describe you as the opposite of a politician, in the commonly accepted sense of the word, for the essence of all politics is membership of a party, whereas with you all parties disappear, consumed by the heat of your love for the fatherland. It was, I think, the misfortune of our great Bismarck that he became, as fate would have it (by no means through innate predisposition), a little too involved in politics. May you be spared this fate.[19]

After making many other such flattering remarks, Chamberlain closed his address by saying:

> My faith in Germandom has never wavered for a moment, though my hopes had, I confess, reached a low ebb. At one blow you have transformed the state of my soul. That Germany in its hour of greatest need has given birth to a Hitler is proof of vitality; your actions offer further evidence, for a man's personality and actions belong together. That the magnificent Ludendorff openly supports you and embraces your movement: what a wonderful combination![20]

Chamberlain's writings apparently made an impression on Hitler's developing thought, since he referred to him approvingly in *Mein Kampf*, which he began writing later the same year. 'Those who had the government of the country in their hands were quite as indifferent to principles of civil wisdom laid down by thinkers like H.S. Chamberlain as our political leaders now are.'[21]

Hitler's approval almost certainly arose from the fact that the ideas contained in Chamberlain's book coincided closely with, and provided an ideological foundation for, his own pathological hatred of Jews. But it wasn't only Hitler who was convinced by Chamberlain's writing. According to Chamberlain's biographer, Geoffrey Field:

> Hitler, Hess, Goebbels, Eckart, Himmler, von Schirach, and above all Rosenberg had read Chamberlain and professed to have been influenced by him. Hans Kerrl, the Minister for Church Affairs, and Hans Schemm, the Bayreuth schoolmaster who became Bavarian *Kultus-minister*, were also firm admirers, while Nazi intellectuals such as Hans F.K. Günther, Alfred Bäumler, Walter Frank, Ernst Krieck, and the Nobel physicist Philipp Lenard showered him with filial respect.[22]

By this curiously roundabout route, the racist ideas of an amateur English biologist, Charles Darwin, were married to the crackpot beliefs of an English eugenicist, Francis Galton, and an English historical fantasist, Chamberlain, to produce the ideological foundations of the future German government – an administration that planned and executed the murder of millions of men, women and children, in the name of racial superiority.

What is perhaps less widely appreciated is that the racist and eugenicist ideas that flourished in Germany between the wars were enthusiastically taken up by scientists and intellectuals in Britain, America and other major countries, where they were put into effect with varying results.

8

Man and Superman

The question most often asked about Nazism is: Whatever possessed Germany, one of the most cultured nations in the world, the home of Luther, Goethe and Beethoven, to go so completely off the rails and descend into uncivilised barbarity in just a few short years?

An important part of the answer is that fascist thinking was emphatically not confined to Germany, but broke out in many modern industrial societies, including Britain, in the years before and after the First World War as a response to the coming of mass culture and industrial urbanisation. And, as described later, Nazi-style thinking – including racial and eugenic ideas – became state policy or was carried into practice in the 20th century by a number of Protestant nations, including Britain, the United States, Australia and Sweden, albeit to varying extremes.

Underlying the rise of fascist ideas was the dramatic explosion of population in Germany, Britain and other European countries, the creation of a mass industrialised society, and the social tensions that this entirely new form of society gave rise to.

The impact of this dramatic population explosion is difficult today to comprehend fully. From the time of the Roman conquest of Britain until around 1800, the average population of Britain, Germany and other European states changed very little. But during the 19th century, due mainly to industrialisation, there was dramatic and continual growth in numbers. The population of England and Wales, for example, was about 9 million in the year 1800, but by 1850 this had doubled to 18 million and by 1911 had doubled again to 36 million.[1] The way in which the population was distributed also changed dramatically. In 1800, 80 per cent of people lived in the country and only 20 per cent in cities and towns. By 1900, 80 per cent of the population lived in urban, mainly industrial, areas that had grown like scars on the emptying countryside.

In Germany, the figures were just as dramatic. In 1800, the country's population was 25 million. By 1850 it had grown to 35 million, and by 1900 had more than doubled to 56 million.[2]

This massive increase in population culminated in the last decades of the 19th century and the first years of the 20th, bringing about dramatic changes felt at every social level.

When society had been stable for such long periods, with an infrastructure that developed slowly and organically, social stresses and strains were usually kept within manageable limits. But when growth was violently accelerated, with populations of many millions doubling in only 50 years, it was inevitable that extraordinary strains would be placed on traditional social relationships, including class relationships. Housing, education, medicine, employment, all had immense pressures put on them. Industrial slums sprang up in every town and city, with attendant increases in disease, in poverty and in crime. Industrialisation was not only the main engine driving the population explosion, it was also one of the main contributors to the growth of social ills such as pollution, occupational disease and injuries, child abuse and alcoholism, all taking place in the continually spreading urban slums.

These ill-effects of rapid industrial and commercial growth became a focus of intense discontent and reaction among writers, artists and philosophers. In some cases, their reaction was a positive one, stirring the educated to campaign on behalf of the poor. W.T. Stead, editor of *The Pall Mall Gazette*, famously campaigned against child pros-titution in Victorian London by 'purchasing' a thirteen-year-old girl to shock the nation's conscience.[3] But in many other cases the response of middle-class intellectuals was nothing more than a selfish cry of despair by people to whom the masses were an eyesore and an inconvenience. The spread of democracy, universal secular education and basic literacy, the advent of tabloid newspapers, photogra-phy, film and radio only made matters worse in their eyes, giving rise to what novelist and playwright J.B. Priestley contemptuously called the 'Admass' society.[4]

As John Carey showed in his book *The Intellectuals and the Masses*, this mass society was deemed by many leading writers and thinkers of the time to consist of pea-brained, barely-educated suburban mediocrities, doomed by both nature and nurture to live out miserable, pathetic lives, their minds made up for them by advertising and the kind of government propaganda served up during the First War to manipulate public opinion.[5]

This state of affairs was perceived by the intelligentsia as not merely inconvenient, threatening to curtail their accus-tomed privileges by a swamping of social facilities and dumbing-down of social norms, but was also of growing concern to them because suffrage was becoming universal, as was the democratic election of popular governments. Mass political movements such as Marxism were spreading their influence everywhere, undermining traditional respect for the authority of Church and state. If the masses responsible for the election of governments and hence for shaping social policies and cultural norms of the future were little better than unthinking media-fodder, then it was up to the gifted, the exceptional, the intellectually aristocratic to speak out and to provide leadership that would prevent Western society sinking into a morass of industrialised mediocrity, ripe for communist takeover.

In effect, the advent of a mass industrialised society, with its resultant downgrading of the status and privileges of those who had previously been society's leaders, was seen by some of those leaders as a declaration of war upon them by the masses. Their response was to declare war in return.

There is no doubt that Nietzsche was one of the earliest and loudest of these voices of protest against perceived mass mediocrity. In *The Will to Power*, he wrote that 'a declaration of war on the masses by higher men is needed', because 'Everywhere the mediocre are combining in order to make themselves master.'[6] But Nietzsche was not the first such voice, nor was he alone.

In 1871, nearly two decades before Nietzsche wrote the words quoted above, French novelist Gustave Flaubert wrote: 'I believe that the mob, the mass, the herd will always be despicable.'[7]

H.G. Wells reckoned that 'the extravagant swarms of new births' was 'the essential disaster of the 19th century'.[8]

George Bernard Shaw, who welcomed Nietzsche's *Thus Spake Zarathustra* as 'the first modern book that can be set above the *Psalms of David*, calmly announced that 'the majority of men at present in Europe have no business to be alive'.[9] Here Shaw was merely echoing his philosophical hero. Nietzsche had written: 'The great majority of men have no right to existence, but are a misfortune to higher men.'[10]

D.H. Lawrence went even further. Lawrence discovered Nietzsche's writings in 1908 and became his most enthusiastic English disciple. 'The mass of mankind', he wrote in the voice of one of his characters, 'is soulless ... Most people are dead, and scurrying and talking in the sleep of death.'[11] As John Carey observes: 'If most people are dead already, then their elimination becomes easier to contemplate since it will not involve any real fatality.'[12]

In *Fantasia of the Unconscious*, Lawrence called for 'three cheers for the inventors of poison gas'.[13] And in a letter to Blanche Jennings, quoted by John Carey, Lawrence explains his plans to dispose of the masses who are already dead: 'If I had my way I would build a lethal chamber as big as the Crystal Palace, with a military band playing softly and a Cinematograph working brightly; then I'd go out into the back streets and main streets and bring them in, all the sick, the halt and the maimed; I would lead them gently and they would smile me a weary thanks; and the band would softly bubble out the "Hallelujah Chorus".'[14]

In the preface to *On the Rocks*, Shaw tells his readers that: 'Extermination must be put on a scientific basis if it is ever to be carried out humanely and apologetically as well as thoroughly ... if we desire a certain type of civilisation and culture, we must exterminate the sort of people who do not fit into it.'[15]

T.S. Eliot's parodies of the lower-middle-class clerk in 'The Love Song of J. Alfred Prufrock' were a reflection of

117

his contempt for the masses. Virginia Woolf, E.M. Forster and Evelyn Waugh similarly created working-class characters and depicted their failed attempts at self-improvement as evidence of their worthlessness as people. Ezra Pound saw humanity as a 'mass of dolts', as 'democracies electing their sewage'.[16]

In the case of writers such as these, even the most vitriolic like Lawrence and Shaw, it is difficult to credit that they seriously considered the murder of their fellow humans. Yet some writers took the question seriously. W.B. Yeats warned that: 'Sooner or later we must limit the families of the unintelligent classes.'[17] And Yeats, and others who thought like him, did not merely call for eugenic solutions but, as described later, they took active steps towards leading society to adopt them.

Other intellectuals in France, Italy, Germany, England and America were just as outspoken about their hatred and contempt for the masses of people and about the problem they represented. Common themes, frequently repeated, are those mentioned earlier: that the masses are already dead from the neck up and that mass extermination, in some future war or natural catastrophe or the gas chamber, would be a desirable thing. The scientific ideas of Darwin and Malthus seemed to point to similar conclusions: among the masses, struggling to survive, individual human life is of no more value than that of an ant in an anthill.

An important factor in understanding the psychology of embryonic fascism and, later, the Nazis, is the question of how exactly intellectuals such as these saw themselves in relation to the masses they despised. Writers such as Lawrence, Wells and Shaw, far from being of aristocratic origins, came from very ordinary working-class or lower-middle-class backgrounds themselves. There was no question of them claiming some aristocratic or royal pedigree. But despite their lowly origins, they saw themselves as natural aristocrats – individuals whose genetic inheritance marked them out from the common herd and endowed them with abilities that made them special and more valuable than common humanity. This idea was one of the most important of Darwin's legacies. It is not pedigree as such that is important; merely genetics. A commoner may command the affection and support due to a king if he has what it takes in his genes.

How should such a natural aristocrat conduct himself? What code of ethics should he follow? Nietzsche answers this question in *The Anti-Christ*:

> What is good? – Whatever augments the feeling of power, the will to power, power itself, in man.
> What is evil? – Whatever springs from weakness.
> What is happiness? – The feeling that power *increases* – that resistance is overcome.
> The weak and the botched shall perish: first principle of *our* charity. And one should help them to it.
> What is more harmful than any vice? – Practical sympathy for the botched and the weak – Christianity ...[18]

It remains true, of course, that while Nietzsche was far from a lone voice, his writing is still the best known source of fascist philosophy, especially his vision of the coming *Übermensch*, usually translated as the superman, who triumphs over his fellow men merely through the exercise of his indomitable will. And because his voice is the best known, Nietzsche is, rightly or wrongly, often regarded as the chief fount of fascist ideas.

But perhaps the most extraordinary aspect of Nietzsche's philosophy and his writings is that, as described earlier, rather than being the product of a unique voice, they were exactly paralleled by intellectual, philosophical and literary developments in Britain. But instead of being perceived as nascent or prototype fascists, these British mirrors of Nietzsche were seen merely as slightly eccentric avant-garde experimental thinkers. And while Nietzsche is now widely seen as the chief herald of Nazism, his British equivalents have merely receded into the cosy glow of the *Oxford Companion to English Literature* as examples of lively literary minds, innocently misdirected by history into lines of thought that were later perverted by unscrupulous foreign politicians.

Man and Superman – the reality

The intellectuals and novelists who looked on the rise of democracy with distaste had few outlets for the war they wished to declare on the masses other than their own writings. But as the 20th century got under way, some leading figures found such an outlet into which to channel their energy.

In 1903, the Sociological Society was founded in London. One of the first speakers to book a slot to address the new society was Francis Galton, who read his paper, 'Eugenics: Its Definition, Scope and Aims' to a meeting held at the London School of Economics. The paper got a very mixed reception and, in the discussion that followed, several social scientists savaged Galton, including Leonard Hobhouse (who became the first professor of sociology in a British university) and prominent sociologist John Mackinnon Robertson, both objecting to Galton's crude attempts to reduce the laws of history to Darwinian selection.[19]

Finding a frosty reception for his ideas among professional scientists, Galton and some like-minded amateur colleagues founded their own society in 1907. At first, they called it the Eugenics Education Society; the 'Education' tag was included in the name to reassure people that the new organisation was merely going to hand out pamphlets and argue from the platform, rather than build gas chambers for the extermination of 'undesirables'. (By 1926, they apparently felt that this first, educational phase was successfully ended, as they changed the name simply to the Eugenics Society.)

Although many mainstream scientists were wary of the over-simplifications of Galton's thinking, the organisation had no difficulty attracting famous names and prominent individuals who needed no scientific evidence because they felt intuitively that the ideas of eugenics were true, in very much the same way that Huxley, Haeckel and other scientists felt intuitively that Darwin's racist views must be true. Indeed, Leonard Darwin, Charles's son, was himself pressed into service as President, and big names like George Bernard Shaw and H.G. Wells graced the platform. Perhaps even more worrying than the eccentric celebrities who put their names on the letter-heading was the very long list of ordinary but highly influential people who signed up to the idea of a national eugenics programme by becoming members of the society.

Hearing about an organisation like the Eugenics Society, one is tempted to think that it must have been that very British institution, a club for cranks, peopled by minor aristocrats with delusions of their own importance, crackpot academics ignored and passed over by their peers, and retired admirals and generals of the 'bring back hanging' temperament. The reality is very much more disturbing.

Many members of the Eugenics Society were medical men and women occupying very senior positions in the academic world, in medicine and in the administration of medicine – a few in government itself. Some appear to have allowed their ideological views on eugenics to influence their views on issues such as medical treatment and welfare services. And actions taken in the name of eugenics are not confined to a remote and ignorant past before world wars, but have continued in recent times. For example, Dr Leonard Arthur was a member of the Eugenics Society and also Medical Registrar at Derbyshire Children's Hospital. In 1980 Arthur ordered 'nursing care only' for John Pearson, who was born a Down's Syndrome baby. Pearson died 60 hours later. The code phrase 'nursing care only' meant sedation, water but no medical treatment. Arthur was charged with murder; though later this was changed to attempted murder on instructions of the judge.[20] The court heard from two doctors in charge of the child that if antibiotics and oxygen had been given, as they would have been to a normal baby, then his life might have been saved. Dr Arthur was acquitted of the charges at Leicester Crown Court in November 1981.[21]

One of the nursing staff who gave evidence, a midwife of eighteen years' experience, told the court that she knew of no cases at the hospital where malformed children who received 'nursing care only' survived.[22]

Just how many cases occurred between 1900 and the present, in which eugenics-minded doctors ordered 'nursing care only' for babies they believed should not continue to live, is now impossible even to estimate. Such cases may be rare, but the activities of some members of the society are still cause for concern, not least because their commitment to the cause of eugenics was not widely known to their contemporaries. Their agenda, if not exactly hidden, was far from common knowledge, unless you happened to belong, like them, to the Eugenics Society and shared their vision of the future of the race. The following are just a few of the most prominent members.

Arthur Balfour was British Prime Minister from 1902 to 1905 and an enthusiastic member of the Eugenics Society. He delivered the opening address at the First International Congress on Eugenics in 1912, where he told delegates from Germany and elsewhere: 'the study of eugenics is one of the greatest and most pressing necessities of our day.' He was later a member of the War Cabinet and chancellor of both Edinburgh and Cambridge Universities. Worryingly, he was also a member of the Medical Research Council from 1924 to 1929.

Men of the Church were prominent in the Eugenics Society. E.W. Barnes, the Bishop of Birmingham from 1924 to 1953, was an active member of the Eugenics Society Consultative Council. In 1933, the Bishop said this to a congregation in Liverpool Cathedral:

> Under the harsh social order which prevailed almost to our own time, those human beings who were manifestly unfitted for the struggle and responsibilities of social life failed to survive. The unfit, the defective and the degenerate were eliminated. But of late at great cost to the community we have not only preserved them, but have also allowed them to propagate their like. I ask you to assent to my own conviction that such blind humanitarianism is neither Christian nor sensible ... As we reflect alike upon the sternness of God and upon the freedom of Christ's teaching from any hint of indulgent good nature, we ought to become willing to accept in our social order measures against which religious sentimentality will raise an outcry. If England ... is to save herself ... and the world ... she must be racially sound.[23]

123

In 1949 he was quoted by *The Times* as saying:

A time was coming when sterilisation of the unfit would be essential to England's social organisation and might well be the complement of the welfare state. ... we must get rid of the slovenly, vicious, idle wasters of the community. Unfortunately the welfare state is only too likely to encourage their increase.[24]

Some medical members of the Eugenics Society were as outspoken as the Bishop of Birmingham about what course society should take to become more efficient. Dr Richard Berry, a member of the Council of the British Medical Association, wrote several papers in the early 1930s on *The Mental Defective: a Problem in Social Inefficiency*. At this time Dr Berry made 'The lethal chamber proposal', in the journal *Eugenics Review* (volume 22, 1930, page 155), in which he 'seriously suggests a lethal chamber, under State control, for the painless extermination of ... [his patients at Stoke Park Colony, Bristol]'.[25]

William Beveridge is best remembered today for his humanitarian work in producing the report on which the National Health Service was founded in 1947. Less well known is that Beveridge was also a member of the Council of the Eugenics Society from the 1930s to the 1950s. When he delivered the Galton Lecture in 1943, 'Eugenic Aspects of Children's Allowances' (*Eugenics Review*, volume 34, 1943, pages 117–23), Beveridge called for higher children's allowances for the rich to be phased in.[26] And in *The Problem of the Unemployed* (1906), Beveridge proposed a novel solution to the 'problem'.

Those men who through general defects are unable to fill such a whole place in industry, are to be recognised

as 'unemployable'. They must become the acknowledged dependents of the State ... maintained adequately
... but with complete and permanent loss of all citizen
rights – including not only the franchise but civil freedom and fatherhood.[27]

Major Leonard Darwin was Charles Darwin's son and was
certainly a chip off the old block, if that phrase is intended
to mean that racist views run in families. He was President
of the Eugenics Society from 1911, soon after it was
founded, until 1943 when he died. He was also President of
the Royal Geographic Society. In an article titled 'Race
Deterioration and Practical Politics', published in *Eugenics
Review* in 1925–26, Darwin wrote:

> Compulsion is now permitted if applying to criminals,
> lunatics, and mental defectives; and this principle must
> be extended to all who, by having offspring, would seri-
> ously damage future generations.[28]

Darwin is here referring to compulsory sterilisation.

One of the best known names in 20th-century science,
Sir Julian Huxley, is also remembered as the first Director
General of UNESCO from 1946 to 1948 and founder of
the World Wildlife Fund. He was Secretary of London's
Zoological Society, and of the Sociological Society, and was
on the executive committee of the Euthanasia Society. In
addition, Huxley was a member of the Eugenics Society
Council and was President from 1959 to 1962.

Like his famous grandfather, Thomas Huxley, Julian was
also a convinced Darwinist. In his *Essays of a Humanist*,
Huxley explained his eugenics views thus:

By social problem group I mean the people, all too familiar to social workers in large cities, who seem to have ceased to care, and just carry on the business of bare existence in the midst of extreme poverty and squalor. All too frequently they have to be supported out of public funds, and become a burden to the community. Unfortunately they are not deterred by the conditions of existence from carrying on with the business of reproduction: and their mean family size is very high, much higher than the average for the whole country.

Intelligence and other tests have revealed that they have a very low average IQ; and the indications are that they are genetically subnormal in many other qualities, such as initiative, pertinacity, general exploratory urge and interest, energy, emotional intensity, and will power. In the main, their misery and improvidence is not their fault but their misfortune: our social system provides the soil on which they can grow and multiply, but with no prospects save poverty and squalor.

Here again, voluntary sterilisation could be useful. But our best hope, I think, must lie in the perfection of new, simple and acceptable methods of birth control, whether by an oral contraceptive or perhaps preferably by immunological methods involving injections. Compulsory or semi-compulsory vaccination, inoculation and isolation are used in respect of many public health risks: I see no reason why similar measures should not be used in respect of this grave problem, grave both for society and for the unfortunate people whose increase has been actually encouraged by our social system.[29]

Probably the most prominent advocate of eugenics was novelist H.G. Wells. Wells was a student of Thomas Huxley at what is today Imperial College, London, where he absorbed both Huxley's passionate belief in Darwinism and his racist outlook. His early science fiction books such as *The War of the Worlds* and *The Island of Doctor Moreau* echo Darwin's picture of the cold indifference of nature to any principle other than the survival of the fittest.

In his 1901 attempt to foresee future human society, *Anticipations*, Wells wrote of 'The swarms of black and brown and dirty-white and yellow people, who do not come into the needs of efficiency.' The world, he said, 'is not a charitable institution and I take it they will have to go. It is their portion to die out and disappear.' Of Britain's African empire, Wells wrote: 'the nigger squats and multiplies in stagnant pools of population.' Wells also speaks of 'People of the Abyss', by which he means the 'great useless masses of people', the 'vicious, helpless pauper masses'. He predicts that only countries that deal with these masses will thrive, and that the 'nation that most resolutely picks over, educates, sterilises, exports or poisons its People of the Abyss' will flourish.[30]

Wells believed that the world of the future would 'be shaped to favour the procreation of what is fine and efficient and beautiful in humanity'. This necessarily meant that for 'the helpless and useless, the men of the New Republic will have little pity and less benevolence'. He despised democracy, saying that:

It has become apparent that whole masses of human population are, as a whole, inferior in their claim on the future, to other masses, that they cannot be given opportunities or trusted with power as the superior peoples are

trusted, that their characteristic weaknesses are conta-
gious and detrimental in the civilizing fabric, and that
the range of incapacity tempts and demoralises the
strong. To give them equality is to sink to their level, to
protect and cherish them is to be swamped by their
fecundity.[31]

Wells translated these beliefs into a programme for social
action that was primarily negative in aspect. It was no use,
he believed, trying to select the best and the brightest.
Society must evolve by getting rid of the unfit.

I believe that now and always the conscious selection of
the best for reproduction will be impossible; that to pro-
pose it is to display a fundamental misunderstanding of
what individuality implies. The way of nature has always
been to slay the hindmost, and there is still no other way,
unless we can prevent those who would become the
hindmost being born. It is in the sterilisation of failure,
and not in the selection of successes for breeding, that
the possibility of an improvement of the human stock
lies.[32]

What is, with hindsight, most striking about Wells' apparently scientific view of the future is that it was completely
without any scientific basis. It was founded on such fundamental misconceptions and myths as the idea that half-
caste children were genetically defective. This is what he
wrote concerning marriages between black and white: 'The
mating of two quite healthy persons may result in disease. I
am told it does so in the case of interbreeding of healthy
white men and healthy black women about the Tanganyka
region; the half-breed children are ugly, sickly, and rarely
live.'[33]

To read such extremist views from such well-known and widely-respected names is rather like discovering that a favourite aunt is an arsonist in her spare time. But perhaps even more shocking is that such views were held and expressed as a matter of routine, in an attempt to 'educate' the British public, not just by celebrities such as those quoted above, but by ordinary men and women who held senior positions in British academic and public life.

From the time of the First War until the 1980s, the Eugenics Society continued to attract prominent and well-placed medical people, who sought to use their positions to introduce eugenics policies. Dr Carlos Blacker, a Secretary of the society, told fellow members in 1951 that Nazi experiments using live people to develop an economical method of mass sterilisation did not work but 'that the continuation of experimentation with one of the sterilisation drugs which were being used by the Nazi doctors would be perfectly in order'. Member of Parliament Major Archibald Church was also a Eugenics Society Council member and, in 1930, sought to introduce a Sterilisation Bill in Parliament, aimed at 'those who are in every way a burden to their parents, a misery to themselves and in my opinion a menace to the social life of the community'. C.D. Darlington was Professor of Botany at Oxford and a Eugenics Society Vice President. In a lecture as recent as 1970 he said that: 'As individuals the unskilled workers ... are not much use to us ... the old settled aristocracies and old unsettled gypsies of Europe were two more such useless groups. At the top and at the bottom of society waste materials accumulate.' Sir Ronald Fisher was a distinguished statistician and geneticist, sometimes called 'the father of statistics', and a Director of the Eugenics Society. Fisher applied sophisticated statistical techniques to genetics to

prove that Darwinism was true – he concluded that 'Natural selection is a mechanism for generating improbability'. Unfortunately he also, on behalf of the tobacco industry, applied the same sophisticated statistical thinking to proving that smoking tobacco was not the cause of lung cancer. Instead, Fisher suggested that the desire to smoke, and getting lung cancer, were both predisposed by genetic factors. Fisher smoked a pipe and died of mouth cancer in 1962.[34]

Prevailing attitudes to the 'masses' were summed up by Mrs Cora Hodson, General Secretary of the society from 1920 to 1931 and editor of *Eugenics Review*. Writing to a member of the society, Wing Commander James, she said: 'I fear some of us will have to stoop to a good deal that is vulgar if we are really to get Eugenics home to the masses, but very possibly they do not matter.' Another woman member was Dr Marie Stopes, famous as the founder of the first birth control clinic in England. She left her substantial property to the society when she died in 1958. In doing so, she cut her son out of her will because, against her wishes, he married a woman who wore glasses and who was therefore, in her view, genetically defective. In 1920, she wrote, in *The Control of Parenthood*, 'Utopia could be reached in my life time had I the power to issue inviolable edicts ... (I would legislate compulsory sterilisation of the insane, feebleminded ... revolutionaries ... half castes.)'[35]

Perhaps the most extraordinary thing about these examples (scores more of which could be given) is that it is so plain from their choice of language that the motivation of these individuals is the very opposite of scientific and that theirs are purely subjective value judgements. In their attempts to characterise those whom they believe to be 'socially undesirable', there is a complete lack of scientific terminology or analysis, and instead only undefined terms like 'feebleminded' ... 'half-castes' .... 'defective' ... 'degenerate' ... 'slovenly, vicious, idle wasters of the community' ... 'irresponsible persons of low intelligence and weak will' ... 'revolutionaries' ...

Eugenics Societies were also founded in other countries, notably Germany, the United States, Australia and Sweden, and there was frequent international contact and cross-fertilisation of ideas between members. Legislation to perform compulsory sterilisation was enacted in all except Britain, where Major Church's proposed laws were thwarted on moral grounds by an alliance of the Labour Party and the Catholic Church.

In the United States, for example, legislation was first introduced in 1909 and continued in force in some states until the late 1960s. During that time, some 60,000 people, many of them black and native American Indians, were compulsorily sterilised. About the same number of people were compulsorily sterilised as 'unfit' in Sweden between 1935 and 1976.[36] In introducing such legislation, the governments of the US, Australia, Sweden and elsewhere were attempting to implement social engineering programmes aimed at 'improving' the breeding stock of their people by eliminating those they considered to be genetically inferior.

On the face of it, Britain's political leaders are to be congratulated for not falling for the pseudo-scientific claptrap of eugenics. But Charles Webster, official historian of the National Health Service, is not so sure. 'In this sorry tale', says Webster, 'the United Kingdom seems to be exonerated since, in common with the Latin countries, it did not introduce sterilisation laws. However, the British collective conscience should not remain untroubled ...'[37]

As Charles Webster observes:

On the basis of [the Eugenics Society's] success in spreading alarm among the higher social classes, the eugenists attracted wide support. This support created an opportunity for decisive intervention on the policy front. The period between 1930 and 1936 marked the high point of the sterilisation campaign in Britain. The cause was powerfully supported within the social establishment, and Britain seemed to be on the brink of introducing one of the most wide-ranging sterilisation laws. But the sterilisation movement collapsed at its last hurdle. The eugenists were over complacent, and tempted to cast their net too widely, thereby opening their vague proposals to criticism from unsympathetic scientists and lawyers. Apart from isolated individuals, the Labour movement was never sympathetic; when it came to a decision, it joined the Catholic Church in opposition. The Conservatives were also reticent owing to their fear of adverse electoral consequences. Finally, the high profile of sterilisation in Nazi ideology frightened away much liberal opinion.

In the UK, eugenic sterilisation seemingly turned out to be little more than a side-show, with no practical impact. The groups vulnerable to such an intervention seemed sufficiently protected by the law. Any doctor performing sterilisation was taking a substantial risk. However, reflecting the passion with which eugenic sterilisation was supported, it is evident that some medical practitioners were willing to defy the law and carry out sterilisation in the interests of what they perceived as the public good. This practice was obviously undertaken with discretion, but there are sufficient traces of its existence to suggest that eugenic sterilisation was current in the UK before World War II. The full evidence of the extent of this practice remains to be uncovered.[38]

Webster describes the practices of medical people who were convinced eugenicists as 'undertaken with discretion'. More plainly they acted in a way that made it difficult or impossible for them to be successfully charged with any kind of offence – such as simply not providing life-saving medical treatment to babies they considered defective. And, while statistics on such cases were kept and are today available from the US, Sweden, Australia, and even Nazi Germany, we shall probably never know how many people lost their lives in Britain in the name of eugenics theories.

9

More English than the English

The idea of the master race, destined by history to rule, became central to Nazi thinking between the wars, both in their domestic and foreign policies. The German intellectuals who held this idea and who promoted it through textbooks and articles may have had what they believed to be a sound theoretical basis for such thinking, but it takes more than just theory for an extremist ideology to become transformed into national policy that is acted upon by the whole state. To be so successful at subverting entire nations, an ideology needs a solid, tangible basis in the everyday life of the people and the nation's leaders and thinkers – such as the oppression and exploitation of the working class serving as the constant spur to communist revolutionaries. So what exactly were the practical, everyday driving forces underlying German belief in their destiny as the master race?

The first such driving force was provided by a passionate, almost subconscious yearning by many members of Germany's governing classes to enter into the same birthright as their close cousins and fellow Aryans who already ruled the most powerful empire in the world – the English.

Historian Barbara Tuchman, writing of American entry to the First World War, described the German ambassador to Mexico in these words:

> ... the blue-eyed, clean shaven [Admiral Paul] von Hintze was considered one of the more agreeable members of the diplomatic corps. Though an ardent Pan-German and Junker into whose mind never entered any question of the divine right of German militarism, he tempered his normal arrogance with amiability ... He was intelligent, sociable, cultivated, spoke English without an accent, and evidently sharing every Prussian's secret ambition to be taken for an English gentleman, dressed in impeccable English clothes.[1]

In British films and books of the 20th century, the typical German officer is depicted as a stiff-necked Prussian militarist, sporting a monocle, clicking the heels of his riding boots, perhaps displaying a touch of Hunnish arrogance while kissing the hand of a beautiful woman. This image, which seems to a British eye so typically German, actually has its origins in the dangerous and deluded love affair between the German ruling classes and all things English. It comes as something of a shock to realise that the monocle, the riding boots, the uniforms fetish, the punctilious courtesy, are affectations that the Germans borrowed from England – a curiously distorted mirror of their perceptions of the English people and their way of life.[2]

To understand how this love affair with England came about, and to grasp the logic and the emotions that fuelled German infatuation with the British and their global empire in the 20th century, it is necessary first to go back to the origins of the German state itself in the 19th.

Germany entered nationhood as it intended to go on – with a calculated Prussian insult to the international community. The country had been finally united by Bismarck through the Franco-Prussian war of 1870, a conflict engineered by the Iron Chancellor to bring about his aim of a federated Germany. After the Prussian army had crushed the French at Sedan, Wilhelm I was crowned Emperor of Germany in the Hall of Mirrors at Versailles, an act of overweening vanity that rankled for a century.

For the moment, Germany was riding high as potentially the most powerful nation in Europe, both industrially and militarily. All that the fledgling nation needed was colonies in Africa and the Far East to compete with Britain, France and the United States in prestige and influence on the world political stage.

But despite its advantages, its natural resources and a string of military successes against Denmark, Austria and France, young Germany had no place of its own as yet in the world community. Its component states each had their distinctive individual tradition and character but the new German nation had little to mark it out as a key actor on the international scene. Well-to-do and influential Germans needed a sophisticated modern image, a lifestyle, a new national identity to weld together their fledgling federation.

In this newly-cosmopolitan frame of mind, German eyes turned to the countries that were currently the most successful global players. After having adopted a somewhat provincial outlook through much of the 19th century, Germany became more open to influences from abroad, and elements of French, Italian and Russian culture began to become commonplace in the salons of Berlin, Europe's newest capital city.

But in searching for a new national identity and the trappings of imperial grandeur, influential Germans looked to one nation above all others, the most powerful nation in the world – England. Indeed, some new Germans were so keen to emulate every form of Englishness that, like Paul von Hintze, they contrived to become more English than the English. This obsessive admiration and desire to emulate became so intense that it would, in decades to come, influence German national life at almost every level and affect profoundly the thinking of senior members of the government and Nazi Party, including Hitler and his closest associates, Hess, Ribbentrop, Himmler, and Goering.

The chief objects of German infatuation were the English aristocracy and ruling elite, who they perceived as being the movers and shakers of the British Empire and as the ideal role model they sought, both in racial pedigree and in management excellence. From the outset, this perception was faulty, not least because the empire was, to a large extent, created and run by non-upper-class, non-English people. In the way that it developed between 1870 and 1940, this flawed perception became one of a number of dangerous delusions – delusions that were ultimately to play a part in wars that cost tens of millions of lives.

Many middle-class Germans of the time were status-conscious, newly enriched by Germany's flourishing industries, and wanted both to underscore their personal success and to stake their nation's claim to a seat at the big table. This *arriviste* social elite welcomed any national movement that gave greater emphasis to social distinctions. One of the great attractions of all things English in the New German mind was that such snobbish emphasis was built in to everything worth importing or emulating from the British Isles. Common people didn't ride to hounds, take tea with cucumber sandwiches in the afternoon, race thoroughbreds or play tennis. More importantly, only the well-bred, the public-school-educated, the sports-minded gentleman was capable of officering an efficient regiment, running a successful business concern, administering an empire. And Britain was seen as the spiritual home of such breeding, such education, the moulding and shaping of such a capable, audacious and enterprising people.

Merely adopt British ways and values, thought the New Germans, and they would be laying the foundations for a future German nation – one capable of world leadership.

In this curious way, social status became synonymous in the German mind with the kind of easy natural authority that leads to managerial, military and political success. But in believing this, Germans were innocently buying into a myth that had been fostered at home and abroad by the English ruling classes about themselves, a myth that proved to be fatally at odds with the real facts.

The living proof of Britain's greatness was its global empire. But the empire that the new Germans admired so much, and which they yearned to imitate, was a splendid and enviable creation only on paper. The thrusting young minds of the Wilhelmstrasse inspected the pink-coloured regions of the map like penniless nephews eagerly appraising the estate of an elderly relative, but the map was an illusion.

On paper, British possessions seemed to them like a series of easy military pickings, rich and ripe for milking; vast natural resources, the wealth of the Indies and Africa and the Far East, unlimited fertile land for farming and rearing animals and a docile population of willing natives as a source of cheap labour to work it all. In the imaginations of the Wilhelmstrasse and in Berlin drawing rooms, this garden of earthly delights was envisaged as being ruled over by the cruellest, most ruthless, most audacious race on earth – the monocle-wearing, riding-crop wielding, public-school-educated, aristocratic English gentleman.

The reality was very different. It was possible to draw coloured maps of land masses thousands of miles apart only because they could be reached by the ships of the British navy and mercantile marine – the map was more a chart of communications than possessions. And moving goods or soldiers between these destinations was as difficult and hazardous a logistical task then as it remains today.

The British Empire that looked so solid and so intentional on the classroom wall was in reality a jumble of rickety, near-bankrupt, under-funded outposts, many of which had become painted pink through little more than an accident. Some had been won by military conquest, and a few had been the subject of heroic battles against other great powers, as when General Wolfe had stormed the Heights of Abraham and wrested control of Canada from the French. Many, however, had been annexed by a rabble of soldiers, acknowledged by their own officers to be undisciplined ruffians, but more powerful than the natives they slaughtered because of the repeating rifles turned out by the factories of Birmingham. Sometimes, the acquisition of territory was motivated by the prospect (real or illusory) of wealth in terms of land, minerals, or other natural resources. Just as often, it was because the territory in question supplied nothing more than a convenient harbour to British naval vessels hunting vulnerable ships from other colonial powers. Often, the mere appearance of a British warship was enough to subdue the local people.

As imperial historian Sir John Seeley observed: 'We seem to have conquered and peopled half the world in a fit of absence of mind.'[3]

A few individuals in Britain made a lot of money out of the empire, chiefly as a market for cheaply made British goods, especially cotton textiles and other mass manufactures. But these individuals were a tiny minority – in the main, a handful of aristocrats, northern manufacturers and City bankers. To a larger number of middle-class British people, farming, soldiering or administrative posts in the empire offered an agreeable lifestyle and a high standard of living, complete with docile servants, on the cheap. The Foreign Office was keen to maintain and preserve the empire because it provided a network of naval bases from which British commercial and military interests could be protected. To the overwhelming majority of British people, the empire was nothing more than a patriotic idea that, like the Union Flag, was regularly run out to be saluted.

As universal state education began to be introduced in Britain from the 1870s onwards, the empire, its peoples, its geography, its raw materials and industries, became subjects studied in Board School classrooms by working-class children who thus learned to feel superior to the natives depicted in the posters on their classroom walls but who, in many cases, were little better off themselves. G.K. Chesterton contemptuously described this educational process as 'training gutter-snipes to sing, "What is the Meaning of Empire Day?"'.[4] But apart from an understandable feeling of national superiority instilled in British schoolchildren, there was in reality little to choose between the singing classrooms of Lambeth and those of Lahore or Ladysmith.

There was just as little financial support for the paupers of Bombay as there was for the poor of London's East End.

No tax revenues streamed into British coffers from abroad – on the contrary, overseas docks and harbours and garrisons were expensive to maintain, and had to be paid for by the local community. Little was left over for welfare or medical assistance or unemployment payments. In some cases, all or part of the bill was picked up by Whitehall – and ultimately by the British taxpayer.

From the point of view of management and control, the empire was an administrative nightmare. Even when Britain was still relatively wealthy and had naval and military resources to spare, before the First World War, policing such a global estate presented immense logistical difficulties, as was shown by the Boer War, for example, in which an uprising by a few thousand armed farmers required most of Britain's spare military resources to contain and took three years to subdue.

If British imperial power was in reality shaky before the First War, it was even shakier after. Writing of the decline of British power, Clive Ponting observes that:

> In reality, the strength of the Empire resembled a Potemkin village. Behind the grandeur of the façade was a lack of substance. The Empire, and in particular Britain, suffered from debilitating political and economic weakness. One fundamental problem was the lack of a coherent political and administrative structure. Little attempt had been made to integrate the various territories and it remained a motley collection of self governing dominions, colonies of various types at various stages of evolution, and territories, such as Egypt, under direct rule. ... The expansion of the Empire in the latter part of the 19th century brought with it a steadily increasing military burden for defence without bringing either a corresponding

increase in internal organisation or the resources needed to meet the threat. The empire contributed little towards imperial defence and on balance was a drain on British resources ... The new areas added after the war only added to the weakness of the whole structure.

The vast extent of the British Empire was, therefore, a source not of strength but of weakness. It left Britain with the task of defending vulnerable territory in every area of the globe. And Britain, a small island off the coast of Europe, with a population of just forty million and dependent on imports for most of its raw materials and half its food, simply did not have the resources to undertake such a vast task.[5]

These were the painful financial, organisational and political realities behind the schoolchildren patriotically singing 'What is the Meaning of Empire Day?' and sticking into their albums colourful postage stamps from far-away places with strange-sounding names.

Given the parlous, rickety state of most of the empire, it is perhaps surprising that any British people could be found willing to leave the comparative security and comfort of the home shores to risk the dangers and difficulties of life in the tropics, even with its opportunities for social climbing, yet hundreds of thousands of empire-builders were willing to go. For some, from the worst of the slums, almost any kind of alternative was preferable, as long as the air and water were clean and the sun shone. In most cases, though, the empire offered the chance of social mobility. For many middle-class people, India, Africa and the Far East offered a far grander lifestyle than they could afford in Woking, Watford or Weybridge, complete with an endless supply of obedient servants. For many, the empire was a mission to be pursued with Christian zeal, bringing cleanliness and Godliness to heathens less fortunate than themselves, and providing positions of social leadership unobtainable at home. And for some – possibly not a few – the empire was their one chance to feel superior to the rest of humanity, and to have someone to look down upon.

When Kipling wrote of 'The white man's burden' in speaking of the empire, it was neither racism nor jingoistic patriotism that motivated him. Rather he wrote as someone who had sweated through the heat and dust of Indian summers himself and who understood the massive economic and physical sacrifices that such climates and such poverty-stricken social infrastructures demanded.

The reality of the pink-shaded regions on countless maps was that India, Africa and other tropical colonial outposts had little to offer to any European, except those willing to endure the heat, discomfort and dangers simply to live a grander lifestyle than they could afford at home, and to make themselves feel superior – an appeal limited to people like the British men and women who queued up to endure such punishment in the name of national greatness. Unfortunately for the world, Wilhelmine Germany harboured precisely the same kind of personalities.

Top Germans wanted to prove to themselves and to the world that they were made of the same stuff as the British. After all, weren't the Germans and the English chips off the same block? Weren't we brothers under the skin?

Quite apart from empire-envy, the German love affair with Englishness expressed itself at several distinct levels. At the most superficial level it involved merely aping British dress, manners, and ways. At a deeper social level it meant importing British customs into Germany and deliberately grafting them wholesale onto German culture in an early form of social engineering experiment. At the deepest level it meant harnessing the German national will and national spirit to ideals and beliefs that were perceived by their leaders to be the guiding principles of British greatness.

As described earlier, Victorian German gentlemen and officers began to sport monocles in the English manner. German aristocrats imported packs of hounds from England, had their pink riding habits made in Savile Row and rode to hounds across the German countryside blowing English hunting horns. Tennis clubs, golf courses and even cricket elevens appeared all over Germany. German schoolboys were lectured on the merits of English habits such as cold baths and early morning exercise. And when Adolf Hitler wished to inculcate nationalist fervour in the young boys and girls of Germany, he turned to Baden-Powell's Boy Scout movement for his model.

But it was at the level of national foreign policy that the German crush on England became most dangerous. For the similarities of German and British aims led Hitler and his fellow Nazis to believe that they had more in common with the British and their empire than with any other nation: that the racial destinies of the two nations were indissolubly linked, and that, in their hearts, the Germans and the British thought as one people. It was this delusion more than any other that led Hitler to believe Britain would stand idly by while he invaded one country after another.

But if many Germans were enamoured of England and its people, to what extent were their feelings reciprocated? Not merely by the unemployed working men who, in frustration, donned black shirts and marched in the East End of London, but by ordinary British men and women? Could Hitler have been right in his assessment of the English temperament? Are we all fascists at heart?

10

Influential Friends

Given the bestial and total nature of the conflict of 1914–18, and the extent to which Anglo-German relations were poisoned by the propaganda war, it would not have been surprising if communications had broken down irretrievably for a generation or more. In fact, not only were the fires of friendship quickly rekindled at both a personal and national level but, within just a few years, prominent Germans were once again casting envious glances at the British Empire and again seeking ways to emulate what they saw as English national superiority on the international stage.

Among post-war Germans who harboured such feelings in the 1920s were the founders of a fledgling political party, the National Socialist German Workers' Party or NSDAP – popularly known as the Nazis – and their young leader, Adolf Hitler.

Paramount among several reasons for this re-emergence of German infatuation with the British was the continuation of pre-war convergence of thinking in the two countries on right-wing political, racial, and nationalist lines. And a key reason for this convergence of thinking was that

147

a right-wing political climate *already* existed in Britain which, in post-war Germany, was now regarded as new and revolutionary.

In an earlier chapter I asked: How could a civilised nation such as Germany descend into barbarity so quickly? Yet Germany was far from alone in the aftermath of the First World War in ridding itself of an outmoded monarchy and replacing it with a totalitarian military dictatorship in the name of modernity and social efficiency. Precisely the same process took place in Austria, Russia, Spain, Italy, Portugal, Turkey, China, Japan and elsewhere. Perhaps the main reason that England remained immune to the contagion of regicide and revolution in the 20th century was that she had already been infected in 1649, and because something closely resembling a fascist state already existed in Britain.

Fascism has been defined as capitalism without parliamentary democracy, but with direct rule by the decree of a powerful elite. By this definition, it is not difficult to argue that Britain's ruling class in the last decades of the 19th century and the first decades of the 20th qualified as a fascist, or quasi-fascist government. It is true that the party in power was in theory chosen democratically by the electorate, but this electorate spoke for only a tiny fraction of the population. In 1901, for example, the British population was 38 million. In the general election held that year, only 3.5 million people voted – less than 10 per cent. In 1910, the population was 42 million but the number of people voting in the general election was still only 6.7 million.[1] In any case, whichever party this unrepresentative electorate chose, the power of determining Britain's domestic and foreign policy remained firmly in the hands of a privileged few, men of high birth and social station who, in the main, came from a very narrow range of social backgrounds and had been educated at Eton or Harrow, Oxford or Cambridge.

Apart from a handful of left-wing firebrands – socialists, Marxists and anarchists – few in Britain objected to the state being run by a powerful elite, just as long as that elite possessed the qualities of the upper-class English gentleman so admired and envied around the world. That such a government qualified as fascist never entered most people's minds.

But when, in Germany in the 1920s, power began to pass from such an aristocratic, privileged elite into the hands of a new kind of elite composed of individuals from humble social backgrounds, by virtue of their personal achievements and gifts, alarm bells started ringing and Britain's ruling classes began to be divided in their support for this new phenomenon.

Quite apart from issues of international politics and national prestige, members of the British governing classes tended to divide in their support for Hitler and the Nazis along lines that involved mainly personal preferences or personal self-interest.

Churchill's attitude to Hitler and the Nazis, like many of England's governing class in the 1920s, was ambivalent. In the early days, he welcomed the appearance of a champion of the right willing to defend Europe against the red menace of Bolshevism. Yet at the same time he detested Hitler personally and his party. Writing in *The Strand Magazine* in 1935, he said:

> One may dislike Hitler's system and yet admire his patriotic achievement. If our country were defeated, I hope we should find a champion as indomitable to restore our

courage and lead us back to our place among the nations. We cannot tell whether Hitler will be the man who will once again let loose upon the world another war in which civilisation will irretrievably succumb, or whether he will go down in history as the man who restored honour and peace of mind to the Great Germanic nation.[2]

Churchill's dislike of Hitler the man seems to arise from a snobbish personal distaste for Hitler's lowly origins. In a speech in 1935, Churchill said:

Then (in 1919) it was that one corporal, a former Austrian house-painter, set out to regain it all. In fifteen years that have followed this resolve he has succeeded in restoring Germany to the most powerful position in Europe, and not only has he restored the position of his country, but he has even, to a very large extent, reversed the results of the Great War (now) the vanquished are in the process of becoming the victors, and the victors the vanquished.

Once again, the ambivalence is there: Churchill admires Hitler's political achievements but is unable to resist the class jibe at 'one corporal, a former Austrian house-painter'.

Some members of the British establishment not only admired Hitler but would have welcomed the devil himself so long as he was against communism and willing to fight the red menace. And some, including the most distinguished elder statesmen, still believed Britain's destiny lay in union with Germany despite the horrors of the First War and regardless of the form its government might take.

Sir Edward Grey, who had fought so hard as Foreign Secretary to avoid the war, wrote in 1925:

> There is something more which I think any far-seeing English statesman must have long desired, and that is that we should not remain permanently isolated on the continent of Europe, and I think that the moment that aspiration was formed it must have appeared evident to everybody that the natural alliance is between ourselves and the great German Empire.
>
> I cannot conceive any point which can arise in the immediate future which would bring ourselves and the Germans into antagonism of interests. On the contrary, I can see many things which must be a cause of anxiety to the statesmen of Europe, but in which our interests are clearly the same as the interests of Germany and in which that understanding of which I have spoken in the case of America might, if extended to Germany, do more, perhaps, than any combination of arms in order to preserve the peace of the world.
>
> If the union between England and America is a powerful factor in the cause of peace, a new Triple Alliance between the Teutonic race and the two branches of the Anglo-Saxon race will be a still more potent influence in the future of the world.[3]

At the same time, belief in white supremacy and in the Aryan master race (an echo of which seems to be present in Grey's words) was as strongly held in Britain as in Germany, and there were many people of every class, especially members of the Eugenics Society, who were willing to give support to racial and eugenic policies. Others were violently anti-Semitic. Many such people made common cause with Hitler, at least intellectually, and still others went further than merely tacitly agreeing with German policies.

Direct flirtation with Nazism in Britain began at the top with Edward, the Prince of Wales, later to become briefly King Edward VIII, and his married mistress, Mrs Wallis Simpson.

When King George V died in 1936, the prospect of ascending the throne precipitated a crisis for Edward. The King of England was also Supreme Governor of the Church of England and hence would be unable to marry a divorced woman, forcing Edward to choose between his throne and the woman he loved. But there was a second problem. Edward had shown himself to be sympathetic to Hitler's government in the three years since it came to power in 1933. He was one of many British aristocrats who were deeply alarmed by the spread of communism and who admired what Hitler was doing in Germany, seeing him as a European saviour. Wallis Simpson shared and encouraged Edward's views on Nazism. She developed a close relationship with the German ambassador in London, Joachim von Ribbentrop, and it has even been suggested that she became his lover. Both British and American intelligence services became alarmed that Mrs Simpson was passing useful information to German intelligence via Ribbentrop.[4]

Shortly after Edward acceded on the death of his father, the German embassy in London sent a cable to Berlin for Hitler's personal attention. Among other things, the telegram told Hitler that 'An alliance between Germany and Britain is for him (the King) an urgent necessity', strongly suggesting that Edward must have conveyed this idea to Ribbentrop himself. At the very least, the existence of a sympathetic English head of state must have encouraged Hitler to believe that Britain would not go to war with Germany, whatever his territorial ambitions in Europe.

Within a year Edward had bowed to pressure from Baldwin's government and abdicated his throne; this may well have been in part because of his Nazi leanings. Within months, in October 1937, Edward and his wife, now Duke and Duchess of Windsor, made a formal visit to Nazi Germany where they met Hitler, dined with Rudolf Hess and were given a guided tour of a concentration camp. At the outbreak of war, Edward was moved from France out of harm's way to become Governor of the Bahamas from 1940–45.

The Duke and Duchess remained under suspicion throughout the war and their activities continued to be monitored by British intelligence and the FBI. The Duke is reported to have told an acquaintance in the Bahamas: 'After the war is over and Hitler will crush the Americans ... We'll take over ... They [the British] don't want me as their King, but I'll be back as their leader.'[5]

A US Naval Intelligence report, revealed in 2003, showed that the Nazis continued to regard the Duke as a potential ally at the height of the war. American agents had discovered that at a conference of German foreign officials in 1941, the Duke of Windsor was described as the best person with whom Hitler could negotiate terms, and 'the logical director of England's destiny after the war'.[6]

Despite Edward's abdication, the groundswell of support for Nazism among leading figures continued to gather pace. Within a few years of Hitler coming to power, several organisations were founded in Britain to foster links with Germany and the Nazis, to which many prominent British people subscribed their names.

The Nordic League was established in 1935, reportedly with the assistance of secret agents from Nazi Germany, sent over for the purpose. Initially, the organisation was known as the White Knights of Britain – a title that managed to combine both racist and anti-Soviet overtones, since 'White' was the epithet widely adopted by the members of the Russian ruling class who survived the revolution of 1917 and subsequently opposed communism. It also attracted many prominent members including Archibald Ramsay, the Conservative MP for Peebles and a deeply religious man, who became its first leader.[7]

In May 1939, Ramsay formed another organisation, which he named the Right Club. His aim was to unify all the different right-wing groups in Britain, or as Ramsay put it, 'co-ordinating the work of all the patriotic societies'.

Ramsay recorded the names of his club's membership in a so-called Red Book – a roll-call of many in the British establishment and aristocracy of the period, including the Duke of Westminster, Baron Redesdale, Lord Sempill, Lord Ronald Graham, Lord Carnegie, the Earl of Galloway, Princess Blucher, Prince Turka Galitzine, and Sir Alexander Walker. The Right Club also forged links with other like-minded pro-fascist organisations, such as the Anglo-German Fellowship, founded by Admiral Sir Barry Domvile, a former Director of Naval Intelligence, and Oswald Mosley's British Union of Fascists.

The activities of Ramsay and his organisations began to alarm some in Whitehall, and he was put under observation by department B5b of MI5, run by Maxwell Knight, and concerned with monitoring political subversion. MI5 managed to penetrate the Right Club with three female agents, Joan Miller, Marjorie Amor and Helen de Munck, who reported on his activities.[8]

Other than political activists like Ramsay, perhaps the most prominent member of right-wing political organisations was Lord Redesdale, who bought the Swinbrook estate in Northumberland, married and had six daughters: Diana, Jessica, Nancy, Unity, Pamela and Deborah Mitford. Redesdale lost much of his fortune in the late 1920s and, becoming embittered, he developed extreme right-wing opinions and became a member of several right-leaning organisations including the Anglo-German Fellowship and The Link. His daughter Diana Mitford married Oswald Mosley, leader of the British Union of Fascists, in 1936. Another daughter, Unity Mitford, went to Nazi Germany and met Adolf Hitler, Heinrich Himmler, Hermann Goering, Joseph Goebbels and other Nazi leaders. Hitler told newspapers in Germany that Unity was 'a perfect specimen of Aryan womanhood'.

When the war broke out in September 1939, Unity Mitford tried to commit suicide by putting a pistol to her head. She survived and returned to England suffering from wounds.

Perhaps surprisingly, Britain's best-known Nazi, Sir Oswald Mosley, was probably the least dangerous of the lot. Although Mosley and his wife, Diana Mitford, had visited Germany many times, were on friendly terms with Hitler, and had been married in Joseph Goebbels' house with Hitler as a wedding guest, Mosley had been dismissed by Hitler as a nonentity. The measures passed by the British Parliament in 1936 prohibiting political parties from wearing uniforms and holding street rallies effectively neutered Mosley and his Blackshirts. Hitler accurately saw that he would never be anything but an insignificant bit-part player in British politics, a conclusion also reached by P.G. Wodehouse, who comprehensively satirised Mosley in the ludicrous persona of Roderick Spode, Earl of Sidcup and leader of the 'Blackshorts' in the piffling world of Bertie Wooster.

Among many PR gaffes, Mosley blotted his copybook irrevocably when he told cinema newsreel audiences that the House of Commons was nothing more than a 'talking shop' that could be dispensed with. Even the most slavish fascist supporter does not want to hear that his or her political opinions are no longer wanted.

But quite apart from racists, anti-Semites, anti-communists, and the fascist-minded, there were plenty of other decent, patriotic British people who believed Germany to be our natural ally. A good example is Sir Ian Hamilton, a professional soldier best known as the commander of the ill-fated Gallipoli expedition in 1915. Before admission to Sandhurst as a young man, Hamilton visited Germany and stayed for some time in Dresden with General Dammers. Here he became fluent in German and made many German friends. After the First War he became president of the Scottish division of the British Legion and wrote books and letters to *The Times* of a pacifist nature, wishing to avoid a repetition of the suffering he had seen during the war at Gallipoli.

He travelled to Munich in 1938, where he visited Hess at his family home. He was also invited by Hitler to visit the Berghof, his mountain retreat in Bavaria, where he stayed as an overnight guest. He was photographed deep in conversation with Hitler on the front cover of the August 1938 edition of *Anglo-German Review*. Rather than pro-Nazi or pro-fascist, Hamilton can perhaps best be described as a deeply patriotic man who also had a high regard for Germany and wished to do anything to avoid another disastrous war. Other British figures similarly sympathetic to

Germany included the Duke of Bedford, the Duke of Buccleuch and the Duke of Montrose.[9]

If many of Britain's aristocracy and governing class were in varying degrees sympathetic to German aims, much of the British press was right behind them – either out of cowardice or out of conviction.

The policy of appeasement of the dictators between 1936 and 1939 was supported and even advocated by many British newspapers and their proprietors. Lord Rothermere, owner of the *Daily Mail*, was openly admiring of Hitler and visited him in Germany. The *Daily Telegraph* had begun to have doubts about appeasement, but when its correspondent in Vienna, Eric Gedye, wrote a book critical of the policy of appeasement in 1938, he was sacked by the *Telegraph*'s editor on the grounds that he was no longer 'impartial'.

The editor of *The Times*, Geoffrey Dawson, and his deputy, Robert Barrington-Ward, were so pro-Hitler that in 1938 they actually urged the Czech government in a leading article to cede the Sudetenland to Germany voluntarily in the interests of peace. But they didn't have things all their own way. Many of *The Times*' senior journalists were outraged by this and besieged Barrington-Ward in his office demanding a stronger line against Hitler. 'Most of the office is against me', Barrington-Ward confided to his diary.

Some of the press, notably Lord Astor, owner of *The Observer*, and publisher Victor Gollancz, detested the Nazis and said so. But broadly speaking the British press, just like the British government, continued to believe in rapprochement with Germany and Italy right up until the moment Hitler's troops marched into Czechoslovakia in spring 1939.

What is most striking about this high level of agreement of the fascist elements in Britain and Germany is that if leading Nazis such as Hitler and Himmler had sat down at a dinner table with many of these prominent British people at any time in the two decades between Hitler's abortive coup in 1923 and the outbreak of war in 1939, they would probably have found themselves in wide agreement over issues of race, international politics, the continuity of the British Empire and the need for German expansionism in the east. The range of personal reactions of prominent Britons to supping with the Nazis would doubtless have diverged greatly over individual issues, ranging from the racism of Redesdale, to the religiosity of Ramsay, to the pacifism of Hamilton, to the admiration of Rothermere, to the hysterical adoration of Unity Mitford. But all of them would very likely have been united in their feeling that the Nazis were like-minded people with whom they could do business.

But – by the same token – the attitudes of senior Nazis like Hitler and Himmler to British aristocrats were no less misguided and irrational. Gaining the approval of people whom he admired and looked up to with unreal expectations convinced Hitler of the rightness of his cause and reinforced his belief that he was walking with destiny.

This strange meeting of minds had consequences that were both tragic and unforeseen. For when men like Redesdale, Ramsay, Domvile and Mosley started believing in the irrational racist theories of Aryanism and eugenics, they automatically became intellectual collaborators with the Nazis. Those who entertained fantasies of racial purity and the master race – whatever their nationality – encouraged each other in an international *folie à deux*. The fact that the democratically elected Chancellor of Germany was a violent anti-Semite encouraged people like Redesdale and Ramsay to think that they were on the right track. What they perhaps did not realise was that Hitler and the Nazis drew exactly the same erroneous conclusion: that the racist policies pursued by English aristocrats, who they believed ruled the world, must be politically desirable and correct and ought to be adopted by any modern, forward-looking government. This meeting of minds gave the Nazis the intellectual respectability they craved and gave them the moral authority and permission to carry out their pathologically misconceived schemes.

There is one final aspect of Anglo-German relations in the 1930s that is perhaps most curious of all. It is that, had Hitler sat down to such a heart-to-heart talk over dinner, not with Britain's fascist elements, but with its actual leaders – such as Churchill, Halifax, Hoare, Chamberlain and Eden – and had both sides managed to overcome their intense mutual suspicion, they, too, would probably have found themselves in agreement with the main planks of Nazi foreign policy, though not, of course, domestic policy.

11

Perfidious Albion

Consider this description of England's military spirit:

> England has always possessed whatever armament she
> happened to need. She always fought with the weapons
> which success demanded. She fought with mercenaries
> as long as mercenaries sufficed; but she reached down
> into the precious blood of the whole nation when only
> such a sacrifice could bring victory; but the determina-
> tion for victory, the tenacity and ruthless pursuit of this
> struggle, remained unchanged.[1]

The prose is almost Churchillian and the writer clearly pos-
sesses a considered understanding of, and admiration for,
English character and military tradition. Perhaps surprisingly, the writer was Adolf Hitler, imprisoned for nine
months in Landsberg Fortress for his abortive coup
attempt and penning the book that accurately foreshad-
owed all his future political strategies, *Mein Kampf*.

Hitler's autobiography is notable for several reasons.
First, he openly and without embellishment or evasion laid
out his entire future geopolitical strategy, a strategy he later
attempted to follow to the letter. Second, he equally frankly

disclosed his evaluation of, and feelings for, the English, and described in detail, several times, the kind of working relationship he wanted to establish with the British Empire.

Mein Kampf (My Struggle) is often dismissed as badly-written drivel, part Nazi propaganda and part the delusory maundering of a madman. One contemporary critic contemptuously referred to its '600 turgid pages'. These descriptions may well be influenced in part by the book's obsessive, carpet-chewing tirades against Jews and others. However, when he is not romanticising his own past or foaming at the mouth against imaginary enemies, Hitler's book is a great deal more literate and more informative than the average political memoirs. In particular it is a great deal better informed on the subject of geo-political strategy.

Early in his book, Hitler re-examines the political strategy of Germany before 1914 and concludes that it was disastrously wrong. Above all, Hitler believed, Germany should have gone to any lengths, paid practically any price, in order to conclude an alliance with England. He wrote:

> All alliances, therefore, should have been viewed exclusively from this standpoint and judged according to their possible utilisation. If land was desired in Europe, it could be obtained by and large only at the expense of Russia, and this meant that the new Reich must again set itself on the march along the road of the Teutonic Knights of old, to obtain by the German sword sod for the German plough and daily bread for the nation. For such a policy there was but one ally in Europe: England. With England alone was it possible, our rear protected, to begin the new Germanic march ... Consequently, no sacrifice should have been too great for winning England's willingness. We should have renounced

colonies and sea power, and spared English industry our competition. Only an absolutely clear orientation could lead to such a goal: renunciation of world trade and colonies; renunciation of a German war fleet; concentration of all the state's instruments of power on the land army. The result, to be sure, would have been a momentary limitation but a great and mighty future.[2]

Not only was Hitler convinced that alliance with England was the only way for Germany to advance strategically; he also believed that such an alliance was realistically feasible:

There was a time when England would have listened to reason on this point, since she was well aware that Germany as a result of her increased population had to seek some way out and either find it with England in Europe or without England in the world. And it can primarily be attributed to this realisation if at the turn of the century London itself attempted to approach Germany. For the first time a thing became evident which in the last years we have had occasion to observe in a truly terrifying fashion. People were unpleasantly affected by the thought of having to pull England's chestnuts out of the fire; as though there ever could be an alliance on any other basis than a mutual business deal. And with England such a deal could very well have been made. British diplomacy was still clever enough to realise that no service can be expected without a return.[3]

The policy that Germany had actually pursued, which Hitler characterised as an attempt at the 'peaceful economic conquest of the world' was the one that inevitably led to war with England, he said – a war that could and should have been avoided.

If, nevertheless, Germany took this road, [economic and industrial expansionism] she should at least have clearly recognised that this development would some day likewise end in struggle. Only children could have thought that they could get their bananas in the 'peaceful contest of nations', by friendly and moral conduct and constant emphasis on their peaceful intentions, as they so high-soundingly and unctuously babbled; in other words, without ever having to take up arms. No: if we chose this road, England would some day inevitably become our enemy. It was more than senseless – but quite in keeping with our own innocence – to wax indignant over the fact that England should one day take the liberty to oppose our peaceful activity with the brutality of a violent egoist.[4]

Talk about the 'peaceful economic conquest of the world', said Hitler, was possibly 'the greatest nonsense which has ever been exalted to be a guiding principle of state policy'. He adds that what made such a policy even more nonsensical was that its supporters pointed to England as being a prime example of the success of such a 'peaceful economic conquest'. England, said Hitler, was an example of the very opposite.

England, in particular, should have been recognised as the striking refutation of this theory; for no people has ever with greater brutality better prepared its economic conquests with the sword, and later ruthlessly defended them than the English nation. Is it not positively the distinguishing feature of British statesmanship to draw economic acquisitions from political strength, and at once to recast every gain in economic strength into political power? And what an error to believe that England is personally too much of a coward to stake her own blood for her economic policy! The fact that the English people possessed no 'people's army' in no way proved the contrary; for what matters is not the momentary military form of the fighting forces, but rather the will and determination to risk those which do exist. England has always possessed whatever armament she happened to need. She always fought with the weapons which success demanded. She fought with mercenaries as long as mercenaries sufficed; but she reached down into the precious blood of the whole nation when only such a sacrifice could bring victory; but the determination for victory, the tenacity and ruthless pursuit of this struggle, remained unchanged.[5]

In this passage Hitler showed in the clearest possible terms how he believed England's empire had come about: not by accident, in a 'fit of absentmindedness', as in the English national myth, but by brutality and ruthlessness. Moreover, he showed that he intended to act in the same ruthless and determined way to secure a German empire – not in remote oceanic provinces but rather by conquest of the peoples of central Eurasia. In other words, he wanted to become like the English and to achieve this aim he was going to act like the English. But, Hitler believed, Germany had an extra ace up its sleeve:

[As the] Englishman had succeeded, we too were bound to succeed, and our definitely greater honesty, the absence in us of that specifically English 'perfidy', was regarded as a very special plus. For it was hoped that this would enable us to win the affection, particularly of the smaller nations, and the confidence of the large ones the more easily.[6]

But as well as the Englishman's cold ruthlessness, according to Hitler, England also had another important weapon in its armoury, which he believed Germany must acquire to become successful.

> Nothing proved the Englishman's superior psychological knowledge of the popular soul better than the motivation that he gave to his struggle. While we fought for bread, England fought for 'freedom'; and not even for her own, no, for that of the small nations. In our country we laughed at this effrontery, or were enraged at it, and thus only demonstrated how empty-headed and stupid the so-called statesmen of Germany had become even before the War. We no longer had the slightest idea concerning the essence of the force that can lead men to their death of their own free will and decision. In 1914 as long as the German people thought they were fighting for ideals, they stood firm; but as soon as they were told to fight for their daily bread, they preferred to give up the game.[7]

It wasn't only when penning geo-political works for posterity that Hitler was openly admiring of the English. His Anglophile leanings were there in his personal life, too. His well-known predilection for taking tea each day at five, complete with cucumber sandwiches and swastikas on the plates and tea cups, was a very non-German habit acquired from the English. He also regularly read English magazines which showed the upper classes relaxing in their country homes, such as *The Tatler*.

And he invited a constant stream of prominent British people to Berlin and to his retreat at the Berghof, in order to cement Anglo-German relations and create a receptive atmosphere for a rapprochement.

According to David Irving:

It was for the British that he had a maudlin, unrequited affection that caused him to pull his punches throughout 1940 to the exasperation of his strategic advisers. As Halder explained Hitler's program to the chief of army intelligence late in January: 'The Fuhrer wants to win the war *militarily*: defeating France and then a grand gesture to Britain. He recognises the need for an empire.'

During lunch at the Chancellery in these weeks of early 1940, Rudolph Hess once enquired, 'Mein Fuhrer, are your views about the British still the same?' Hitler gloomily sighed, 'If only the British knew how *little* I ask of them!'

How he liked to leaf through the glossy pages of *The Tatler*, studying the British aristocracy in their natural habitat! Once he was overheard to say, 'Those are valuable specimens – those are the ones I am going to make peace with.'[8]

What is perhaps most interesting of all about *Mein Kampf* is that, towards the end of the book, Hitler makes it plain that not only should Germany have concluded a partnership agreement with Britain at any cost before 1914, in order to prevent a war, but that this was still the correct future course for post-war Germany.

I should not like to conclude these reflections without pointing once again to the sole alliance possibility that exists for us at the moment in Europe. In the previous chapter on the alliance problem I have already designated England and Italy as the only two states in Europe with which a closer relationship would be desirable and promising for us. Here I shall briefly touch on the military importance of such an alliance.

The military consequences of concluding this alliance would in every respect be the opposite of the consequences of an alliance with Russia. The most important consideration, first of all, is the fact that in itself an approach to England and Italy in no way conjures up a war danger. France, the sole power that could conceivably oppose the alliance, would not be in a position to do so. And consequently the alliance would give Germany the possibility of peacefully making those preparations for a reckoning with France, which would have to be made in any event within the scope of such a coalition. For the significant feature of such an alliance lies precisely in the fact that upon its conclusion Germany would not suddenly be exposed to a hostile invasion, but that the opposing alliance would break of its own accord; the Entente, to which we owe such infinite misfortune, would be dissolved, and hence France, the mortal enemy of our nation, would be isolated. Even if this success is limited at first to moral effect, it would suffice to give Germany freedom of movement to an extent which today is scarcely conceivable. For the law of action would be in the hands of the new European Anglo-German-Italian alliance and no longer with France.

The further result would be that at one stroke Germany would be freed from her unfavourable strategic position. The most powerful protection on our flank on the one hand, complete guarantee of our food and raw materials on the other, would be the beneficial effect of the new constellation of states. But almost more important would be the fact that the new league would embrace states that in technical productivity almost complement one another in many respects. For the first time Germany would have allies who would not drain our own economy like leeches, but could and would contribute their share to the richest supplementation of our technical armament.

And do not overlook the final fact that in both cases we should be dealing with allies who cannot be compared with Turkey or present-day Russia. The greatest world power on earth and a youthful national state would offer different premises for a struggle in Europe than the putrid state corpses with which Germany allied herself in the last war.

Assuredly, as I emphasised in the last chapter, the difficulties opposing such an alliance are great. But was the formation of the Entente, for instance, any less difficult? What the genius of a King Edward VII achieved, in part almost counter to natural interests, we, too, must and will achieve, provided we are so inspired by our awareness of the necessity of such a development that with astute self-control we determine our actions accordingly. And this will become possible in the moment when, imbued with admonishing distress, we pursue, not the diplomatic aimlessness of the last decades, but a conscious and determined course, and stick to it.[9]

So it was that, from the outset, the leader of the resurgent German nation and Nazi Party was a self-confessed Anglophile whose primary foreign policy aim was an alliance with Britain. In this, Hitler was keeping faith with the foreign policy of Germany for the past hundred years, excepting only the disastrous aberration of 1914–18, when the Anglo-German alliance flickered and was temporarily extinguished.

But if Hitler was a committed true believer in an Anglo-German alliance, why did such a partnership not come about? Was it because he was unable to convince his fellow Nazis of the central importance of such a strategy? Was it because his fellow Nazis failed to share his passion for Britain and the British?

12

The Playing Fields of Eton

Even allowing for the inevitable distortions of our perceptions by wartime Allied propaganda, there is a fundamental misconception about the Nazi leadership that I
sense remains widespread even today: the idea that senior
Nazis had little real understanding of the British and were
out of touch with what was really going on in Britain. More
than one historian has painted a picture of senior figures in
Berlin scrabbling through the British daily newspapers in
search of clues to events in Whitehall.

In fact, something pretty nearly the opposite of this was
the case. Like Hitler, many top Nazis were Anglophiles who
had British friends, who cultivated a keen understanding of
Britain and her way of life, and who had many firm
communications links to London. This group included
Hess, Goering, Ribbentrop, Speer, Heydrich, Doenitz, Jodl,
Economics Minister Schacht and other, less well-known
figures who were nonetheless part of Hitler's immediate
circle, such as Karl Haushofer, Ernst Hanfstaengl and
Ernst Bohle.

From the very earliest days of the Nazi Party in Munich,
Hitler's staunchest supporter, and the man he appointed

Deputy Leader of the Nazi Party, was Rudolf Hess. Hess is usually remembered today merely as the madman who flew to Britain in 1941 and spent the rest of his life in prison. But until that episode, Hess occupied a position of importance and power and was considered an indispensable aide by Hitler, at whose side Hess was almost invariably photographed on state occasions.

In his book, *The Hitler/Hess Deception*, Martin Allen says:

Rudolph Hess was not a monumentally important personality in National Socialism, but it is certainly the case that had he never existed, or had he been killed during the First World War, the course of world history during the inter war years may well have taken a very different path. His introduction of Adolph Hitler to Professor Karl Haushofer, Germany's leading expert on geopolitics, was to have profound consequences.

Haushofer would provide Hitler with the theoretical concepts of Nazi expansionism, German ethnicity and *lebensraum*, or living space, for the German people. Furthermore in the years to come his son Albrecht would provide important assistance to Hitler and Hess, inexorably advancing the Nazis' aims of territorial expansion within Europe, according to his father's plans for a Greater Germany. By the late 1930s Albrecht Haushofer would become the hidden hand of Hess and his Fuhrer in pursuing the Nazis' foreign policy objectives.[1]

These two men, Hess and Haushofer, were to have more influence than any other over Hitler's strategic thinking and his ideas on geopolitics both before and during the existence of the Third Reich. Both men were fluent English-speakers, actively pro-British, with extensive friends and political contacts in the British Isles. And both had absorbed some radical new British ideas on geopolitics that were to shape Nazi thinking.

Hess had seen action fighting for Germany in many theatres from 1914 to 1918, including Ypres and Verdun as well as the Eastern Front. In 1918 he managed to join Germany's newly-formed Air Corps, in which he trained to become a fighter pilot and flew Fokker triplanes during the last weeks of war. After the war, Hess joined the Thule Society, a part-mystical, part-political Munich club that was the forerunner of the Nazi Party. In the summer of 1919, a fellow member introduced him over dinner to Professor Karl Haushofer. Haushofer was a rare individual. As well as being professor of geopolitics at Munich University he was also a general who had commanded the Thirteenth Bavarian Division during the First World War. His theories on geopolitics were no ivory-tower pipe-dreams, but grounded in his first-hand experience of modern war in all its horrors. Martin Allen explains the significance of Haushofer:

> Geopolitics was the theory, as promulgated by Haushofer, that in the future the world would be restructured into an age of great land empires, dominated by 'the Heartland', an area 'invulnerable to sea-power in Central Europe and Asia.' This, Haushofer asserted, would revolutionise the world's balance of power, ushering in a 'new age' of stability, peace and prosperity for all.

Where had this startling concept originated? Allen explains:

> In 1904, the eminent British geographer H.J. Mackinder had written a paper titled 'The Geographical Pivot of

History', which Haushofer had read avidly, particularly the paragraph that declared: 'The spaces within the Russian Empire and Mongolia are so vast, and their potentialities in population, wheat, cotton, fuel and metals so incalculably great, that it is inevitable that a vast economic world, more or less apart, will there develop inaccessible to Oceanic commerce.'[2]

In a by-now well established process in which English concepts were 'Germanised', Haushofer took Mackinder's geographical ideas and added to them a new dimension – German ethnicity. Haushofer said that the realisation of Mackinder's new Euro-Asian empire would come about only when Europe was redefined along ethnic lines so that there was a suitable single ethnic bloc, dominating the whole of central Europe. That ethnic group, believed Haushofer, was destined to be the Germanic peoples.

Hess was quickly converted to Haushofer's theories and rapidly became a close friend of the entire Haushofer family: the Professor, his wife Martha, and their two sons, Albrecht and Heinz. Hess had much in common with the Haushofers besides political ideas, for all of them were Anglophiles who had visited England and spoke fluent English.

Hess got on particularly well with Haushofer's elder son, Albrecht, an intelligent young man of seventeen. A friendship swiftly developed that would last the rest of their lives. In a foretaste of events to come, Hess would comment: 'I sometimes go for a walk with [Albrecht] and we speak English together.'

After five months of congenial friendship with Karl Haushofer – the relationship having quickly developed into one of devoted protégé and mentor – Hess quit his job at a

Munich textile importers to enrol at Munich University as a student of geographical politics under Karl Haushofer.[3]

Karl Haushofer served in the Bavarian army as a young man in the 1880s and later joined the Foreign Service, serving in Germany's embassy in Japan and becoming fluent in Japanese, as well as visiting India, China, Korea and Russia. In the 1890s he returned to Germany and took up a post with the General Staff, teaching at the Military Academy. After his marriage in 1896, he joined the academic world where he wished to develop his new ideas on geographical politics.

> In 1898 the Haushofers visited Britain, where Karl was to conduct a series of lectures on 'Internationalism'. It was during this trip that he first learnt of a theory that he would one day develop into geopolitics. During this trip he also made several important contacts that would stand him in good stead in the coming years. In London, he met the Colonial Secretary Joseph Chamberlain (father of Neville Chamberlain) considered at the time to be very much the coming man of British politics. After this the Haushofers planned to travel on to Cambridge, where Karl was due to give a lecture. However, they went first to Oxford where Karl made the acquaintance of a young Scot by the name of Halford Mackinder, a geography don who was developing an exciting new theory concerning the Eurasian 'Heartland' … which, he claimed, would by natural ascendancy eventually gain superiority over the 'maritime lands'.[4]

The Haushofers made another important friendship when they travelled to Cambridge. Karl was due to speak to the Cambridge Foreign Science Students' Committee, and the secretary of this group was a Cambridge lecturer named

Herbert Roberts. The Haushofers became friends with him, his wife Violet and their son Patrick, a friendship that would last 40 years, the Robertses often visiting Germany and the Haushofers often staying in Cambridge.

Twenty years later, the First World War now over, Karl Haushofer became a member of Munich University's Department of Geography with the title Professor General in deference to his wartime stint in command of an artillery regiment. At the university he lectured on the new science of geopolitics, which he defined as 'a science concerned with the dependence of the domestic and foreign politics of peoples upon the physical environment'.[5]

The friendship between Hess and Haushofer was to have fateful consequences. In the spring of 1921, Hess persuaded the Professor to accompany him to a working-class district of Munich to hear a young political firebrand speak out about the injustices of the Versailles Treaty and the evils of communism. The speaker was Adolf Hitler. Hess appears to have been sold on Hitler from the start. Haushofer was less sure to begin with, but eventually he, too, gave his support to Hitler becoming leader of the fledgling National Socialist Workers' Party.

How close the relationship became between Hitler and the Haushofers (despite the fact that Martha was of Jewish parents) can be judged from Hitler's actions two years later, following the failure of his attempt to stage a coup in 1923. After a street gun battle in central Munich between Nazis and army, it was to the Haushofers' flat that Hitler fled to hide up for the night.[6]

After the failure of the putsch, Hitler and Hess were both sentenced to a term of imprisonment in Landsberg Fortress near Munich. And it was during his time in prison that Hitler wrote *Mein Kampf*. Hess acted as his secretary, taking the book down as Hitler dictated it. But Hitler was not merely dictating his political beliefs while imprisoned; he was also learning about international politics from Hess and, ultimately, from Haushofer. Thus there are three distinct voices in *Mein Kampf*: Hitler's, Hess's and Haushofer's. All three were admirers of the English and their empire.

It is against this background that one must see *Mein Kampf*'s admiration for the British Empire and its insistence that Germany's principal territorial claims lay in the east, not in Europe.

During Professor Haushofer's interrogation by American Intelligence in 1945, he was asked: 'isn't it true that Hess collaborated with Hitler in writing *Mein Kampf*?' The by now very elderly Haushofer replied unhesitatingly: 'As far as I know Hess actually dictated many of the chapters in that book.'[7]

Haushofer's son, Albrecht, was also to have an important influence on Hitler and other top Nazis. During the 1930s he travelled the world, lecturing in South America, India, China, Japan and Egypt.

Despite Albrecht's range of contacts across the world, the country that he – and also Hitler and Hess – had a predominant interest in cultivating was not an ocean or a continent away. It was a rather staid, old-fashioned, class-structured little nation a mere 350 miles from Germany's Western frontiers. It did however possess one of the world's great empires, and was one of the world's major powers. Albrecht Haushofer was Germany's foremost expert on Britain.[8]

Through the Haushofers' family connections with Patrick Roberts, Albrecht met many important members of the British ruling class.

> By the mid-1930s Albrecht Haushofer's range of aristocratic and political contacts had completely opened up British society to him, such that he had dined and smoked after-dinner cigars with such pillars of the British establishment as Stanley Baldwin, Ramsay Macdonald, Neville Chamberlain, Lord Dunglass (Alec Douglas-Home) Sir John Simon, Anthony Eden, Lord Halifax and, perhaps most intriguingly of all, Winston Churchill.[9]

An example of Albrecht Haushofer's importance to the Nazi government occurred in 1935 when Germany re-introduced conscription, a move that alarmed Whitehall to such an extent that Foreign Secretary Sir John Simon was dispatched with Anthony Eden to fly to Berlin to find out what Hitler was going to do next.

> Hitler, for his part, was deeply worried by the British reaction, and was indeed ' putting on a brave face'. He absolutely did not want a conflict with the British and made no secret of the fact that he considered the English to be Germany's 'Aryan cousins'. He therefore desperately wanted to persuade Britain's politicians to let him do exactly as he wanted, without a war which he knew Germany would lose at that time.

In a confidential meeting on Saturday 23 March 1935, held at his Reich Chancellery Office, Hitler met with Hess, Phillipp Bouhler, the Chancellery head and party business manager, and Albrecht Haushofer, attending as a specialist on English affairs, to decide the course of action. It was concluded that an Anglo-German diplomatic banquet would provide the best low-key opportunity for Hitler to argue his case for Germany's need to throw off the shackles of Versailles. To Haushofer fell the task of drawing up the guest list, devising the seating plan and advising Hitler during his meeting with Simon and Eden.

At the banquet the guests were placed so that Eden was seated close to Hitler, separated from him only by Lady Phipps, the British Ambassador's wife, while Sir John Simon was placed opposite the German Fuhrer. Other British guests included leading Tory politician Viscount Cranborne, the new Ambassador to Berlin Sir Eric Phipps and his predecessor Sir John Seymour, while the top Germans present included Goering, Hess, Goebbels and von Neurath. There were, however, no military men, no SS or Schutzstaffel, and certainly no one whose presence would have hinted at the darker side of Nazism, such Himmler or Heydrich. This was a diplomatic dinner aimed at defusing a sensitive international situation, not an occasion for military intimidation. However, as Goebbels later noted, Hitler did speak 'out against Russia [and] has laid a cuckoo's egg which is intended to hatch into an Anglo-German entente.'[10]

This policy of *England-Politik* began to be realised later in 1935, the year that the two countries signed the Anglo-German Naval Agreement which tore up the limitations placed on German military shipbuilding contained in the Versailles Treaty. In 1937, Hitler's 'cuckoo's egg' policy had fully hatched, because when Lord Halifax visited Germany and met Hitler, he noted: 'Unless I am wholly deceived, the Germans speaking generally, from Hitler to the man in the street, do want friendly relations with Great Britain. There are no doubt many who don't: and the leading men may be deliberately throwing dust in our eyes. But I don't think so ...'[11]

As well as these heartfelt connections and links to Britain at the very top of Nazi Germany, there were many other senior party officials and government ministers with similar Anglophile links. Among them was a fascinating and enigmatic character, Ernst Bohle.

One of the Nazis' most important Foreign Office departments was the *Auslandorganization*, which was responsible for the political well-being of Germans living outside the Reich. This department reported directly to Rudolf Hess, and at its head was Ernst Bohle.

Bohle was born in Bradford, Yorkshire in 1903. When he was still a child his parents emigrated from England to South Africa. Later, he studied economics and political science at the University of Cologne. Because of his birth and early upbringing here, Bohle spoke perfect English. Amazingly, until as late as 1937, by which time he was already very senior in the Nazi government, he remained a British citizen.

Having gained his doctorate in commerce in 1923, Bohle's early career had been in the import and export business, based first in Rotterdam and then in Hamburg. In 1931 he had seen an advertisement in a newspaper for a post within the Nazi Party's new foreign policy office ... Bohle thus had a common background with Hess. They were both *Auslanders* by birth, they had both begun their careers in commerce, and had both worked in the import trade in Hamburg. As a result the two got on very well together, often sharing jokes about past experience that others in the Nazi Party were unable to understand. By 1932 Bohle was heading the small but increasingly important *Auslandorganization*, where he remained for the next ten years, nine of them under one superior – Rudolph Hess.[12]

Because of his languages and foreign affairs expertise, Bohle was drafted into the German Foreign Ministry, becoming a Secretary of State in the Foreign Office in January 1937. The same year he visited London with the aim of furthering a long-term Anglo-German peace accord. While in England he, like Haushofer before him, made the acquaintance of many politically powerful people, including Winston Churchill, with whom he was photographed.

Bohle was not only an Anglophile like his superior, Hess, but also appears to have been someone who genuinely wished to work hard in the cause of peace. Of his trip, he later commented: 'I personally didn't believe in war, and I made that pretty public in my speech in London in 1937.'

Hermann Goering was a fluent English-speaker who retained the respect of a First World War fighter ace for his former opponents in the Royal Flying Corps (and later the RAF). This attraction of opposites was to prove potentially important in Anglo-German relations once the Second World War had started, since, as described later, several of the important moves to sign a peace treaty between Britain and Germany were either initiated by Goering or emanated from the Air Ministry in Whitehall and would have landed on his desk. More importantly, Goering was perceived in London as being a relatively 'moderate' politician who might take Hitler's place as Chancellor in a general settle-ment. The most important peace overtures instigated by

Germany to Britain in 1939 were those of Birger Dahlerus, the influential Swedish businessman who was a personal friend of Goering, who had lived and worked in Sweden between the wars.

Heinrich Himmler was not an English-speaker, nor a noted Anglophile, but he followed the lead of Hitler in admiring what they both saw as the ruthlessness and hardness of the English ruling classes.

On occasions, Himmler's responses showed that he, too, was an innocent victim of the myths of the aristocratic Englishman. He prescribed a regulation diet of porridge for breakfast for his SS men on health grounds. When some SS wives questioned whether such a diet might not make them fat, Himmler reassured them by pointing to Anthony Eden and Nevile Henderson, British ambassador to Berlin, both men of enviably slim build and both, said Himmler, members of the English aristocracy, 'in which society nothing whatever is ever eaten for breakfast but porridge'.[13] That a handful of shy, tweed-wearing, inbred individuals should inspire such admiration and even awe in one of the worst mass-murderers the world has ever known is a curious tribute to the English public-school system.

One of Himmler's primary concerns was to locate and recruit young men and women considered to be of 'pure Aryan' blood to join the ranks of the SS and produce Aryan children for the Reich. Hitler and Himmler looked once again to England to find inspiration. The Scouting movement was started in England in 1907 by General Robert Baden-Powell. Only two years later, there were Scouts in Ireland, Australia, Canada, New Zealand and South Africa, and Baden-Powell was summoned to Windsor where he was knighted by King Edward VII. By the time the Nazis came to power in 1933, Scouting was a global phenomenon with an astonishing 1 million Scouts and Guides in Britain alone. The same year, Hitler ordered the formation of the Hitler Jugend (or Youth) movement, based on closely similar lines, with its quasi-military uniform, military drilling and organisation, training in outdoor activities, and its emphasis on the toughening up of youngsters to military-style discipline. Above all, Hitler wished to emulate the central ethic of British Scouting in the 1930s – that youngsters can best serve their country by being prepared for military conflict from a young age, to be ready for national service when grown up.[14]

The Nazi Party's youth movement was formed with the aims of encouraging physical training, Nazi ideology and racial concepts, as well as absolute obedience to Hitler and the party. Once Hitler had assumed complete control over the German state, he made the Hitler Jugend the country's sole youth movement, banning Scouting and other youth groups. The Nazis organised German youngsters into two branches of the Hitler Jugend, one branch for boys and one for girls. Membership was eventually made compulsory, and all boys had to report to a neighbourhood office to have their racial background checked and to be registered for membership.

Hitler's aims here were primarily military. In a speech in 1935, he said: 'He alone, who owns the youth, gains the Future.'[15] By the late 1930s, this prediction was coming true and the Hitler Youth movement was providing a steady stream of conscripts both for the Wehrmacht and for Himmler's SS.

It would be easy to conclude that Hitler's aims in founding the Hitler Youth and Baden-Powell's in founding the Scouts were radically different: the former warlike, the latter peaceful. In fact Baden-Powell's aims were explicitly those of providing early military training in order to prepare the next generation for a future war. He says in *Scouting for Boys*: 'Every boy ought to learn how to shoot and obey orders, else he is no more good when war breaks out than an old woman.'[16]

There is, of course, a radical difference between the two movements in that there was and is no compulsion in Scouting, no automatic conscription to the armed services and no racial checks or discrimination on racial grounds. But it remains a fact that most Scout meetings closed with a prayer that was taken straight from the Protestant prayer book, a custom that must have made many Jews and Catholics in the 1930s question whether they would be welcome in such a movement. The seriousness with which Hitler and other top Nazis treated the Hitler Jugend was one more example of Nazi admiration for English institutions being so great that they were taken up and transplanted wholesale into German daily life in a way that affected literally millions of German families.

Hjalmar Schacht was another Anglophile senior Nazi. His father, who had lived in the United States, christened him Hjalmar Horace Greely Schacht after the American radical journalist and campaigner against slavery. Schacht was the financial genius who conquered Germany's hyper-inflation after the First War and became President of the German National Bank and, later, Hitler's Minister of Economics. He spoke and wrote perfect English and toured the US in the 1930s making many speeches and radio broadcasts and writing articles in American newspapers. Schacht was instrumental in enabling Hitler to come to power since he persuaded many wealthy German industrialists to support the Nazis financially. Like Hitler, he believed strongly in alliance with Britain and the United States.[17]

1. Kaiser Wilhelm II prepares to hunt with the royal hounds in the English manner in Brandenberg, November 1895.

2. British guests and observers during the German army manoeuvres of 1906: Winston Churchill, junior minister at the Colonial Office (front left) with the Earl of Lonsdale (smoking a cigar) and General Ian Hamilton (third from right).

3. King Edward VII and Kaiser Wilhelm. Although appearing in public here in civilian clothes, Edward was a Field Marshal in the German army, a uniform he wore on military occasions.

4. British tourists outside Thomas Cook's Berlin office, c.1910. Germany was Britain's favourite overseas holiday destination.

Imperial War
Museum

5. A Boer commando. An armed revolt by a few thousand
    farmers in South Africa in 1899 tied up all of Britain's imperial
    military resources for three years. This is the face of the enemy
    that made headlines in Britain for so long.

Imperial War
Museum

6. Lord Milner, Britain's High Commissioner to South Africa,
    and his military staff. Milner engineered the Boer War with the
    aim of extending British imperial rule from Cairo to the Cape.

Imperial War Museum

7. British soldiers clearing a farm at Winburg. 'Clearing' was the
    euphemism for the illegal forced eviction of Boer women and
    children to 'concentration camps' and the torching of their
    homes – the very atrocity that Britain accused Germany of
    twelve years later. More than 26,000 Boer women and children
    and 14,000 black Africans died in the camps from lack of
    proper food and medical treatment.

Imperial War Museum

8. A refugee Boer family, surrounded by their possessions at a
    railway station. They have been dispossessed of their home by
    Britain's war of imperial expansion in Africa.

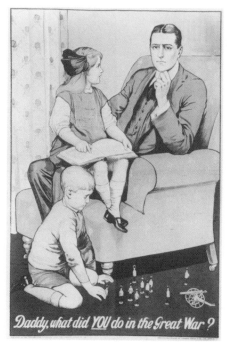

Imperial War Museum

TAKE UP THE
SWORD OF JUSTICE

9, 10. British propaganda was skilful both in its emotional appeal and in seizing the moral high ground. Here Britannia calls for justice over the sinking of the passenger liner *Lusitania* by a German U-boat.

Imperial War Museum

11. The German war machine according to the US Committee on Public Information.

Imperial War Museum

Author's collection

12. The reality. A German private, Nicolas Gruber, sends home a picture postcard of himself and comrades in 1915.

Imperial War Museum

13. This poster is a work of pure imagination by British Intelligence. It's difficult to see what effect it is intended to have, other than to instil in British people a lifelong hatred of Germans.

14. Once the Bryce Report on German 'atrocities' had been published, its main allegations were later turned into visual form as shown in this poster. Germans are depicted bayoneting babies, torching a poor home, and drunkenly eyeing up a helpless girl preparatory to rape.

Imperial War Museum

15. Ernest Brooks, the first British official war photographer to be appointed by Wellington House. Charles Masterman decreed that no pictures of dead bodies should be published. None were.

16. A corporal of the Hampshires releasing a leaflet balloon. Leaflets were regularly dropped by propaganda units over German lines.

17. President Wilson leaves Versailles having handed the German delegation the terms of the Treaty, 7 May 1919. Wilson's press officer at the peace conference, who set up his many photo opportunities, was Edward Bernays, who later founded the public relations industry.

18. Hitler and Rudolph Hess (second from right) on their release from Landsberg prison in 1924. At Landsberg, Hitler wrote *Mein Kampf* with the help of Hess and Albrecht Haushofer, professor of geopolitics at Munich University. Both Hess and Haushofer were fluent English-speakers and, like Hitler, passionate Anglophiles, who argued for strategic alliance with the British Empire.

19. The Reichstag fire, 1933. The Nazis blamed the communists and the international press blamed the Nazis. Yet a British reporter was on the scene within minutes and found that it was the work of a single fanatic, Marinus van de Lubbe.

Imperial War Museum

Imperial War Museum

20. Hitler Youth. Hitler and Himmler modelled their youth movement on Britain's Boy Scouts.

21. Joachim von Ribbentrop leaving the German embassy in London on his way to Buckingham Palace, 1936. Ribbentrop infuriated British opinion by giving the Nazi salute to the King.

Imperial War Museum

Imperial War Museum

22. Hitler in conversation with British ambassador Sir Nevile Henderson at a Berlin reception. Henderson cabled the Foreign Office in 1939: 'If we handle him [Hitler] right, my belief is that he will become gradually more pacific. But if we treat him as a pariah or mad dog we shall turn him finally and irrevocably into one.'

23. Goebbels opening the 16th Radio and TV Show in July 1939 and watching the German television service. He was among the first politicians to appreciate the importance of radio, and here appears to be weighing up the potential of TV.

24. Goebbels swaps propaganda ideas with Italian Culture Minister Alessandro Pavolini in June 1941.

25. Hitler, in country tweeds, inspects the table setting for tea in the Berghof. He took tea and cakes every afternoon in the English manner.

26. Neville Chamberlain, French Prime Minister Daladier, Hitler and Mussolini on signing the Munich Agreement, September 1938. Chamberlain's attempts to come to terms with Hitler were too little, too late.

Imperial War Museum

27. By 1941, as Britain stood alone, the Red Menace had become our only ally in fighting Nazism, so communism was no longer un-British.

Imperial War Museum

28. Winston Churchill gives the victory sign at No. 10 Downing Street. Churchill promised to 'fight on the beaches', yet there were no fewer than sixteen separately identifiable attempts to conclude peace with Germany between September 1939 and September 1940.

29. William Beveridge, author of the report that led to the post-war National Health Service. Best remembered today as a humanitarian, Beveridge was also a eugenicist who once wrote that unemployed men should lose the vote, their freedom and the right to fatherhood.

30. Army Bureau of Current Affairs lecture, April 1943. A medical officer lectures serving soldiers on plans for a post-war National Health Service. *British Way and Purpose* pamphlets were produced for use in such lectures so that the men in uniform knew what they were fighting for.

31. Albert Speer (left) puts some distance between himself and Admiral Doenitz and General Jodl on being taken into custody by the British army in 1945. Speer and Doenitz were spared at Nuremberg but Jodl was hanged, although he was not a Nazi.

32. Churchill poses for a photograph sitting on one of the chairs from Hitler's bunker in Berlin, 1945.

However, although Schacht supported Hitler's political ideas, he did not go along with Hitler's violent anti-Semitism and he publicly disagreed with what he called 'unlawful activities' against Jews. In August 1935 he made a speech denouncing the rabid anti-Semitism of Julius Streicher and the articles he had been writing in *Der Stürmer*. He pointed out that Jews had fought bravely in the German army in the First World War and deserved to be treated fairly. Schacht also disagreed with the amounts being spent on armaments.

In November 1937, Schacht resigned as Minister of Economics, although he kept his position as President of the Reichsbank where he continued to oppose expenditures for armaments. Eventually, in January 1939, Hitler removed Schacht from power. In 1944, he was arrested and charged with being involved in the July Plot to kill Hitler (although he had actually refused to take part). He was sent to Dachau concentration camp but survived the war. Schacht was then arrested by the Allies and accused of crimes against humanity at the Nuremberg war crimes trial. He was found not guilty.

The other major Anglophile in Hitler's immediate circle was Joachim von Ribbentrop. Anglophile is perhaps not the precise term for Ribbentrop, since his attitudes towards the British seem to have been ambivalent. Ribbentrop was educated at boarding school in Switzerland but also spent some time in England as a child and learned to speak English fluently. In 1911, he started work in London as a clerk with a German importing company. A year or so later he moved to Canada where he worked on the reconstruction of the Quebec Bridge and the Canadian Pacific Railroad. He then moved into the United States where his English was good enough for him to be employed as a journalist in both New York and Boston.[18]

He served in the German army during the First War, was wounded in action and decorated. In 1917 he joined the War Ministry, and he was a member of the German delegation that attended the Paris Peace Conference. After leaving the German army, Ribbentrop worked as a salesman for the French champagne company Pommery in the Rhineland.

Ribbentrop joined the Nazi Party in 1932 and rose with astounding speed through its ranks. Within a year he had become Hitler's foreign policy adviser and by 1936 was appointed German ambassador to London. In 1938, Hitler appointed him Foreign Minister and he began to negotiate treaties directly with Russia and Britain.

Ribbentrop spent little time in London during his spell as ambassador, and when he was here he managed to infuriate many with whom he came in contact. He gave the Nazi salute to King George V when presenting his credentials, posted SS men on guard outside the German embassy and swept around London in his German limo, flying swastika flags.

On the other hand he loved the social-climbing opportunities that being in London offered and, when there, never missed an opportunity to rub shoulders with the English aristocracy. The rituals of polite English society appealed to him – he was an inveterate kisser of ladies' hands, imagining that this behaviour was widespread in England. He was also a snob who was not actually entitled to the 'von' he inserted in his name. He was distantly related to a real von Ribbentrop and was said to have paid the elderly relative a sum of money to adopt him legally, thus giving him the right to call himself von Ribbentrop. Just how much he had to pay for those three letters isn't known, but he evidently considered the price worth it.

His English social contacts, with the future Edward VIII and Wallis Simpson and with aristocrats who admired Hitler, were an important element in convincing the Nazis that an accommodation with England was just as feasible as the non-aggression pact that Ribbentrop had already miraculously signed with Russia. Having someone he trusted implicitly in the heart of London, drinking champagne with the very people that he could only read about in English glossy magazines, made Hitler feel increasingly confident that he could 'settle accounts' with France without interference.

From 1920 to 1937, the man who acted as Hitler's personal private secretary and personal press officer was Dr Ernst 'Putzi' Hanfstaengl, the son of a wealthy Munich publisher and an American mother. Hanfstaengl went to America as a young man and studied at Harvard University, where he graduated in 1909. He stayed in the US as a journalist and did not return to Germany until 1919. He became an early convert to Nazism and one of Hitler's financial supporters, donating the money to buy the party newspaper *Volkische Beobachter*.[19]

Hanfstaengl was an old party stalwart who took part in the 'Beer Hall putsch' in 1923, the first occasion on which Hitler and the fledgling Nazis attempted to come to power. When the coup failed, Hanfstaengl hid Hitler in one of his country homes. The two men remained close, Hanfstaengl advising Hitler on press matters and on issues in Britain and America. In 1931 Hanfstaengl was appointed foreign press chief of the Nazi Party and tried to use his contacts in Britain and America to improve Hitler's press image abroad. He later quarrelled with Goebbels and fled from

Germany to the United States in 1937, believing his life was in danger. Although not present during the war years, Hanfstaengl kept Hitler and other top Nazis briefed on events in London and Washington throughout the inter-war years.

Other senior members of both the Nazi Party and the German armed services were fluent English-speakers and had English contacts. They included Hitler's Armaments Minister, Albert Speer, Heinrich Himmler's SS deputy and head of the Gestapo, Reinhard Heydrich, who spoke both English and French, Commander-in-Chief of the German navy, Karl Doenitz, and Alfred Jodl, Chief of Operations of the armed forces high command.

Finally there is the bizarre fact that Hitler himself had English relatives. His elder brother Alois came to England around 1909, where he met and married an Irish girl, Bridget Dowling. They were married in London in 1910 and later set up home in Liverpool, where Bridget gave birth to a son, William Patrick Hitler. Bridget claimed in her memoirs (written in the 1930s to cash in on the Führer's popularity) that Adolf had visited them in Liverpool in 1913, shortly before the First World War, but this is almost certainly false (though the image of Hitler cheering on the Reds from the terraces of Anfield is a difficult one to erase from the mind).

But if German ruling circles between the wars contained so many Anglophile Nazis, many of whom wished to see the re-establishment of the traditionally close relations enjoyed by the two countries, what was the position in Britain at this time? Were the British governing classes completely deluded about the Nazis?

It was no secret, either in Whitehall or in Berlin, that there were senior members of the government and the ruling classes who were willing to consider seriously an agreement with Germany, as late as summer 1940.

The policy of appeasement that had been followed by successive governments in the 1930s was not a policy of choice but one of necessity. Without powerful allies, with dwindling finances and with the few military resources she possessed already stretched to breaking point, Britain was simply unable to oppose Hitler. Playing for time, and hoping that something would turn up, was the only feasible option. An alliance with Hitler, and perhaps Mussolini too, was a key that would unlock entirely new strategic possibilities for Britain and empire. There were also plenty of politicians in Britain who genuinely believed that the Versailles Treaty had been too harsh on Germany and who wanted to accommodate Germany within a workable international system. This group even included figures such as Churchill, and the genuine desire for fairness prompted British attempts at diplomatic conciliation such as the Treaty of Locarno in 1925. The same desire for an accommodation was also one of the roots of the policy of appeasement.

If Britain's policy of appeasement was dictated by political necessity, it was by no means unwelcome to some leading British politicians who had a real desire to restore the very close relationships that once existed between Britain and Germany and to use that relationship as the basis for a new world order.

It was an open secret that Lord Halifax, Foreign Secretary under Chamberlain, and his trusted lieutenant Rab Butler, were disposed to consider a deal with the German government – though whether with Hitler is less clear. Another well-known appeaser was Sir Samuel Hoare, whose unlikely face appeared on the famous cover of *Time* magazine on 23 September 1935. Hoare had been appointed Foreign Secretary by Prime Minister Stanley Baldwin only three months earlier but had become man of the moment because Italy had invaded Ethiopia. Together with Pierre Laval, the French Prime Minister, Hoare had cut-and-pasted together a messy secret agreement that gave Italy virtually all of the territory that it had conquered illegally. When details of the Hoare-Laval Pact were leaked to the press in December 1935, Hoare was once again in the news, accused by Churchill and others of rank appeasement of totalitarian dictators, and this time was forced to resign. Hoare's pro-appeasement stance meant that Neville Chamberlain brought him back into government in 1936 as First Lord of the Admiralty and the following year promoted him to Home Secretary. On the outbreak of war, Chamberlain included him in the War Cabinet.

When Churchill became Prime Minister in May 1940, he lost no time in getting rid of men whose presence he believed would signal a desire to make peace to Hitler. He sent Samuel Hoare to Madrid as British ambassador to Spain and Lord Halifax to Washington as Britain's American ambassador. It seems that Churchill also quashed peace overtures that had originated in London from 'Air Ministry circles'. Just who these top RAF officers or civil servants were is not clear, although the peace feelers were quickly amputated by Churchill and the War Cabinet.

A key question at this time was: Who exactly did Hitler imagine he was going to do business with in Britain? Who were the 'valuable types' he admired in the pages of *The Tatler* that he believed would be receptive to a deal to carve up the world into two parallel empires, one land-based, one sea-based?

Whatever Berlin may have imagined, the model Englishmen that Hitler thought he could do business with did not exist in reality, but only as a cleverly constructed myth that Hitler and the other Anglophile top Nazis had innocently bought into. This myth was a rich, complex, shape-shifting legend endlessly adapted to different political and propaganda purposes, but it had certain fixed themes that can still be discerned today: the stiff upper lip; playing a straight bat; championing the underdog and not kicking a man when he is down, or punching below the belt; taking everything that fate can throw at you and still doing your duty to King and Country without complaint and with no thought of personal reward other than a job well done. Kipling's famous poem 'If' is an anthem to these admired national qualities of Britishness.

One key part of the rich mythology of British military history is summed up in the idea that 'The battle of Waterloo was won on the playing fields of Eton'. This patriotic metaphor expresses the idea, widely-held in the 19th century, that great military victories such as Waterloo were won primarily by the coolness, courage, determination and fighting skill of the public-school-educated officer class who were the backbone of the British army; that the qualities instilled in English gentlemen by the fine traditions of English public schools such as Eton were the qualities needed to beat an enemy as formidable as Napoleon and France's Grande Armée – qualities such as personal courage, a sporting outlook, an immunity to sentimentality, and a selfless dedication to one's country and one's fellow countrymen.

This picture of the sportingly heroic English gentleman crops up again and again in English myths of the past two centuries, and became the central feature of many a well-loved and often-told tale. From the Indian Raj comes the young subaltern, armed with nothing more than a walking stick, who quells a native mutiny with his stern glare. From the First World War comes the madcap young officer who goes over the top kicking a football across no-man's-land, heedless of shot and shell.

From the Second War comes the army newsreel film of General Montgomery arriving in North Africa to take charge of the Eighth Army, calling his officers and men to draw near around him and then casually telling them: 'You men are going to knock Rommel for six!'

It is impossible not a feel a buzz of pride when seeing such calm, cold-blooded insouciance in the face of a mighty and implacable enemy.

Equally, it seems on the face of it to be beyond all reason that Hitler's favourite film was *The Lives of a Bengal Lancer*, a preposterous 1935 Hollywood pastiche in which American screen idols Gary Cooper and Franchot Tone play English officers stationed on India's North West Frontier, overcoming the wiles of scheming natives with British pluck while keeping a stiff upper lip. It beggars belief that someone as intellectually and politically sophisticated as Hitler could allow himself to fall victim to such crudely-drawn propaganda stereotypes. Part of the attraction for such a film, I suspect, was precisely this view of the sporting gentleman determined to do the decent thing and assert his no-nonsense English authority on the situation, armed only with a walking stick, whatever frightful tricks the treacherous natives of the lower orders may resort to.

Even with its racist overtones, this remains an attractive and comforting idea, an idea that was fostered by the English ruling class and, equally, bought into by Englishmen and women of all classes who, like Hitler, flocked to cinemas to watch films like *The Lives of Bengal Lancer*, as well as countries like Germany, keen to emulate such cool imperial heroics.

It is certainly true to say that Eton and the other first-rank public schools, such as Harrow, Rugby and Winchester, produced a disproportionate number of the British Empire's political and administrative leaders and of its senior military and naval officers in the 19th and early 20th century. But it is equally true to say that the basis of this pre-eminence was privilege based on social class rather than on merit or natural ability as the 'playing fields of Eton' myth tries to imply. It is also the case that a significant number of empire-builders and successful military leaders did not come from public schools but from a range of more modest backgrounds, and an equally significant number came from Scotland, Wales and Ireland.

But whatever the real facts, when influential individuals at home or abroad – such as Hitler and the Nazis – perceived the sporting, public-school Englishman to be an able administrator and first-rate military mind, they were merely subscribing to a national myth that was fostered to bolster British prestige around the world, especially in remote areas of India and Africa where it was necessary to hold down a superior native population largely by bluff.

More importantly – and this, I believe, is a key point in understanding Nazi psychology – when Hitler and his colleagues bought into the urban myth of the English gentleman, they laid themselves open to infatuation with, admiration of and, ultimately, dialogue with precisely the wrong kind of ally: the reactionary, fascist-minded aristocrats like Lord Redesdale, Sir Barry Domvile and Sir Oswald Mosley, with whom they believed they could do business.

Politics always makes strange bedfellows, but in this Tragedy of Errors the unholy alliance of disappointed English aristocracy and aspirant racial masters managed to convince themselves that they were spiritual and ethnic soul-mates, whose goals were identical.

More tragically still, they collaborated with each other in an attempt to reach a political rapprochement between the Germans and the English that would enable the two 'Aryan' nations to carve up the world between them into an empire that would last forever – as when Rudolf Hess flew to Scotland, imagining that he would conclude a peace agreement with influential pro-Germans.

Most tragic of all, it led Hitler to think that if only he could bypass Churchill and get through to the right people in London, he would get the same nod of aristocratic assent that he had already received in Germany; and that assent would give him the green light to act as the English had acted for centuries – to roam the world enslaving nations and peoples as the whim took him, just like the English, meeting anyone who opposed him with brutal military reprisals, just like the English, and converting the culture of every nation he touched to conform to his own national ideology, just like the English.

13

Mass Observations

If many prominent British aristocrats and intellectuals were inclined to side with Hitler and the Nazis in their views, what did the ordinary man and woman in the street think of them? Until the mid-1930s, statesmen of every democratic nation paid lip service on a daily basis to 'public opinion', a phrase that also appeared regularly in the daily newspapers. Paradoxically, while press and politicians insisted that they placed great store by public opinion, there was in fact no mechanism for determining just what that opinion might be, apart from the very imperfect sampling of noisy special-interest groups and the winner-take-all verdict of the ballot box every four years, in which an unrepresentative minority voted.

By the end of the 1920s, the marketing techniques practised by Edward Bernays had become developed to a highly sophisticated level; and by 1930, at least one New York advertising agency, Young & Rubicam, had hired its own director of market research, Dr George Gallup.[1] Random sampling techniques that would allow market research to be conducted economically had been developed in England in 1915 by A.L. Bowley.[2] Unfortunately these were unknown to statesman Robert Cecil, who left the Conservative Party in 1934, founded the International Peace Campaign, and organised what he called 'the Peace Ballot', a gigantic house-to-house survey that polled some 11.5 million replies, showing a 90 per cent majority in favour of disarmament.[3] This is very likely the biggest survey that ever has been or ever will be carried out. For Bowley's statistical methods meant that this result could have been determined with a high level of confidence from a sample of fewer than 2,000 people, just as long as they were chosen to be representative of the population as a whole.

Gallup developed Bowley's sampling methods and originated many of the methodologies and techniques used today in advertising and audience research. By 1936, he had developed his research techniques to the point where he was able to predict correctly that Franklin Roosevelt would defeat Kansas governor Alfred Landon in the Presidential election, even though a seemingly authoritative poll by *Literary Digest* had predicted a landslide win for Landon. (The *Digest*'s survey had been based on lists of registered owners of telephones and motor cars, most of whom favoured Landon; Roosevelt was elected by people too poor to own phones or cars.)[4]

It was in the following year, 1937, that someone for the first time in this country seriously questioned whether the British press actually represented accurately the views of British men and women. Three like-minded young men, Tom Harrison, Charles Madge and Humphrey Jennings, met through having written to the weekly socialist magazine *New Statesman*. Harrison was a self-taught anthropologist, Madge a Fleet Street journalist and poet, and Jennings a writer and film-maker. They set up the first English survey organisation, Mass-Observation, with the aim, they wrote in *New Statesman*, of creating an 'anthropology of our-selves' – a study of the everyday lives of ordinary people in Britain.[5]

The fledgling organisation recruited a team of paid observers and a panel of volunteer writers to study the lives and opinions of ordinary people. People's conversations and behaviour were recorded in a variety of settings – in the street, in the pub, at dance halls and cinemas, in churches and chapels, at meetings and public events, at work in the cotton mills and on holiday in Blackpool.

As one of its first major projects, Mass-Observation carried out a detailed study of a typical northern working-class town, Bolton – referred to in reports as 'Worktown'. A team of investigators was sent to live in a terraced house in Bolton and to melt into the urban landscape while keeping their pencils and notebooks at the ready. These observers – mainly working-class clerks recruited by Harrison, Madge and Jennings for the purpose – attempted to join in the life of the local community, visiting pubs and clubs, noting down overheard snippets of conversation and finding out what the workers really thought about their political leaders and the international situation.

The early work of Mass-Observation, from 1937 to the outbreak of war in 1939, is of special interest, since policies and politics had not assumed such importance, nor international events moved so fast, since August 1914. This early research was turned into a best-selling early Penguin paperback in 1939, titled *Britain by Mass-Observation*, by Harrison and Madge. Writing of this early work in the introduction to a 1986 reprint, Angus Calder observed that

> Mass-Observation was part of the broad movement, typified by Orwell, of conscience-stricken middle-class

intellectuals trying, in days of wide unemployment, to meet and understand the working class. Though the air of 'slumming' and condescension which such an enterprise can convey still sometimes arouses prejudice against M-O, the motivations of those involved surely deserve respect. However the very concept of 'mass' now seems dated and unhelpful. It is never wholly clear, from *Britain* or from other M-O publications, whether the primary aim was observation *of* the masses or *by* the masses.[6]

What the early work of Mass-Observation showed very clearly was that the suspicions of the three young founders were entirely justified. The British press did not represent public opinion accurately – indeed it quickly became obvious that neither Fleet Street nor Whitehall had a clue what British men and women were thinking and feeling about the international situation. According to Harrison and Madge:

The attitude of the masses to Crisis is very imperfectly understood by the minority who control the sources of opinion. Baldwin steered through the Abdication Crisis, and Chamberlain through the War Crisis of September 1938: how they were able to do it is a question worth more serious enquiry than it has yet received. If one was to believe, for example, all that was said by 'intelligent people' about the state of public opinion at these times, the only answer to the question would be that a miracle happened in each case. But in fact these 'intelligent people' have a deep-seated tendency to base their estimates of public opinion not on factual observation but on their own personal judgment. Their judgment is usually wrong, because they do not realise that their picture of the world is different from that of the mass of the people.[7]

One of Mass-Observation's earliest discoveries was that most people rely on newspapers more than any other source when forming their opinions (35 per cent), and yet, dependent as they are on the press, people distrust it. 'It is', say the authors, 'like being led through a strange country by a guide who may turn out to be a gangster in disguise.'

Another curious and counter-intuitive finding was that even though international affairs were becoming more dramatic all the time, people's interest in such matters was declining. 'At the present stage of Western civilisation', said the authors, 'changes are taking place with such rapidity that there is in a sense a continuous crisis. In Fleet Street or Whitehall this is obvious enough, but the further you move from such centres, the less real does this conception of crisis appear. ... [A]s one crisis succeeds another, one might expect that this interest would grow. But when M-O asked 460 people if their interest in crises was increasing or decreasing, the results pointed quite clearly to a decrease of interest.'

The qualitative responses were also illuminating:

Social worker, female, 28. 'Decreasing, because the help-lessness of the individual appals me.'

Deputy registrar, female, 26. 'Decreasing interest. It's too blasted uncomfortable.'

Clerk, 18. 'I take little interest in any of the accounts of crises – I am getting tired of people talking about wars in Spain and China, and if people start talking about another war I feel like saying "For goodness sake shut up".'[8]

In view of these and many similar vox pop replies, the authors warn that: 'This decreasing interest is highly significant as a reflection of the stage our society has reached. It is partly a defence against nervous strain, partly a kind of fatalism, partly a mistrust of newspaper information. Broadly speaking it is a symptom of a serious breakdown in the relation between the individual and society.' Harrison and Madge place the blame for this breakdown squarely on the press.

> Opinion is made in two ways. It is made by each single person looking at the facts, as far as they are available, and then framing his own judgment on them. It is also made by the reaction of each single person to the opinions of other people. ... It is here that the newspapers play an important role. For the newspapers not only state *their* version of the facts – they also state *their* version of the public opinion of the moment.[9]

They quote an interview with a 45-year-old man in New Cross in September 1938 regarding the Czech crisis. 'I'm just a working-class man and I'm as entitled to an opinion as anyone else. We've let them down [the Czechs] good and proper. That is the opinion of all working-class people. You should read the *Star* tonight and see for yourself.'

'The only means', say Harrison and Madge, 'by which this man can tell what others like himself are thinking (apart from the few he meets and talks to) is through the newspapers and their estimates of public opinion. It is their function to give these estimates, and they have an obvious responsibility to see that what they say about opinion is firmly founded on fact, and that it is stated as clearly as possible. Unfortunately, although the papers are always playing up to the desire for this kind of information, they take little trouble to be factual with it.'

The newspaper mentioned by the man in New Cross, the *Star*, had covered the Czech crisis with regular articles written by its editor, R.G. Cruikshank, whom Harrison and Madge approved of as 'intelligent' and 'progressive minded', quoting one such article titled 'My Country'. In this, Cruikshank depicts England in the kind of 'precious stone set in a silver sea' terms that editors sometimes give way to in moments of crisis. They also mention that 'Cruikshank had had long talks with mass-observers, with whose aims he was in sympathy and with whose point of view he approximates in this article'. Despite this convergence of views – or perhaps because they felt free to criticise a friendly voice without rancour – Harrison and Madge insist that

> In making these key statements about public opinion it is *not enough* to rely on personal impressions and 'such tokens as come, through letters and by word of mouth.' Why cannot the great newspapers, with all the machinery at their disposal, make some effort to be scientific on this all-important question? By failing to do so, they forfeit their potential right to act as the voice of everyman – they have to be counted among the forces which make for confusion. In the same article Cruikshank goes on to say:
>
> "To those who are sick at heart – and I know that they are many – I should like to say, if they will let me, 'Keep steady!' The worst of all surrenders is to lose confidence in one's country. Remember that the people of England have not yet been heard from. They will speak in due season."

Why, one is bound to ask, shouldn't they speak now, if the newspapers were really prepared to let them do so?[10]

But if the press was to blame for misleading the man and woman in the street about the real state of public opinion, Mass-Observation also blamed politicians both for failing to tell people the facts and for their poor showing in the public mind for what little the public did know of their efforts.

People in a London borough were asked the question, 'What do you think about the country's foreign policy?' in March 1938. Of those who answered, 28 per cent said they were satisfied with government policy, 32 per cent were not satisfied and 40 per cent gave replies that showed ignorance, uncertainty and bewilderment – most succinctly expressed by the respondent who said: 'It's a fucking mess, ain't it?' Just as worrying was that 35 per cent of those polled refused to express any opinion at all.

Though Mass-Observation provided the first real indication of public opinion on a range of important contemporary issues, one question that M-O did not ask the man and woman in the street – perhaps because it was too sensitive in the late 1930s – was 'What political party do you support?'

Were the voters in the street leaning towards the rightist politics of Berlin? Or leftwards to Moscow? Or did they look to Whitehall and its apparently moderate, centrist politics? Even in the absence of polling results on purely political questions, there are some useful indicators.

The majority of fascist and right-wing political organisations in Britain between 1919 and 1939 were elitist affairs with memberships numbering only in the hundreds.

Mosley's British Union of Fascists on the other hand was a populist mass party aimed at the man and woman in street. From its founding in 1931, the party grew very rapidly and by 1934 had some 50,000 registered members – a level of growth that the Labour and Conservative parties could only look upon with envy.

As a point of comparison, registered individual membership of the Labour Party, since its foundation in 1900, had grown to 380,000 in 1934, while that of the British Communist Party was around the 50,000 mark, also built up slowly over many years.

However, 1934 saw the high-water mark of popular fascist politics in Britain. Mosley's declared anti-Semitism and well-publicised ugly street fights meant that people deserted the party in droves and, in 1936, new legislation against uniforms and street marches effectively made the party illegal.

As far as the British public was concerned, then, there was little prospect of a Nazi-style government being returned on a popular vote, despite the considerable support for Nazi ideas that existed among some members of the governing classes. But if the public was not inclined to back fascism, it was also lukewarm about the Conservative-led government of National Unity that governed Britain from 1935 until the outbreak of war. On specific issues, public dissatisfaction with the lack of openness by government was very marked. Take for instance the resignation of Anthony Eden as Foreign Secretary in 1938. In reality, Eden resigned because Chamberlain had gone behind his back to open negotiations with Mussolini who was threatening British interests in Egypt. Eden saw this as appeasement of the fascist dictators. That one of the government's brightest stars should resign from such a sensitive post as

Foreign Affairs on what was possibly the eve of war was a subject in which almost everyone had an interest. Yet Eden's real reasons were covered up by the government in the interests of national and party unity. When Mass-Observation asked people all over the country if they were following the news of the resignation, no less than 82 per cent said they were. However, 43 per cent of these believed some but not all of what they were being told, while 21 per cent didn't believe any of it.

Given this kind of – to put it mildly – ambivalence in the popular attitude to government openness and truthfulness, one might have expected warning bells to have sounded in Whitehall. After all, if war were to come, as seemed increasingly likely, then the government would have to depend totally on the willing cooperation of the ordinary population for even the simplest of daily tasks to be carried out. If people were actively opposed to war and to government policies about war, then the government had a big problem.

At the end of August 1938, this was precisely the issue that Mass-Observation put to its sample audiences. They asked people: 'What do you suggest the ordinary man or woman should do, if anything, in face of a danger of war?' The answers were divided by researchers into four categories (younger men, older men, younger women, older women) and there was a marked division of opinion among those questioned. Overall, though, about a quarter said they would work for peace by means such as joining the Peace Pledge Union or becoming a conscientious objector. Around the same number said they would cooperate with the authorities (the existing government) by joining the ARP or Territorials or simply following orders. Around 15 per cent said they would carry on by keeping their head and going about 'business as usual', while about a quarter expressed negative ideas such as 'nothing', 'don't know', 'die', or 'look after myself'.

Even more telling, the researchers asked the crunch question: 'What will you actually do if war breaks out?' Here, things looked superficially rather better for the government, but still gave cause for concern. A little less than half of those questioned said they would cooperate with the government by joining the armed services, volunteering for medical duty and the like. About 10 per cent or so offered qualified cooperation, such as expecting to be conscripted, or supporting only humanitarian work, or saying they would follow their conscience. A roughly similar number said they would actively oppose the government by conscientious objection, passive resistance or revolutionary action. Another 10 per cent or so said they didn't know what they would do, and a similar number said they would try to get out of the way or look after themselves.

These figures must, paradoxically, have given Whitehall both cause for satisfaction and cause for concern. More than half of those questioned (about 58 per cent) said they would cooperate with the government in the event of war. But the necessary corollary was that not far short of half the population was undecided, lukewarm, unsure, or even in a sizeable minority of cases actively opposed to following government orders. Far from providing sure grounds for planning the next moves, these findings must have made Whitehall realise that they couldn't count on the whole nation or anything like the whole nation being fully behind them when it came to war with Hitler.

Part Three

Crimes Against Humanity, 1939–45

14

Finest Hour

All British people, myself included, can feel justifiably proud of Britain's lone stand against Hitler and Nazi military might in 1940, our 'finest hour'. It's impossible to listen to Churchill's speech promising to 'Fight on the beaches' without a lump in your throat. But there can be little doubt that the courageous truth is thickly encrusted with retrospective myth-making. Between September 1939 and July 1940, the 'phoney war', there were no fewer than sixteen separately identifiable sets of negotiations between London and Berlin, some direct, some through various intermediaries, all aimed at arriving at a negotiated peace settlement. Clive Ponting, in his book *1940: Myth and Reality*, says:

> British peace efforts in the period 1939–1940 remain a highly sensitive subject for British governments, even though all the participants are now dead. Persistent diplomatic efforts to reach peace with Germany are not part of the mythology of 1940 and have been eclipsed by the belligerent rhetoric of the period. Any dent in the belief that Britain displayed an uncompromising

'bulldog spirit' throughout 1940 and never considered any possibility other than fighting on to total victory is still regarded as severely damaging to Britain's self image and the myth of 'Their Finest Hour'.[1]

Indeed, attempts to reach a negotiated accommodation with Hitler and Mussolini had begun well before the outbreak of war. In 1938, Neville Chamberlain wrote: 'In the absence of any powerful ally, and until our armaments are completed, we must adjust our foreign policy to our circumstances.'

What he meant by this was brokering a deal of some kind with Italy or Germany. Foreign Secretary Anthony Eden disliked both Hitler and Mussolini and trusted neither, but thought Germany a better bet. Chamberlain, however, favoured getting an agreement with Italy first, and he secretly opened negotiations with the Italians behind Eden's back. It was this issue that caused Eden to resign in February 1938. In the event, nothing came of these overtures towards Italy.

In 1939, during the Polish crisis, Chamberlain made a major effort to conclude peace with Hitler. He organised a four-day peace conference in London in July, at which he offered the Germans a massive loan to ease their economic transition back to a peacetime state in return for a general European settlement and disarmament. Indeed, the British offered much more even than this Danegeld: they held out the possibility of an Anglo-German non-aggression treaty along with cooperation in foreign trade.[2] It seems likely that Britain would even have offered to stop backing the Poles if Germany would consent to an agreement. It is now clear, though, that Hitler and his army had already gone too far in their military preparations for invading Poland to pull back,

so the peace plan was too little, too late, and Europe went
to war for the second time in twenty years.

According to Ponting:

> Britain therefore entered the Second World War in an
> extremely weak position. Successive governments had
> found no way of resolving the potentially fatal amalgam
> of pressures undermining Britain's ability to defend
> itself and the Empire. Britain was still responsible for the
> defence of territory and interests in every part of the
> world. It had to face one actual plus two likely enemies
> but only had the economic and industrial resources to
> provide an adequate defence against one of them. The
> major rearmament programme under way since 1934
> was already straining the economy to breaking point but
> had not acted as an effective deterrent. Britain had been
> unable to find any way of reducing the number of ene-
> mies it faced.[3]

After war had begun, the British government hoped that
economic pressure could destabilise the German economy
and lead to the fall of the Nazi regime. No economy, they
believed, not even Germany with its increasingly powerful
industrial base, could keep itself on a wartime footing
indefinitely. In fact, this hope was mere illusion – Germany
was so strong economically that it did not even bother to
switch to a full wartime footing until 1943. But illusory or
not, Britain's only strategy was playing for time, so that it
can plausibly be argued that all the peace negotiations
entered into over the next year were simply a means to
string Hitler along. It would also have been negligent not to
have explored every possible alternative to a shooting war.

A further dimension to some of these peace negotiations
was recently suggested by Martin Allen in *The Hitler/Hess*

Deception: British Intelligence's Best-Kept Secret of the Second World War. Allen brings forward persuasive evidence to suggest that the Political Warfare Executive – the part of the Special Operations Executive that dealt in black propaganda – was tasked by the government with carrying out deception operations aimed at deluding Germany into thinking a negotiated peace might be possible, in order to buy time and delay any planned attack on Britain for as long as possible. It was as a result of this intelligence deception, says Allen, that Rudolf Hess flew to Britain under the illusion that he was coming to sign a peace accord.[4]

But genuine or no, all the attempts at peace that were floated by either side foundered on the same reef. The British government would conclude a peace with Germany but not with Hitler, while the Nazis would conclude a peace with Britain, but not with Churchill. Did Britain have a war leader in prospect who could break the deadlock? A man who could unite Britain and still do a deal with Hitler? There was indeed such a man, awaiting the call.

In 1936, Lloyd George had been invited to visit Germany twice by senior Nazis. No doubt this was perceived as a major PR coup, as he had been basking for twenty years in his reputation as the war leader who won the First World War for Britain. While in Germany he was invited by Hitler to visit him at the Berghof. At 5.30, very much as in England, Hitler and his guests sat down to tea, sandwiches and cakes. The two men were photographed and filmed, obviously getting on well together. On his return to England, Lloyd George wrote an article for Beaverbrook's *Daily Express*. Lloyd George told his readers:

It is not the Germany of the first decade that followed the war – broken, dejected and bowed down with a sense of apprehension and impotence. It is now full of hope and confidence, and of a renewed sense of determination to lead its own life without interference from any influence outside its own frontiers. One man has accomplished this miracle. He is a born leader of men. A magnetic and dynamic personality with a single-minded purpose, a resolute will and a dauntless heart.[5]

He went on to say that Hitler had no territorial ambitions in Europe. Clive Ponting explains:

Although out of office for almost twenty years, Lloyd George had not lost his political ambition and in 1940 would have been the almost certain choice as Prime Minister if Churchill had failed and peace with Germany became inevitable. As the acclaimed leader from the First World War, he could have played the role of Marshal Petain in Britain and tried to rally the nation in defeat. He had been pessimistic from the start about the possibility of victory. Early in 1940 he talked to Cecil King of the *Daily Mirror* about 'this damn crazy war,' in which he did not expect either side to achieve victory after a long-drawn-out conflict. He preferred to keep his freedom of action rather than join Churchill's government. King reported, after a conversation with him on 15 May that '[he] expects that Churchill will get into a mess and that he, the victor of the last war, will be called in too late and will have no alternative but to sue for peace.'[6]

Churchill had succeeded Chamberlain as Prime Minister in May 1940. Though his position as war leader became unassailable later on, he was initially viewed with wide mistrust and uncertainty, even by some of his close colleagues such as Lord Halifax and Rab Butler. It was not until July 1940 that Churchill was confident enough to announce unequivocally his policy of fighting on, in the expectation that, eventually, the United States would enter the war on Britain's side. During the first two months that Churchill was in office, the option of making peace was considered twice by the Cabinet.

Before this, however, Churchill's first task was to try to shore up France, now feeling the full might of the Nazi war machine and its Blitzkrieg methods. Churchill fulfilled British obligations to France as fully as was possible, sending valuable and scarce fighting resources across the Channel, much of which was to end up on the beaches of Dunkirk. Some in France predictably carped that Britain did not do more, or speculated that Britain, too, would soon fall.

Even before war was declared, in February 1939, Prime Minister Daladier told William Bullitt, the US ambassador in Paris, what he really thought of England, which Bullitt duly reported back home:

> He considered Chamberlain a desiccated stick; the King a moron; and the Queen an excessively ambitious woman who would be ready to sacrifice every other country in the world in order that she might remain Queen Elizabeth of England ... he considered Eden a young idiot ... he felt England had become so feeble and senile that the British would give away every possession of their friends rather than stand up to Germany and Italy.[7]

Given this bad blood, it was hardly surprising that many people in England were unsympathetic to the French, even when they had been crushed by the Wehrmacht.

Rab Butler's Parliamentary Private Secretary, Henry 'Chips' Channon, wrote in his diary: 'The Third French Republic has ceased to exist and I don't care; it was graft-ridden, incompetent, Communistic and corrupt and had outlived its day.'[8] It would not have been too difficult to find many others in Whitehall who agreed with these sentiments.

Inevitably, however, it was not long after that many in Whitehall also began to think the unthinkable and ask themselves what possible basis there could be for a negotiated peace. Clive Ponting says:

> At the beginning of October, Joseph Kennedy, the American ambassador in London, reported to Washington that Churchill was talking about accepting an armistice with Germany if offered reasonable terms. What sort of deal did the government have in mind? In other words what were Britain's war aims in the Autumn of 1939? The British government never did manage to define clearly what it would want to achieve in a peace conference. Restoration of Poland, as the ostensible cause of the war, was, in some form, essential although the status of Danzig and the [Polish] corridor might be altered. But how could Poland be restored with the Soviet Union occupying the eastern part of the country? And what about Czechoslovakia? Were the Munich settlement and the German take-over of March 1939 to be reversed? Provided these issues could be resolved satisfactorily, the British government felt it had few quarrels with Germany and would be quite willing, as long as the Germans renounced future aggression, to concede effective German domination of central and south-eastern Europe.[9]

The kind of terms Germany might demand were already familiar to Churchill. In his history of the Second World War, Churchill describes how, in 1937, he had held an extended conversation with Joachim von Ribbentrop, Germany's ambassador to Britain at the time. Ribbentrop was remarkably frank during the discussion, explaining to Churchill that

> Germany sought the friendship of England ... Germany would stand guard for the British Empire in all its greatness and extent ... What was required was that Britain give Germany a free hand in the East of Europe. She must have her Lebensraum, or living-space, for her increasing population. Therefore, Poland and the Danzig Corridor must be absorbed. White Russia and the Ukraine were indispensable to the future life of the German Reich of more than seventy million souls. Nothing less would suffice. All that he asked of the British Commonwealth and Empire was not to interfere. There was a large map on the wall, and the Ambassador several times led me to it to illustrate his projects.[10]

Now, in the autumn of 1939 alone there were at least five officially approved approaches to Germany to explore possible peace terms. The most promising were the contacts that came about through the offices of a Swedish businessman, Birger Dahlerus, who was a personal friend of Hermann Goering. Dahlerus flew to Britain in August and again in September, when he met Chamberlain and Halifax. The talks foundered for the usual reason: Britain would deal only with a new regime in Germany, not with Hitler. In the end it was the Germans who called the talks off.

The Americans also tried to kick-start negotiations. Early in 1940, Roosevelt sent his Assistant Secretary of State, Sumner Welles, to London and Berlin to see what grounds existed for a negotiated peace. 'The Welles mission', says Ponting, petered out,

> ... but that did not discourage Butler. Even after the German conquest of Norway and Denmark he put out more feelers at the end of April through the British minister in Bern, Sir David Kelly, to dissident German elements led by Prince von Hohenloe in the hope that they might be encouraged to lead a coup against Hitler and enable peace to be made with a new conservative regime.[11]

On 26 May, with things worsening by the hour in France and the French government on the point of capitulation, the War Cabinet met under Churchill. One of the main topics of discussion was how Britain might obtain a negotiated peace with Germany. Importantly, they seriously discussed for the first time what Britain might have to give Germany and Italy in return for peace. Clive Ponting describes what must have been a tense meeting.

> There was general agreement that Mussolini would want Gibraltar, Malta and Suez and Chamberlain thought he might well add Somaliland, Kenya and Uganda to the list. It was more difficult to see what might have to be conceded to Hitler. The war cabinet were united in agreeing that Britain could not accept any form of disarmament in a peace settlement but that the return of the former German colonies taken away in the Versailles settlement was acceptable. At one point Halifax asked Churchill directly 'whether, if he was satisfied that

matters vital to the independence of this country were unaffected, he would be willing to discuss terms.' Churchill's reply shows none of the signs of the determined attitude he displayed in public and the image he cultivated after the war. It reveals little difference between his views and those of Halifax, and shows he was prepared to give up parts of the empire if a peace settlement were possible. He replied to Halifax's query by saying that 'he would be thankful to get out of our present difficulties on such terms, provided we retained the essentials and the elements of our vital strength, even at the cost of some cession of territory.' Neville Chamberlain's diary records the response in more specific terms than the civil service minutes. He quotes Churchill as saying that 'if we could get out of this jam by giving up Malta and Gibraltar and some African colonies he would jump at it.'[12]

The next day, 27 May, the War Cabinet met again and Churchill argued in favour, not of continuing the war until victory, but of trying to get through the next two to three months before making a decision on whether or not to ask for peace.

He was quite prepared for concessions to achieve peace. 'If Herr Hitler was prepared to make peace on the terms of the restoration of German colonies and the overlordship of central Europe, that was one thing.' But as Churchill pointed out, acceptance of such a limited restoration of German strength after their stunning military victories was 'most unlikely'. Nevertheless he revealed that though he was not prepared to ask Hitler for peace terms, he would discuss any offer that was made. Halifax thought that the situation was not so bad that it was best to try to see if a reasonable offer would be made by Germany before the Allied position collapsed irretrievably.[13]

Ironically, although Churchill thought this basis for peace was 'most unlikely', it seems to be pretty much what Hitler himself was in fact thinking at this time. For while Churchill and his War Cabinet had to face the unpleasant fact of Britain's virtual bankruptcy and impotence, this weakness was unknown to the Germans, who still perceived Britain as a world power that must be courted and won over diplomatically.

And there was a second factor that must have loomed large in Hitler's calculations now. He was uncomfortably aware that his victory in France had been due not only to military skill but also to a large dose of luck. Up until almost the eve of the attack, the German high command had been planning a virtual re-run of the 1914 Schlieffen plan, which would very probably have had similar results to 1914 and degenerated into a deadly slogging match. It was only at the last minute that Hitler overruled the high command and insisted on an attack much like the successful advance of 1870 which had smashed the French at Sedan. The trick worked a second time and in very much the same way.

The popular idea of a 'lightning war' spearheaded by Panzer tanks filling up at French petrol stations as they rolled through village after village was largely the stuff of myth. In reality, Hitler and his generals had been constantly terrified throughout the French campaign that the armoured columns were getting too far ahead of supporting troops and would get cut off, and the high command was constantly on the field telephone ordering the Panzers to halt their advance while the foot-slogging, largely horse-drawn infantry, creeping slowly along behind, caught up with them.

Ponting summarises the official position in 1940 thus:

> It is clear from the widespread evidence of war cabinet discussions and approaches via the Swedes and the Americans that in May and June 1940 not only did Britain seriously consider making peace with Germany, but that some members of the government went as far as to ask what terms the Germans would offer. Within the war cabinet there was a spectrum of views: from Halifax who favoured trying to make peace before the military situation became even worse; to Churchill, who wanted to fight on for a few months. It was also clear from the war cabinet discussions that in May and June 1940 their policy was not an absolute commitment to fight on to victory. Instead they adopted a more short-term aim of preparing to resist any German invasion in the hope that Germany might collapse quickly or, if it did not, that Britain would at any rate be able to obtain better peace terms later on in the year, once any invasion had been repulsed, than in the immediate aftermath of the collapse of France.[14]

From the third week of June 1940, for almost a month until the middle of July, Hitler was sufficiently unconcerned about the state of the war that he held no military conferences and did not discuss any possible invasion of Britain. From this show of almost English coolness it seems clear that he believed that the British would have no alternative now but to come to terms with him. Those terms would have been the ones he had already published in *Mein Kampf* and which Ribbentrop had expounded at length to

Churchill before the war – a non-aggression alliance under which Britain kept its empire in return for giving Germany a free hand in Europe. The next military discussion that Hitler had about England was on 13 July, when one of his generals afterwards noted:

> The Führer is most preoccupied with the question of why England does not want to step on the path of peace. Like us he sees the answer to the question in the hopes which England puts upon Russia. He therefore reckons to have to force England to make peace. But he does not like it very much. Reason: if we smash England militarily, the British Empire will collapse. Germany will not benefit from this. With German blood we would obtain something whose beneficiaries would only be Japan, America and others.[15]

When exactly did Hitler finally give up all hope of making peace with Britain? His last attempt seems to have been in the first week of September 1940, a full year after the war had started.

The War Cabinet was astonished to receive a 'Most Secret' encrypted telegram from Victor Mallet, British ambassador to Sweden, with unexpected news. Mallet had been contacted by a Berlin barrister named Dr Ludwig Weissauer who, said Mallet, 'is understood to be a direct emissary of Hitler'. Weissauer, explained the ambassador, 'wishes me to meet him very secretly order to ... talk on the subject of peace'.

At first, this approach was treated with some suspicion, as though the work of a crank. But Ludwig Weissauer turned out to be none other than the chief legal counsel to the Nazi Party and Hitler's own personal legal adviser.

Mallet went on to say that the emissary wished any conversations that took place to remain secret and said he would report back directly to Hitler in person. This strongly suggested that the initiative had originated with Hitler himself.[16]

In the end this approach came to nothing, like all the others. The War Cabinet instructed Mallet to ignore the message. But it is the clearest indication that Hitler's words in *Mein Kampf* were not mere rhetoric. He believed profoundly that an Anglo-German alliance was essential and was prepared to go the last mile to try to conclude such an agreement. Now he was compelled to realise that there would be no negotiated peace. Like the German government of 1914, he found himself in the place he had wanted to avoid above all: a fight to the finish against France and Britain on one side and potentially against Russia on the other. Thus, it was not until late in 1940, when the bombs started falling both on London and Berlin, that Hitler finally accepted that he was never going to conclude a negotiated peace with Britain, that Churchill was probably leader for the duration and that the only way he could bring Britain to the negotiating table would be to conquer Russia. Hitler thus decided to implement his eastern strategy anyway on the grounds that, once Russia was defeated, Britain's last hope would have been destroyed and Britain would then have no alternative but to get rid of Churchill, appoint Lloyd George or a similar figure as Prime Minister and sue for peace.

Seen in retrospect, the first year of the Second World War, the phoney war, was an almost incredible slow-motion charade of stilted manners, repressed emotions, counterfeit courtesies, and misunderstood gestures. The Wehrmacht and the Luftwaffe, the most powerful military force in

Europe, casually batted aside and crushed the armies of Poland, Holland, Belgium and France in a matter of weeks, yet did not pursue and destroy the British army on the beaches of Dunkirk, and even restrained itself from bombing British cities until the RAF started a nightly bombing campaign of the Ruhr. One has to ask why the German high command repeatedly exercised this restraint in what was plainly a total war. And the only logical answer is that they were carrying out the orders of Hitler and his fellow leaders of the Nazi government, who continued to hope for a reconciliation with Britain, even when they had shattered the peace of half the world and threatened to dominate the remaining half. Such was the depth of Hitler's feeling for Britain, and the British way of life.

15

The British Way

Soon after the Second World War started, senior figures in the British government began to feel nervous about the social effects of the war. It was plain from the nation's experience in the First World War that this conflict must last several years, would consume a significant amount of national resources, and would involve millions of British people being given military training and risking their lives. How long would it be before these millions of ordinary people started asking difficult questions? Questions like: What exactly are we fighting for? Why are we fighting for it? And even: Is it worth fighting for?

The fledgling opinion poll company, Mass-Observation, was finding on the streets that what the British ruling class had considered self-evident for many decades could no longer be taken for granted.[1] British people were by no means unanimously behind the government in their support for war. The phrase 'British way of life' might have been familiar enough in everyday conversation, but many ordinary people were unable to say with any precision what was special or worth preserving about the British way of life, or even what the British way of life was exactly.

The government was particularly concerned about the large numbers of young men being called up into the armed services. They were being asked to forget their personal ambitions of marriage and work and dedicate themselves to their country's service for some years. Many would be asked to go on active service in theatres of war and take part in actions that were bound to result in many deaths and injuries. Would these young men respond when the time came?

It wasn't merely working-class recruits whose loyalty was questioned. The notorious Oxford Union debate in 1933 in which a majority of undergraduates supported the motion 'That this House will under no circumstances fight for its King and Country', meant that even sections of the young officer class were suspect as well.[2]

And it wasn't only their willingness to fight that was in question. The armed services had become a fertile breeding ground for social and political discontent and for competing ideologies, including fascism and Marxism, both of which had gained many thousands of converts among British people in the 1930s. Many ordinary British men and women felt that they had more in common with Hitler and the Germans than with the French or the Poles. Supporting fascist ideas was by no means unthinkable, as long as those ideas had a veneer of Britishness. When the government arrested Sir Oswald Mosley and locked him away in Wormwood Scrubs for the duration, it was precisely because his British Union of Fascists had attracted support from tens of thousands of ordinary members of the working class – men who would now be called up into the British army to fight against ordinary German working men who were also fascists.

Similarly, by 1941, Russia had ceased to be a foreign bogeyman and had become our heroic ally whose way of life was also under threat from militaristic Nazis and thus must be as worthwhile preserving as our own. It was no longer unpatriotic or un-British to be a Marxist or a hard-left socialist.

With this fog of ideological ambivalence swirling around its ears, the government felt compelled to act to ensure as far as possible that the British people would fight for King and Country and that they would be in no doubt what they were fighting to protect. Under instructions from Whitehall, the army commissioned some of Britain's leading academics and professional writers to produce a series of eighteen educational pamphlets setting out clearly and unambiguously exactly who we are, why our way of life is important, and why it should be protected against Nazi Germany. In 1943, these pamphlets were gathered together and republished into an army educational handbook entitled *The British Way and Purpose*.[3]

Tens of thousands of copies of this book, with its distinctive red binding, were printed and published during the war and distributed for use by British servicemen in educational classes and discussion groups. Copies can still be found today in second-hand bookshops up and down the country. The book makes fascinating reading as a snapshot of the national psyche in the early 1940s, and is a remarkable document in several ways.

The first is that, for some bizarre reason, the army authorities decided that it should be classified as a 'Restricted' military document that must not 'be communicated, either directly or indirectly, to the press or to any person not authorised to receive it'. This is perhaps a measure of the seriousness with which Whitehall treated its publication, and a measure, too, of its nervousness at what might happen if the enemy obtained copies of this book and decided, for its own propaganda purpose, to deconstruct the myths it contained. Yet there is something absurdly comical about the army trying to prevent the British press from learning what its armed forces were fighting to protect.

The second remarkable feature is the mismatch between what the book was intended to achieve and how its authors set about achieving that goal. Many prominent academics and writers toiled over its construction. And, since many of the issues dealt with were highly sensitive political matters, it seems only too probable that senior civil servants – perhaps even ministers – were also involved in its production. Their remit was to produce a purely factual text, setting out in clear terms the administrative structure of Britain and the benefits of that structure for British people. Simply put, their aim was to tell the British soldier what he was fighting for. But when it came to spelling out in detail the exact nature of the famous British Way of Life, the celebrity authors were no clearer than the man in the street answering a Mass-Observation questionnaire. It was easy enough to explain how Britain was divided up administratively, how local government and the court system worked and how Parliament was elected. But it proved very much more difficult to explain exactly why this system was democratic, or just, or socially fair, or even better than any alternative system such as National Socialism or Marxism. It was quickly realised that facts alone were not enough; the arts of the spin doctor would be required.

Spin entered the text both in terms of the material chosen for inclusion and the material that was omitted. Thus *British Way and Purpose* is strong on describing how important equality before the law is to the British way, but nowhere does the book mention that the British way of life was critically dependent on the 1 million men who worked in its coal mines, who lost their lives at the rate of 1,000 every year, who were likely to contract agonising respiratory diseases and suffer an early death, but who would be sacked when they could no longer work and who would receive no compensation either from their employers or from the state.[4]

Finding themselves hard pressed to identify and analyse anything factually resembling a British Way of Life, these encyclopaedists naturally turned instead to the mythical British way of life that the English governing classes had fostered at home and abroad for a century.

This myth had many roots and flourished in many forms, but in all of them the British were essentially fair, sporting, tolerant, democratic and inclusive, taking the part of the underdog, helping those less fortunate. British sense of long traditions – especially those of parliamentary democracy and British justice – meant that Britons took things steadily and refused to panic, were slow to anger and slow to judge. But British perseverance and backbone would see Britain through a long hard fight. Throughout it all, the British sense of fair play meant that Britons would keep a straight bat, whatever frightfulness the enemy might resort to, and would ensure that Britain always protected the weak while standing up to bullies.

These underlying myths were now spun into a straightforward series of texts that said to the ordinary working man: 'This is you, too. You are part of this. This is your heritage.'

The roots of the British myth that ultimately ended up encoded into wartime military pamphlets were many and diverse. Contributions came from the contemporary imperialist interpretation of British history, from the educational system, from the government itself and from the mystique of the royal family. Perhaps the most potent source of all was that of popular culture and the urban myths it nourished, whether in café society or the slums of the East End – the patriotic inner vision shared alike by Pearly.King and Mayfair Toff – that Vera Lynn sang to, that Kipling wrote for, and that Edward Elgar appealed to with 'Land of Hope and Glory'.

British Way and Purpose (*BWP*) is a historical document of extraordinary interest in several distinct ways. It is a brilliantly clever piece of nationalist propaganda, still moving and effective today. It is a fascinating snapshot of exactly how the war generation saw themselves. Above all, when deconstructed, it tells us exactly what the rulers of England in 1940 were most sensitive about, the weak spots in the national psyche. As an almost unconscious vision of what Britain should be and might still be, it is to historical analysis what a dream is to a Freudian psychoanalyst.

Its cleverness as propaganda lies in the fact that it highlights the calm modesty and self-effacing moderateness of the British people, and it achieves this by speaking in precisely the same kind of moderate, self-effacing voice. This implicitly contrasts British ways with the strident, noisy, boastful manner of Goebbels and the Nazis. *BWP*, in an understated British kind of way, is the very opposite of a torchlit goose-stepping procession with banners and military bands and all that such pomp and paraphernalia stand for.

Like all effective propaganda, *BWP* relies mainly on the truth, or at least keeps the truth within call at all times. In this way it disarms criticism from the outset. In the very first pamphlet, sociologist Arthur Owen (later to become

Assistant Secretary-General in charge of Economic Affairs at the UN) admits that Britain has much unfulfilled promise.

> Compared with what we have reason to fear if the Nazis have their way, the condition of Britain is almost heavenly. Once the need for such a dire comparison has been eliminated by victory, however, few people are likely to confuse masses without work, half-derelict mining communities, the slums of Glasgow, the under-sized bodies of ill-nourished children, or the shocking scars on the loveliness of the English countryside with any heavenly thing. The fact is that, in spite of all the social progress in the years between the wars, there is still a great deal which cries out to be remedied in the condition of Britain.[5]

The cleverness of this admission is that it makes the social defects of Britain the enemy of the new citizen army along with the Nazis, who have now become the main obstacle standing between us and progress. It implies that the benefit of pulling together to defeat the Nazis will be that we can then all turn our new-found collective strength to improving society. But, of course, we can't start to sort out the problems in our own backyard until we have sorted out Hitler first.

BWP is careful not to tell lies, but it does casually perpetuate a number of useful national myths. In outlining how Britain is governed, it emphasises again and again that Britain has first and foremost a representative system of democratic government. The first chapter takes as its epigram the famous quotation from Abraham Lincoln's Gettysburg address about 'government of the people, by the people, for the people', implying that this is what its armed services are defending.

A little later it says that 'citizens send representatives chosen by ballot from a list of candidates [as Councillors and MPs]', and that 'these representatives ... tend to reflect in Parliament and Council chamber the prevailing political opinions and wishes of the people to whose judgement they will again have to submit themselves after a period of years'.[6]

The reality, then and now, is that those elected to Parliament or local council are not representatives, but delegates. They are under no compulsion to represent the views of their constituents or to vote in any way other than how their party whips tell them, in return for places or preference – which is in fact how almost all of them actually vote. This undemocratic defect alone is one of the principal explanations of the 'masses of unemployed, the half-derelict mining communities, the slums of Glasgow, the ill-nourished children and the shocking scars on the loveliness of the English countryside' which persist despite a thousand years of democracy.

Speaking of the similarities and differences between Britain and the United States, *BWP* says that

The American people are used to a written constitution, interpreted by a Supreme Court, the British people to a mainly unwritten constitution, in which whatever Parliament says goes. ... One nation likes its obligations to be set down in black and white; the other has a passion for vagueness.[7]

Having a 'passion for vagueness' is one way of interpreting the lack of a written constitution in Britain, and the freedom this gives the government to push through any legislation it pleases for any expedient reason that may arise, such as abandoning the centuries-old right to trial by jury, without any right of appeal, for individuals whom the government alone considers merit such treatment, as recent British governments have done.

When it came to sensitive and socially divisive subjects, *BWP*'s strategy was to deal with the issues by implying that they were the residual problems of the bad old days that would all be somehow solved once the war was over. This, for instance, is what it has to say about public schools:

> The public schools have a famous tradition; they have educated thousands of men who have given the most distinguished service to their country. But it is now widely felt, even by the schools themselves, that such privileged places do not fit into a democracy; that, by their exclusiveness, which depends on wealth rather than ability, they preserve and intensify the division of social classes. It is further argued that as 'leaders' have in the past come mainly from these schools, the nation loses by drawing on such a restricted source. It seems likely that the public schools will after the war be brought, in some way that has not yet been worked out, into the national system of secondary education.[8]

This was a usefully vague promise, given that lads from the slums of London and Glasgow are going to feel less like fighting and dying if the post-war country will continue to be run by the old school tie brigade (which is largely what happened in 1945, despite the socialist label of the new government).

By far the trickiest question that *BWP* had to deal with was the subject of the empire. How could Britain oppose the wish of Germany – a larger and wealthier nation – to have colonies, given that we ruled much of the earth? Why should ordinary British working men fight and die when

233

Britain squandered its resources on imperial dreams instead of dealing with the pressing problems at home – unemployment, education, health, housing? Why should Tommy Atkins die on some foreign shore just so that the manufacturers and bankers who ran the empire could continue to get richer? And what about the democratic rights of those that Britain ruled over?

It doesn't take much reading between the lines to realise that the authors, and those who briefed them, followed a few generally agreed lines of explanation, because the same arguments crop up again and again on the half-dozen occasions that *BWP* returns to the subject. There are simple explanations for everything.

First there is the simple explanation as to why we have an empire in the first place. It is the one given by distinguished 19th-century historian Sir John Seeley: 'We seem to have conquered and peopled half the world in a fit of absence of mind.'[9]

Britain didn't really intend to acquire an empire; it just sort of happened while we weren't paying attention. There we were, minding our own business, absent-mindedly sailing the oceans in our triple-decker 74-gun warships, the most powerful weapons of mass destruction on earth, and one-quarter of the earth's land mass accidentally came under our military domination.

Here, for example, is *BWP*'s explanation by Sir Reginald Coupland, Professor of Colonial History at Oxford, as to how Britain came to rule in India.

The English went to India in Queen Elizabeth's days to trade, and for about 150 years they stayed there as traders, not as conquerors or rulers. But the collapse of the 'Mogul' Empire in the 18th century led to such anarchy and chaos that the British trading company, which had become a wealthy and powerful organisation, was forced, if only to defend its trade and counter the moves of the rival French company, to take part in the struggle for power. Once in, there was no getting out. The result, to put it in a sentence, was the gradual extension of British rule till, by about the middle of the last century, it covered the whole of India.[10]

So, there you have it; once in, there was no getting out. We didn't want to be there, ruling India, but we had no real alternative.

Second, there is the simple explanation of how we happened to acquire control of large portions of the earth's surface despite our avowed wish *not* to have an empire. It is because the squabbling natives who lived in the places we visited were not mature enough to settle their differences themselves and pleaded with the wiser, cooler heads of Britain to step in and use our experience to rule on their behalf. Being a technically and socially advanced country, it is Britain's moral duty to assist people who are less fortunate than ourselves in that they were born with black or brown skins and hence are less intelligent, eugenically inferior, and thus not yet fit to run their own affairs.

Thirdly, there is the reason why we cannot be said to be exploiting the people in the empire territories. We do not exact taxes from the peoples of the empire. That would be unfair, because most of them are very poor. We help them out by importing goods from them, goods we need such as sugar, wheat, rubber, iron ore, spices, bananas, and such like. We pay them good prices for their products by their local standards. Of course, you can't compare wages in, say, India or Africa with wages in Britain because our standards of living are so much higher, so we only pay them relatively small sums for their goods. And in return, we export to them quality British goods at affordable prices – it's a win-win situation for everyone!

And finally there is the reason that we continue to possess a global empire, even though we don't want one and it is only a financial and administrative burden on us. It is in order to protect the people of the empire under the British flag. No foreign power can move in and exploit the natives while they are protected by British military power, *Pax Britannica*. As long as they're British, they're safe. It would be reckless and irresponsible if Britain were simply to abandon these backward people to their fate – they would soon be gobbled up by sharks like the Germans, the French or the Americans. Or else they would simply fight among themselves. Put simply, it's our historical duty to deploy British naval power, British legal traditions, and British standards of government to protect the overseas children of the Queen Empress from corruption, squalor and imperialist predators.

Looking back to 1940 with the benefit of hindsight, through an intervening generation of peace won by those who fought Nazism then, was there ever really a British Way and Purpose? Or was there nothing more than a concoction of national prejudices and government spin, dressed up for morale-boosting public consumption?

Certainly the idealistic claims of *British Way and Purpose* are difficult to justify by modern standards. Britain lacked a written constitution then and still does today. This omission was passed off in *BWP* as a mysterious collective understanding that gives Britain its key strength. In reality, it is a convenient black hole at the centre of Britain's legal system that enables the government of the day to govern out of expediency, rather than law or principle, and without reference to the people of Britain. In 1944 the lack of a constitution enabled the War Cabinet unilaterally to give orders for the mass destruction of women and children in German cities. In 2003 the same lack of constitutional accountability enabled the Blair government unilaterally to give orders for the mass destruction of women and children in Iraqi cities.

When the Nazis bombed Guernica, it was the occasion for a Picasso masterpiece, rightly marking a barbaric outrage against civilisation. When the British bombed Dresden, it was a fair and just response of a nation that believed in playing a straight bat and championing the underdog. Such is the power of national myth.

The tragedy is that lies blossom perennially on war and rumours of war. As John Bright observed: 'You will find wars are supported by a class of argument which, after the war is over, the people find were arguments they should never have listened to.'[11]

16

Black Games

Propaganda in the Second World War was a very different game from that of the First – though just as black. The organisations were much the same, and indeed the departmental plans and memoranda from 1914–18 were rapidly taken down from the shelves and dusted off. But the primary means of communication had changed from posters and pamphlets to radio broadcasts and cinema newsreels. More significantly, the population of 1939 was nothing like as naive as that of twenty years earlier and was far less easy to bamboozle. Newspapers continued to be important in influencing opinion, but many had supported appeasement and now faced the uphill task of regaining the public's trust. But for all media the central problem continued to be the same as in the First War: do you tell the public the truth, the whole truth and nothing but the truth? Or do you aim instead to keep up public morale through deception?

In John Ford's classic western film *The Man Who Shot Liberty Valance*, US Senator James Stewart reveals the true facts about a long-romanticised incident in frontier history to newspaper editor Carleton Young, but the newspaperman

239

declines to print the new facts. 'This is the west, sir', he tells Stewart. 'When the legend becomes fact, print the legend.'[1]

The polar opposite of this cynical viewpoint is represented by the famous dictum of C.P. Scott, editor of the *Manchester Guardian*: 'Comment is free but facts are sacred', a lofty goal that generations of idealistic young reporters have tried to live up to.[2]

The reality of newspaper reporting for much of the first half of the 20th century, both in peace and war, hovered uncomfortably somewhere between these two extremes, oscillating between fact and myth depending often on the expediencies of government policy in Germany and England.

Take the case of the Reichstag fire in 1933. Hitler was appointed Chancellor in January and the Reichstag was dissolved preparatory to new elections to be held in March. On 27 February, fire broke out in the empty Reichstag building and a 24-year-old Dutch communist hitch-hiker, Marinus van de Lubbe, was caught red-handed at the scene and arrested for arson.

Charge and counter-charge of conspiracies filled the headlines in London and Berlin. Hitler and the Nazi hierarchy blamed the communists for conspiring to take over Germany by revolution and ordered the suppression of the Communist Party. This enabled the Nazis to gain seats at their expense in the March elections, which assisted them in coming to total power that year, with apparent legitimacy. Communists and others internationally blamed the Nazis for setting up the fire in order to discredit the communists and thus seize power. Leaders of the communists were put on trial in Berlin and van de Lubbe was found guilty, while a mock 'counter trial' was held in London and found the Nazis guilty. Even C.P. Scott's *Manchester*

Guardian followed the line that it was the Nazis who had set the fire in order to blame the communists, showing that facts may be sacred but they are sometimes conveniently flexible, too.

What is perhaps most extraordinary about this fog of myth and counter-myth surrounding the incident is that a British reporter of impeccable credentials was on the spot within minutes of the fire starting and was in a unique position to know the true facts, yet his story was largely ignored.

Sefton Delmer, a British journalist who had been born in Berlin and spoke perfect German, was the Berlin bureau chief for Express Newspapers in 1933. His office was a mile and half from the Reichstag building and when the alarm was raised he ran there to find out what was happening.

A policeman on the scene told him that van de Lubbe had been caught and arrested. Minutes later, cars arrived with Hitler and Goebbels and the party entered the building. Delmer, who had met and interviewed both Nazi leaders many times, attached himself to the party and blagged his way in. He heard Goering, who as police chief was already on the scene, reporting to Hitler and says he felt certain that the shock and anger of all the Nazis present was genuine and not merely an act.[3]

'What was the truth about the Reichstag fire?', Delmer wrote in 1961.

I have always believed that neither the Nazis nor the Communists laid and lit this fire, but that both exploited it for their political warfare. The Nazis did so for the immediate objective of suppressing all opposition to themselves in Germany, the Communists for the long term objective of rallying the world against the Nazis.

My own view I put forward in an article on Hitler and the Reichstag fire in 1939, when I said, 'I rather suspect there was really just one incendiary who lit that fire – the lunatic van der Lubbe.' Today I no longer suspect, I am sure of it.

Even today, when the 'Hitler, Göring and Goebbels did it' legend has been thoroughly exploded as a result of the meticulous and painstaking historical investigation done by the German writer Fritz Tobias, I fear it will still live on among the historical lumber filling the minds of most people.[4]

Partly because of his reports exonerating Hitler of complicity, Delmer was suspected by British Intelligence of being in the pay of the Nazis. In fact, far from being sympathetic, Delmer joined British Intelligence at the outbreak of war, and was responsible for heading British black propaganda radio operations against the Germans for the remainder of the war.

Early in 1941, Delmer joined the Political Intelligence Department of the Foreign Office, under the Minister of Economic Warfare, Hugh Dalton.[5] This department's role was to conduct psychological warfare against the Germans. Dalton was worried about several spoof radio stations that Goebbels had set up in Berlin, purporting to be pirate radio stations broadcasting from somewhere inside the British Isles. These 'black' stations called themselves 'New British Broadcasting Service', 'Radio Caledonia' and 'The Worker's Challenge'. This last station purported to be the voice of discontented British workers opposed to the war. In reality it was scripted by William Joyce ('Lord Haw Haw') and voiced by unfortunate British prisoners of war combed out of the POW camps. For some months, though, to Churchill's annoyance, they had caused elderly listeners in Tunbridge Wells and Cheltenham to fume at the demands and threats in cockney accents of the 'workers', liberally sprinkled with the kind of offensive Anglo-Saxon four-letter words never heard on the BBC.

The Political Intelligence Department was tasked by Dalton with replying in kind by launching a short-wave station that would pretend to be broadcasting from somewhere inside Hitler's Europe.

Delmer created a 'German' radio station called Gustav Siegfried Eins (a call sign equivalent to today's 'Golf Sierra One'), and to front it he invented a far more credible character than Goebbels' foul-mouthed leftist cockneys. He came up with 'The Chef', an elderly military man of high rank, broadly sympathetic to the Nazis as the opponents of Bolshevism but full of complaints about the corruption and pettiness of individual Nazi officials and the egotistical activities of Nazi leaders like Goering. Delmer also added a stroke of genius. He had 'The Chef' constantly complain about the prevalence of pornography and licentious goings-on in wartime Germany, often going into graphic detail. German listeners, especially in the armed forces, tuned in regularly to hear the latest juicy titbits.

Delmer described how he went about getting listeners. 'I decided to use radio-pornography to catch their attention. My "Chef" became a kind of radio Streicher, except that the victims of his pornographic tirades were Nazis, not Jews. The recipe was an instant success. One unfortunate young German woman, denounced by the Chef for having insulted the honour of the German army by using an officer's steel helmet as a chamber pot during a sexual orgy (our intelligence claimed she was an informant of the Gestapo) is still angry with me today because of the stream of telephone calls she received from listeners denouncing her in the harshest terms. The American military attachés included the broadcasts of the Chef in their dispatches to Washington as evidence of the growing rift between the army and the National Socialist party.'[6]

In an echo of the First War propaganda duel, Delmer's project was subtle and sophisticated where the German black radio efforts were crude and their messages poorly targeted.

'[W]e did not use pornography', Delmer wrote, 'because we thought it would have a deleterious effect on our German listeners. We used it simply for its listener appeal – just as some popular newspapers use scabrous stories and pictures of scantily clad models to increase their circulation. And we took great care not to let it seem that the Chef enjoyed the bawdy details of what he revealed of the licentious sexual excesses of Hitler's "elite". He never sniggered over them. His denunciations were filled with the indignation and horror of a Salvation Army evangelist. He was a puritan die-hard of the old Prussian army revolted by the depravity and corruption of the party functionaries and determined to expose and chastise them.'[7]

As in cases cited in earlier chapters, the mechanism of successful propaganda was so subtle and sophisticated that even some of those closely involved with black propaganda did not fully understand it. Delmer was constantly pestered by agents in the Special Operations Executive to produce printed pornography to distribute overseas in order to undermine German morale. But he included pornography in his broadcasts not because he believed it would in any way reflect badly on the Nazis, but merely because he knew it would attract listeners – just as the red-top tabloids today include their Page 3 nudes to attract readers. For the same

reasons Delmer was reluctant to spend much of his department's resources on printed pornography, and produced
only three items – only two of which were ever distributed.
It was not, he said, 'because I was squeamish, but simply
because I did not think the effort involved on our part
would be justified by the subversive effect on the
Germans'.[8]

Perhaps the most curious aspect of the 'black' radio war
is the contrast that it highlights between Goebbels the brilliant peacetime propagandist, who made Hitler a national
hero, and Goebbels the wartime propaganda supremo who
constantly struggled to keep up with the Allies and was
almost always beaten at his own game. As described in the
next chapter, the techniques that Goebbels perfected on the
unsophisticated audiences of the 1930s no longer worked
in the cynical, war-weary 1940s. As in the case of 'black'
radio stations, Goebbels continued to be innovative and
original, but his execution was heavy-handed and misguided and his strategy rebounded on him badly in the end.
He had broken one of his own cardinal rules – make sure
your propaganda is boomerang-proof.

By 1944 Delmer's radio stations were so successful that
he launched two others, Atlantiksender and Soldatensender
Calais. Now, he also had a powerful 600-kilowatt medium-
wave transmitter at his disposal, purpose-designed and
built by RCA, so that his broadcasts could be heard all over
the Third Reich by audiences potentially numbering in the
millions. But regardless of the effects his broadcasts had on
morale, they played a key tactical operational role in support of the D-Day landings in June 1944. Delmer's stations
broadcast urgent messages to German listeners telling
them not to stay in their homes but to pack their belongings
and take to the streets, thus adding to the queues of

refugees already choking German roads and making it increasingly difficult for the German army to conduct defensive operations.

German radio stations frantically responded with official broadcasts explaining that enemy radio stations were sending counterfeit messages that should be ignored and people should stay at home – a gift to Delmer's black stations, which simply broadcast official-sounding messages saying that the enemy was broadcasting counterfeit messages which should be ignored. The resulting mass confusion was precisely what Churchill intended, and it contributed to the collapse of order in Germany.

There was one final echo of the First War propaganda conflict and a final act of subtlety by Whitehall in the black radio war. Because he now possessed a powerful radio transmitter that could reach the whole of Europe and could counterfeit practically any German station at will, Delmer proposed to Churchill and the chiefs of staff that he broadcast a fake announcement that Hitler was dead and the war over. His proposal was turned down, partly because it was realised that it would cause as much confusion among Allied troops as it would among the Germans. But, more importantly, there were those who recalled the end of the First War when Lord Northcliffe had publicly claimed credit for hoodwinking the Germans by the propaganda he had directed at them. Gloating like this made it possible for some Germans to claim that they had not been beaten fairly in the field, but merely tricked into defeat by British lies, providing a basis to claim a re-match. Whitehall did not want it to be possible for anyone in future to say that Hitler had merely been tricked into defeat.

17

The Pied Piper

Mass-Observation's early surveys had shown that, in the years immediately preceding the Second World War, the people of Britain were uncertain and divided. By contrast, the majority of Germans were united as never before, behind a leader and a government that commanded nationwide approval and support. This consensus of national purpose and vision was largely due to one man with an extraordinary gift for tapping into the unconscious mind of the masses of German people and weaving public policies out of the dreams he found there – Joseph Goebbels.

Because of his success at manipulating public opinion, both at home and abroad, Goebbels soon became a personal target for British Intelligence's black propaganda campaigns, both before and during the Second World War. Not surprisingly, few historians or writers have cared to spend much time or effort disentangling the real person from the layers of intelligence myth, and today the most widely received image of Goebbels is the blackened view, distorted like a half-burned photograph. In this view, Goebbels is denied any credit for originality or talent, other than an instinctive, rat-like cunning. He is said to have relied on lies as his main means of communication with the German people – the bigger the lie the better. He is thought of as an unscrupulous opportunist, more interested in blonde German film stars than in the doctrines of National Socialism, and as someone who flourished only because he was protected in Hitler's shadow, incapable of surviving alone. That, ultimately, he was a self-deluding fanatic who took the easy way out.

This view, of course, begs the question: how could such a person as this achieve such extraordinary results? For even if his inadequacies have been exaggerated by black propaganda, the fact remains that it is the contradictions in Goebbels' personal life that are most puzzling of all. That a small, sickly cripple with an unappealing, ferret-like face should become, first, a hero to Berliners and then a national figure. That such an unlikely figure should become the standard-bearer of the Reich in the darkest days of war. And that Goebbels, the master of spin, should step through the political minefield of peacetime putting barely a foot wrong, yet – as soon as war began – somehow become transformed into Goebbels the Mister Magoo of PR, staggering from one media crisis to another.

The big question, of course, is how on earth did he do it? How did someone with no military training and little business or political experience become Gauleiter of Berlin and orchestrator of one of the most powerful propaganda machines in history? What was his secret?

There is no doubt that Goebbels was among the first European politicians – probably *the* first – to realise the importance of the propaganda discoveries of Edward Bernays. Unlike many people who had read *Propaganda* and *Crystallizing Public Opinion* in the 1920s and concluded that the essence of spin was just a matter of being clever at deceiving people, Goebbels realised that Bernays was on to something fundamentally important about human nature and about unconscious motivations: that the way to reach people and gain their support was to understand their deepest aspirations and to persuade them that they can achieve those goals by signing up wholeheartedly to your candidate, your policy, your party.

Goebbels learned from Bernays that the first rule of marketing is to understand very carefully what exactly it is that your target audience wants at the deepest level, then to find ways of giving your product the appearance of meeting those deepest, often unconscious needs, and finally targeting your audience with sales messages telling them they can have what they want simply by switching to your product. Soap powder or motor cars, holidays or houses, movie stars or politicians, the product or service was unimportant. Only the process of engineering consent matters, and that remains the same whatever the audience, whatever the product.

The important aspect of this approach is that it does not involve directly engaging either the press or the public, but is designed essentially to work indirectly, by remote control. Through organising a 'freedom march' of women smokers in New York, Bernays made smoking symbolic of feminist aspirations. By letting slip President Wilson's itinerary in Paris, Bernays ensured there would be cheering crowds to greet him wherever he went and press photographers on hand to testify to Wilson's popularity for mass newspaper audiences. By associating Hitler in the public mind with the German nation itself, and Hitler's personal will with the national will to greatness, Goebbels inspired the kind of fanatical loyalty and dedication that the British reserved for their King and their flag.

For me, the most amazing aspect of Bernays – the arche-typal PR man – is his admission that he had not spoken directly to the press for 50 years or more.[1] Isn't manipulat-ing journalists what PR is all about? Don't PR men twist the press around their finger with free booze, foreign trips and lashings of soft soap? That is certainly how many PR people (and some journalists) in both Europe and the US still do business. But this view fundamentally misses the importance of engineering events so that other influencers will do the job of selling to the press for you, out of convic-tion rather than a sense of obligation, from the heart rather than the head.

Armed with Bernays' magic formula, Goebbels set about transforming Nazi politics in the late 1920s from a series of street clashes by disorganised rabbles into a disci-plined modern political party.

Everything that Goebbels did was the result of careful analysis and careful targeting – he left nothing to chance. In the 1930s (as Mass-Observation's research had shown in Britain) the primary medium of information for the over-whelming majority of people was the newspapers. The press was complemented by radio broadcasts and cinema newsreels. Long before the Nazis came to power in 1933, Goebbels published his own newspapers – making sure they contained stories his readers wanted, just like today's tabloids; the Nazi equivalent of 'Freddie Starr ate my ham-ster'. Though a willing disciple of Bernays' indirect meth-ods, Goebbels also made sure that every avenue of mass communications was tamed in the service of the state. Once in power, he took control of every medium, organis-ing a department and expert officials to oversee each one. He then made sure that all media broadcast the same core messages, so that they reinforced each other in the public mind. This 'confirmation' of one medium by another was especially powerful in forming a consensus of public opinion and eliminating dissenting voices.

Goebbels recognised and actively promoted the medium of radio at a time when very few politicians had cottoned on to its power. It was a medium that also fitted well with the Nazis' semi-mystical belief in the power of the spoken word in raising consciousness. Shortly after coming to power in 1933, he opened the 10th Radio Show in Berlin and took the opportunity to promote a cheap radio receiver that every German home could afford, the *Volksempfänger*. He told his audience that:

> The radio will be for the 20th century what the press was for the 19th century. ... Its discovery and application are of truly revolutionary significance for contemporary community life. Future generations may conclude that the radio had as great an intellectual and spiritual impact on the masses as the printing press had before the beginning of the Reformation.[2]

These are not the words or the vision of a cunning opportunist with a third-rate mind, but those of someone who understood the impact of new technology and its application to modern life.

Goebbels originated techniques that today are taken for granted by every political party. He argued that every aspect of policy must be examined from the point of view of presentation to the public and – if necessary – policy must be re-shaped to ensure public acceptance. He insisted that every member of the government stay 'on message' whenever and wherever they spoke or wrote. To ensure this harmony of media messages he wrote and circulated policy position papers, together with prepared answers to tricky questions. If the Nazis had bad or unpalatable news, he would sometimes 'bury' it by keeping the news for release until some other major story captured the headlines. And he would make sure that editors of Nazi-controlled newspapers knew which stance to take on international issues. Equally, he took care to know what news would please the crowds and made sure there was a supply of suitably good news on hand, manufactured if necessary. And he topped off this routine spoonfeeding with occasional national spectaculars and political rallies attended by hand-picked audiences at which every word and gesture was carefully rehearsed in advance, designed to provide a national 'feel-good' factor.

To anyone even vaguely familiar with the 'pager' culture of New Labour's media machine and the activities of media manipulators like Alistair Campbell, Peter Mandelson and Jo Moore (9/11 was 'a good day to bury bad news'), it's clear that Goebbels was an early adopter of the modern way of doing things, and his activities now seem routine. But to his contemporaries in the 1930s – both in Germany and abroad – they appeared Machiavellian and deeply shocking.

US Secretary of State Henry L. Stimpson had declared of spying as recently as 1929 that 'Gentlemen do not read each other's mail'. In 1942, when War Cabinet member Stafford Cripps learned that the Political Warfare Executive was broadcasting black propaganda, including pornography, to Germany, he told Foreign Secretary Anthony Eden: 'If this is the sort of thing we have to do to win the war, I would rather lose it!'

Fortunately for the Allied war effort, not every member of the British or US government was so naive or so squeamish. Yet views such as these were still commonly held, and it was against this sort of background that Goebbels and his Propaganda Ministry were judged by their contemporaries. Even some top Nazis were nervous about Goebbels' methods – in some cases the same people who were later to embark on genocide. It required very little effort to depict Goebbels as a man completely without conscience or honour, and that is exactly how he was portrayed by the British press and the communist press abroad.

Probably the greatest success of British home front propaganda during the Second World War was in fostering the widespread belief that, while the German public was easily taken in by government propaganda, the British public was immune to such attempts to manipulate it, and that the free men and women of Britain made up their own minds about the meaning of current events, unlike subservient Germans.

In fact, contrary to the picture painted by Allied propaganda, Goebbels rarely resorted to lies as a media technique. There was nothing ethical about this; he was merely following Bernays' advice – that the simplest and easiest way to get people to listen to you and believe what you tell them is to make certain they know you are telling them the truth. He knew also that his enemies – especially the British press – would delight in ensuring that the German people were informed about any bad news that befell them. Grasping the nettle of being the one to bear bad news gained the priceless advantages of appearing strong and confident as well as truthful, while avoiding being cornered by foreign journalists, keen to make the Nazis look like fools or knaves.

Goebbels took this policy of truth-telling as the basis of his relationship with the German public to almost fanatical lengths. When, for example, the German army suffered a catastrophic military defeat at Stalingrad, Goebbels told the German public about it in excruciating detail. In February 1943 he told a Berlin audience: 'My task is to give you an unvarnished picture of the situation, and to draw the hard conclusions that will guide the actions of the German government, but also of the German people.'[3] He told them:

> There is no point in disputing the seriousness of the situation. I do not want to give you a false impression of the situation that could lead to false conclusions, perhaps giving the German people a false sense of security that is altogether inappropriate in the present situation. The storm raging against our venerable continent from the steppes this winter overshadows all previous human and historical experience. The German army and its allies are the only possible defence.[4]

He also plainly told his audience that they could lose the war against Russia unless the whole country mobilised for war.

Goebbels was criticised for this policy of outspokenness by many in the Nazi Party. There were constant appeals to Hitler by the armed services to get Goebbels to shut up in public, but it appears that Hitler rarely if ever interfered.

One curious aspect of this pathological honesty is that it led Goebbels to spell out to the German people exactly what he was doing and why. In England and America, 'propaganda' had become a dirty word by 1919 and was scarcely mentioned at all in public except in a pejorative sense. As described in an earlier chapter, when Edward Bernays injudiciously used the word in a press release about President Wilson's visit to the 1919 Peace Conference, he called down the wrath of press and

Congress on his head. The word had exactly the same unpleasant and dangerous connotations in Germany, yet Goebbels revelled in it. He called himself 'Minister of Propaganda' and his organisation the 'Propaganda Ministry'. He wrote articles for popular consumption with titles like 'Political Propaganda' and even made a speech to the assembled thousands at the 1934 Nuremberg rally, 'On Propaganda', in which he blatantly recommended the German model to the rest of the world.[5]

Goebbels' national oversight of propaganda extended at one and the same time to the most banal crudity and to a level of subtlety that escapes most PR people even today. In 1930, Goebbels' Reich Propaganda Office circulated advice to party members on the most effective forms of propaganda. His pamphlet contained the advice that: 'Flyers in various colours, but with identical slogans, some with caricatures, spread through entire city districts are effective.' He then provided an example of an effective flyer: 'Become a National Socialist, all else is shit.' This and other slogans, he helpfully pointed out, 'can be ordered from the propaganda department'.[6]

Against the astonishing crudity of such posters must be placed advice of the following kind, from the same document, showing an attention to detail that was far beyond even the propaganda agents of Perfidious Albion:

> Leaflets, free newspapers and brochures should be distributed only in such places where it is likely that they will be read immediately. Good places are in train stations, for those going to a train, not coming from one. People will read on the train, but not on the street.

Because he possessed a real talent for PR on a national scale – perhaps the first German in the 20th century to do so – Goebbels understood intuitively exactly why and how Britain had won the propaganda war in 1914–18. His propaganda speeches on the subject, though containing his own brand of spin and an unmistakable note of bitterness, still make slightly uncomfortable reading today. In 1939, some months before the Second World War, he told his listeners:

> The English are well known throughout the world for their lack of political scruples. They are experts at the art of hiding their misdeeds behind a facade of virtue. They have been at it for centuries, and it has become such a part of their nature that they hardly notice it any longer. They carry on with such a pious expression and deadly seriousness that they even convince themselves that they are the exemplars of political virtue. They do not admit their hypocrisy to themselves ... They not only behave as if they were the model of piety and virtue – they really believe that they are.[7]

Goebbels had plainly devoted his analytical skills to understanding exactly what Charles Masterman had accomplished and, more importantly, how he had achieved it.

> English propaganda turned the whole world against us. One had not thought them capable of it. The experts found its planning and execution brilliant. English propaganda was limited to a few powerful slogans. With devilish depravity, they were spread systematically throughout the entire world and pounded into the brains of millions of people. At the end, they were helpless victims of mass hypnosis.
>
> There were really only a few slogans that the English spread throughout the world. They spoke of children's

hands chopped off, eyes poked out, women raped, and old people tortured.

Long years of anti-German propaganda campaign persuaded the whole world that Germany was a nation of barbarians, uncivilised and inhumane, and that it was the moral and cultural obligation of the rest of the earth to destroy Germany and to break its power. Only then could the world know peace and friendship. That made it easy for the rest of the world to join England in fighting Germany.[8]

Goebbels' assessment of his own genius as a propagandist was that it is an innate talent. As early as 1928, he gave a speech to an audience of party members in Berlin on 'Knowledge and Propaganda' in which he remarked:

[T]here is no ABC of propaganda. One can make propaganda, or one cannot. Propaganda is an art. Any reasonably normal person can learn to play the violin to a certain degree, but then his teacher will say: 'This is as far as it goes. Only a genius can learn what remains. You are not a genius, so be content with what you have learned.' I can certainly teach any reasonable person the absolute basics of propaganda. But I will soon recognise the limits. One is either a propagandist, or one is not.[9]

It is often thought that PR people are the epitome of insincerity, and Goebbels' name is still often invoked as being synonymous with hypocrisy and empty words. In reality, Goebbels committed the cardinal sin of public relations – he believed his own press releases. In 1945, with the Red Army at the gates of Berlin, he and his wife chose death with Hitler in the Chancellery bunker. Hitler swallowed cyanide and shot himself after appointing the faithful

Goebbels his successor as leader of Germany. Less than a day later, pausing only to draft a press release about his appointment that the press would never print, Goebbels and his family took poison. Goebbels was thus rewarded for his loyalty by becoming Führer of the Third Reich for a few brief hours, until the cyanide pill did its work and the world's press began to print the kind of headlines he had worked so tirelessly to prevent.

18

Business as Usual

At the height of the Second World War, in May 1944, as
British and American troops were fighting and dying
in Italy and the Far East, the American president of the
Bank for International Settlements, Thomas Harrington
McKittrick, met his fellow directors around the boardroom
table in Basle, Switzerland. Also sitting around the table
were German, Japanese, Italian, British and American executive staff. While their fellow countrymen died fighting
each other, the bank's officials had met to discuss something that transcended total war – money.

To understand how this extraordinary situation came
about, you have to go back 30 years to the previous world
war.

At Vimy Ridge on the Western Front in 1916, the Allied
and German trenches were only fifteen metres apart at
their nearest point – close enough for men on both sides to
see each other's faces and hear each other's voices. The men
who served their fortnightly turn here, on both sides of the
line, were compelled to confront the reality of war in a way
that generals and politicians never were – an intimacy that
had unexpected consequences. According to men who

served at this hot spot, the usual first action of incoming troops of both sides on taking up their tour of duty was to throw gifts over to the opposing trenches – cigarettes, tobacco, beer, wine, sausages. These peaceful missiles carried a message that was neither written nor spoken, but was universally understood: 'We won't start anything if you don't.'[*1]

Emperors may speak of conquest and presidents may talk of democracy, but the man in the muddy trench has an altogether more realistic view of the world. This realistic view was not confined to the old sweats in the trenches, but was shared in the boardrooms of the world's largest commercial and industrial corporations. But rather than promises to keep their distance, the tacit message of some European and US businessmen on the outbreak of war was just the opposite: 'We're happy to do business as usual – and keep quiet about it – if you'll do the same.'

The international nature of trade in the 20th century meant that war required special legislation, ostensibly to relieve companies of being guilty of breach of contract, or of becoming unwitting traitors to their countries, but also to prevent unscrupulous traders from cashing in. Britain passed a 'Trading with the Enemy' Act in 1914 and the US did the same in 1917. The immediate effect of this legislation was to cancel all pre-war international contracts with enemy countries and to prohibit any further trade with them until the cessation of hostilities. There was also the question of enemy subsidiaries to consider.

Take for example Siemens, which in 1914 was the world's biggest electrical concern with sister companies in

*This situation changed dramatically the following year, when 20,000 Canadian troops overwhelmed the German defences at Vimy Ridge in the single biggest breakthrough of the war.

Germany and England that were both wealthy and success-ful. But the firm's main business then was electrical com-munications – telephone, telegraphs, and especially the business of undersea cables, which had assumed crucial strategic significance in the first propaganda war. In addi-tion, Siemens held scores of important basic UK patents in strategic electrical and communications technologies. The British government decided it was expedient to nationalise the British end of the company and to expropriate all its assets and patents. The family firm in Germany received no compensation.[2]

The 'Trading with the Enemy' Acts also had another effect that the governments of Britain and the US felt desir-able in that it effectively censored German language mate-rial. Publishers could no longer import German books, magazines or newspapers or even commission German language news and features. In the US, this resulted in hun-dreds of German language newspapers, in German-speak-ing states such as Oregon, Minnesota and Pennsylvania, going out of business. Another consequence of the wave of patriotic fervour that swept the US was that German busi-nesses changed their names and even German foods were Americanised. Sauerkraut became liberty cabbage, ham-burgers became liberty sandwiches, and German measles became liberty measles. There are towns in Oregon and Minnesota today called Liberty that, until 1917, were named Berlin, Munich or Vienna.[3]

Twenty years later, when the Second World War started, major British and US corporations found themselves in the same position all over again, except that now they had become more sophisticated, their operations were even more globalised and more deeply embedded in the economies of overseas countries, and their illegal activities even harder to track. Most crucial of all, they had a much higher level of overseas interest to protect.

According to Charles Higham in his book *Trading with the Enemy*, US overseas investments in Germany in 1941 amounted to 'an estimated total of $475 million. Standard Oil of New Jersey had $120 million invested there; General Motors had $35 million; IBM had $30 million; and Ford had $17.5 million.'[4]

In theory, under German war legislation, these assets should have been confiscated and nationalised for the German war effort. In practice they were protected from seizure by the Nazis by being put into special holding companies, their revenue accumulating until the war's end. This by itself was no great crime, since the loss of such investment could have injured America's economy and weakened the American war effort. But it meant in practice that American-owned companies continued to turn out products that would aid the German war machine.

Ford Motor Company's French subsidiary turned out vehicles for the Wehrmacht.[5] Standard Oil shipped fuel through neutral Switzerland to the German forces and the Allies alike.[6] International Telephone and Telegraph (ITT) managed Nazi military communications with the help of its US president.[7] And IBM Germany supplied punched card equipment to enable the SS to document the Reich's Jewish citizens.[8]

In part this trading 'across the lines' resulted from an ethical relativism arising from industry's increased international complexity. But in some cases there was also an ideological predisposition to cooperate. Henry Ford, for example, was an ardent admirer of Nazism who had been awarded a medal by Hitler personally in 1937 for his contribution to the Third Reich. Thomas Watson, legendary boss of IBM, was another admirer of Nazi drive and efficiency and another US captain of industry honoured by Hitler with a medal. And some senior Nazis had a personal financial stake in overseas industrial companies.

If industry was more complicated than in 1914 because of its international nature, banking and finance were infinitely more complex in the Second World War thanks to the creation in 1930 of the Bank for International Settlements. Based in Basle, the bank was jointly owned by the Bank of England, the German Reichsbank, First National Bank of New York, the Bank of Italy, the Bank of France, and other central banks. The main inspiration for the bank was Hjalmar Schacht, the Nazi Economics Minister who had defeated hyper-inflation and put the German economy back on its feet. The ostensible purpose of the bank was to provide the Allies with reparations to be paid by Germany for the First World War. But as Higham points out, the bank's function was soon turned on its head and it became 'a money funnel for American and British funds to flow into Hitler's coffers and to help Hitler build up his war machine'.

Schacht foresaw that war might come again, so he arranged that the various governments signed up to a founding charter for the bank guaranteeing that it would remain immune to seizure, closure, or censure, even if its owners were at war with each other. Because of this remarkable international status which made it invulnerable to anything as prosaic as a world war, the principals who owned the bank – both Allies and Axis – continued to meet each year during the war to decide financial matters.

As described earlier, in May 1944, while fighting raged, the bank's principals met in Basle under its American president, Thomas Harrington McKittrick. One subject under discussion was the $378 million in gold that had been sent to the bank by the Nazi government after Pearl Harbor for use by its leaders after the war – gold that had been looted from the national banks of occupied Austria, Holland, Belgium and Czechoslovakia.[9]

Even before the outbreak of war in 1939, the Bank for International Settlements had invested millions in Germany, while, in turn, the Germans had deposited large sums in looted gold in the bank. If it occurred to anyone on either side that there was anything legally or ethically wrong with this arrangement, no one attempted to do anything about it. The bank's charter and infinitely elastic respect for the convenience of Swiss banking laws enabled all parties to turn a blind eye to the blatantly treasonable proceedings.

The extent of the inextricable links between international banking and international industry is well illustrated by the interests of the Rockefeller family. These included ownership of Chase National Bank (now Chase Manhattan Bank) as well as Standard Oil of New Jersey (active throughout the world including Germany), Swedish ball bearing manufacturer SKF, and international communications giant International Telephone and Telegraph (ITT). One of the principal investors in Standard Oil Germany was Heinrich Himmler's Gestapo, whose representatives Karl Lindemann and Emil Hefferich were senior executives of the company (and who, in turn, were close friends and colleagues of Baron von Schröder of the Bank for International Settlements).[10]

In 1936, Rockefeller formed a joint venture with New York bank Schroder's to finance the Third Reich. The partners in Schroder, Rockefeller and Company included Avery Rockefeller, nephew of John D., Baron Bruno von Schröder in London, and Kurt von Schröder of the Bank for International Settlements and the Gestapo in Cologne. Avery Rockefeller owned 42 per cent of Schroder, Rockefeller, and Baron Bruno and his cousin 47 per cent.[11]

Even in cases where it did not suit the government of Britain or Germany to turn a blind eye, they were often unwilling or even powerless to act. According to Charles Higham, this was the case with the giant telecommunications corporation, ITT.

> [I]n the case of ITT, perhaps the most flagrant of the corporations in its outright dealings with the enemy, Hitler and his postmaster general, the venerable Wilhelm Ohnesorge, strove to impound the German end of the business. But even they were powerless in such a situation: the Gestapo leader of counterintelligence, Walter Schellenberg, was a prominent director and shareholder of ITT by arrangement with New York – and even Hitler dared not cross the Gestapo.[12]

It might be imagined that these connections were on paper only and that, apart from providing banking facilities, there was no funny business behind enemy lines. But consider the events of early 1942 when Karl Lindemann, Rockefeller-Standard Oil's representative in Berlin, held a series of urgent meetings with two directors of the American ITT Corporation: Walter Schellenberg, head of the Gestapo's counterintelligence service (SD), and Baron Kurt von Schröder of the Bank for International Settlements and the Stein Bank. 'The result of these meetings', says Higham,

> was that Gerhardt Westrick, the crippled boss of ITT in Nazi Germany, got aboard an ITT Focke-Wulf bomber and flew to Madrid for a meeting in March with

Sosthenes Behn, American ITT chief. In the sumptuous Royal Suite of Madrid's Ritz Hotel, the tall, sharp-faced Behn and the heavily limping Westrick sat down for lunch to discuss how best they could improve ITT's links with the Gestapo, and its improvement of the whole Nazi system of telephones, teleprinters, aircraft intercoms, submarine and ship phones, electric buoys, alarm systems, radio and radar parts, and fuses for artillery shells, as well as the Focke-Wulf bombers that were taking thousands of American lives.[13]

It's difficult to blame a commercial corporation for wishing to save itself from being taken over and snuffed out, as the British branch of Siemens was in 1914. Losing everything and ending up broke is not an attractive option. What both world wars showed was that the price of survival was active and willing collaboration with the enemy, which is treason, whatever the label and whatever the reason. Large corporations have proved to be immune to charges of treason, or to the consequences of such charges, simply because they have proved to be more powerful and more durable than their governments.

Motives that have led corporations in the past to reject patriotism and give in to treason are just as powerful today. According to a report issued by the US Treasury, more than 100 banks, retailers, and other organisations have been fined in recent years for trading with nations accused of sponsoring terrorism. On the list of companies named since 1998 are Ikea, Citibank, and Goodyear Tire & Rubber.[14]

The US Treasury had in fact kept these and other names secret, but was compelled to release details after two watchdog groups sued the government under the Freedom of

Information Act. Information on more than 180 other fines is expected to be released soon, according to the *New York Times*.

The *Wall Street Journal* has pointed out that Halliburton Co., the oil-services firm once headed by US Vice President Dick Cheney, apparently violated the law by opening an office in Tehran in 2000, while Cheney headed the company. Even in the 21st century, business is still business.[15]

19

Class Distinction

In earlier chapters I pointed to the many similarities that existed in British and German society between the wars in terms of their common political philosophy and the fundamentally fascist nature of both societies. These similarities were masked at the time and since, because they were overlaid by a single factor that far outweighed them all – class structure.

Beneath the liberal democratic façade, most members of the governing classes in Britain in the 1920s and 30s were elitist, right-wing, racist, mainly eugenicist in outlook, kept in office by a small, unrepresentative electorate, committed to the maintenance of an overseas empire, and to the domestic status quo, by brutal military repression – a description that applies equally well to the aims of the Nazis. But whereas the majority of Nazis came from a middle-class or working-class background, the majority of Britain's leaders had aristocratic or upper-middle-class origins.

This class contrast was perhaps the single most important factor that generated and maintained deep suspicions between the two governments. And nowhere was this clash of classes more evident than in the two national leaders who came to dominate the prosecution and conduct of the Second World War. Winston Churchill and Adolf Hitler were polar opposites in ways that were virtually guaranteed to enrage and antagonise each of them. But it was not so much the differences in personality that caused the deep antipathy between the two leaders – in fact, the two were very similar in many important respects. Rather, it was at the deepest and most primitive emotional level that the two scorned and despised one another, and the issue that more than any other fuelled that scorn and hatred was class.

The driving force of Churchill's life was that he was an English aristocrat, born to be a member of the ruling class. To be sure, there were many 'ifs' and 'buts' surrounding that title – he was half American, without any money of his own, and without an inherited title. He was compelled to make his own way in the world and was treated as a poor relation by some of Britain's wealthiest and most powerful aristocrats, and with suspicion by many British statesmen who perceived him as an adventurer. But Churchill felt from the outset that the seeds of greatness were in him, and he never lost sight of the great future he felt sure they must portend. He was the grandson of a duke, and a descendant of the great John Churchill, first Duke of Marlborough – indeed, he had been born at Blenheim Palace. His father, Lord Randolph Churchill, had been Chancellor of the Exchequer.

Despite his patrician origins, Churchill was in many respects a liberal democrat by nature. Clive Ponting cites a telling example from 1940 when Churchill was still First Lord of the Admiralty. He discovered that, despite the acute shortage of naval officers, three boys who had been placed fifth, eighth and seventeenth out of 400 candidates had been rejected by the Navy selection board as 'unfit for naval service'. Churchill insisted on interviewing the boys personally and discovered that one had a slight cockney accent while the other two had been considered to have socially inferior origins, one being the son of a chief petty officer and the other the son of a Merchant Navy engineer. Churchill, in effect, told the Navy Board to stop being snobs and ordered that all three boys be accepted for officer training.[1]

When it came to social welfare and legislation he was a committed liberal who genuinely wanted to improve the lot of ordinary people. He was Lloyd George's most trusted and committed lieutenant in pushing through revolutionary social legislation, such as the 1911 National Insurance Act, against conservative opposition.

But in many other respects, Churchill was an unreconstructed patrician politician of the old school, and could be as authoritarian as Hitler. He regarded virtually any attempt by organised labour to press its case for better wages and conditions – for example by strike action – as communist subversion and anarchy, which could legitimately be put down by police and armed soldiers.

In 1910, as Home Secretary, Churchill ordered 600 Metropolitan Police into Tonypandy in the Rhondda Valley to deal with 30,000 striking coal miners. Strikers and their families were attacked by police and one striker was killed. Churchill then ordered the army into Tonypandy, and sent to command them General Nevil Macready, who later commanded the notoriously brutal Black and Tans in Ireland. Troops remained in the valleys for a year, suppressing the strike. The following year, in the dock strike of 1911, Churchill mobilised troops to crush the strike, and in Liverpool and Llanelli troops opened fire on strikers.[2]

Hitler brought out all of Churchill's most snobbish instincts. To Churchill, Hitler was no more than a jumped-up working-class oik with ideas above his station; no better than the street agitators whose heads he ordered the police to knock together. Perhaps one of his most prophetic moments came in 1935, when he wrote about Hitler's abilities and ambitions:

> Then (in 1919) it was that one corporal, a former Austrian house-painter, set out to regain it all. In fifteen years that have followed this resolve he has succeeded in restoring Germany to the most powerful position in Europe, and not only has he restored the position of his country, but he has even, to a very large extent, reversed the results of the Great War (now) the vanquished are in the process of becoming the victors, and the victors the vanquished. When Hitler began, Germany lay prostrate at the feet of the Allies. He may yet see the day when what is left of Europe will be prostrate at the feet of Germany. Whatever else may be thought of these exploits, they are certainly among the most remarkable in the whole history of the world.[3]

Here, Churchill pays the greatest compliment to Hitler. He describes the achievements of Hitler the politician as among the most remarkable in the whole history of the world. And yet, even while paying this compliment he is unable to resist belittling Hitler the man by incorrectly describing him as a 'former Austrian house-painter'. What, I wonder, would Churchill have said of Hitler in 1935 if, like Bismarck, one of his illustrious predecessors as Chancellor, he had been 'von' Hitler and a prince of royal German blood?

Churchill continually referred to Hitler as 'Corporal Hitler', again belittling Hitler's lowly origins and position. This is all the more surprising since Churchill was himself a soldier who had served in action on the Western Front, just like Hitler, and who must have known that Hitler was decorated several times for acts of courage under fire.

But, curiously, it wasn't Hitler's personal qualities that Churchill disliked, merely his social background. In 1937, Churchill wrote a book titled *Great Contemporaries*, in which he penned essays on world figures of the day such as Joseph Chamberlain, Herbert Asquith and Arthur Balfour. He included Hitler in his book, and wrote: 'Those who have met Herr Hitler face to face in public business or on social terms have found a highly competent, cool, well-informed functionary with an agreeable manner, a disarming smile, and few have been unaffected by a subtle personal magnetism.'[4]

As Andrew Roberts pointed out in *Hitler and Churchill*: 'Churchill had the moral courage to keep the sentence in the 1941 reprint of *Great Contemporaries*.'[5] But as the war got under way, Churchill continued to make belittling personal remarks about Hitler's background and education. He referred to him as a 'blood-thirsty guttersnipe': blood-thirsty, certainly – but a guttersnipe? What can this possibly mean other than that Hitler's origins were humble? And why should this count against him? Again, in a BBC broadcast in 1942, after Hitler had made the strategic mistake of attacking Russia, Churchill said:

Then Hitler made his second great blunder. He forgot about the winter. There is a winter, you know, in Russia. For a good many months the temperature is apt to fall very low. There is snow, there is frost, and all that. Hitler forgot about the Russian winter. He must have been very loosely educated. We all heard about it at school; but he forgot it. I have never made such a bad mistake as that.[6]

One can almost hear Churchill adding under his breath: 'Because I went to public school.'

In some respects, Churchill's snobbish feelings about Hitler were not so wide of the mark. Hitler had escaped from his lower-class roots and loved nothing more than to rub shoulders with the rich, the beautiful and the powerful – he social-climbed with the best of them. Unlike some of his colleagues, notably Goering, Hitler did not seek power in order to line his own pockets, yet he hardly stinted himself in terms of the places he provided for himself to live and work, such as the Berghof and the Berlin Chancellery, and although his tastes in food and drink were simple, his taste for ceremony and a grandiose lifestyle were as great as any other world leader.

Whenever Hitler spoke of Churchill it was with the same deep hatred. In January 1942 he told his fellow Nazis: 'I never met an Englishman who didn't speak of Churchill with disapproval. Never one who didn't say he was off his head.'[7]

Later the same year, Hitler told Rommel at dinner:

Churchill is the very corrupt type of journalist. There's not a worse prostitute in politics. He himself has written that it's unimaginable what can be done in war with the help of lies. He's an utterly amoral repulsive creature. I'm convinced that he has a place of refuge ready beyond the Atlantic. He obviously won't seek sanctuary in Canada. In Canada he'd be beaten up. He'll go to his friends the Yankees.[8]

It seems to me that Hitler brought out the worst, as well as the best, in Churchill, and knowing this wounded Churchill still further. Hitler, on the other hand, would have loved to have been born with Churchill's social and educational advantages.

One tiny incident stands out above all others in my mind as revealing Churchill's real feelings about Hitler. In 1945, with Germany defeated, Churchill travelled to Potsdam for the Big Three conference on the future of Europe, with Stalin and Truman. On the way he did a little sightseeing and visited Berlin to inspect the ruins of Hitler's Chancellery and bunker complex. There was little to be seen on the surface of the bunker, other than a pile of rubble. But while Churchill was there, at his enemy's lair, he made a point of being photographed sitting on a chair brought up from Hitler's underground bunker and placed on the pile of rubble. The chair was from Hitler's study and had very likely been used by Hitler himself at some time. The victorious look on Churchill's face says everything about what for him was clearly a crowning moment of the sweetest triumph as he sat on his vanquished adversary's seat.

The war for him had not merely been about defeating Nazism and making the world safe for democracy; it had been personal. And the silly look on Churchill's face says not merely 'I won', but also 'The right people are in charge again'.

This is the only occasion of which I am aware when Churchill publicly behaved in such a petty way. To my mind it is quite out of character with the world statesman who wrote: 'In war: resolution. In defeat: defiance. In victory: magnanimity. In peace: goodwill.' And yet, the very fact that this gesture was so out of character shows how deeply motivated it must have been, and how powerless even

275

someone of Churchill's indomitable will was to resist dancing on his enemy's grave when that enemy was 'a former
house-painter' and corporal who had dared to challenge
Britain's right to rule the world.

There is one final irony that emerges from a comparison
of the personal qualities of Hitler and Churchill. Hitler and
his fellow Nazis believed that they were the heralds of a new era,
in which the supermen of the master race would re-order
the world for the good of mankind. They saw themselves as
just such new men. As one who believed profoundly in
democracy, Churchill considered such talk of supermen
and master races as elitist nonsense – nothing more than
the excuses of old-fashioned tyrants through the ages.

Yet, ironically, the war between Britain and Germany
was a titanic contest that demanded of national leaders just
the kind of superhuman qualities that the Nazis aspired to.
Conducting the leadership of their respective countries for
six long, bitter years of total war required exceptional abilities and moral strength to endure an ordeal from which
there was no escape until one or other was utterly defeated.
But in this ultimate conflict, it was Churchill, not Hitler,
who proved to have the superior qualities.

General Alan Brooke, who as Chief of the Imperial
General Staff worked more closely with Churchill through
the war than anyone else, writing in 1945, thanked God for
the 'opportunity of working alongside such a man, and of
having my eyes opened to the fact that such supermen exist
on this earth'.[9]

It was not the Wagnerian hero of ice and steel who tri-
umphed, but the slightly dog-eared Englishman with his
bow-tie, his glass of whisky, and his unshakeable conviction
that the British Island Race were the right people to run
things.

20

Judgement at Nuremberg

Even though *British Way and Purpose* was produced as early as 1941, when the war looked to be going badly for Britain, the document nevertheless contained an intriguing question regarding the post-war world of the future. What should be done with Hitler and the leaders of Nazi Germany, once the war was won?

Merely asking the question at all had an obvious propaganda value; it wasn't *if* we win the war, it was what are we going to do *when* we have won the war and our minds turn again to resuming normal life?

But, as well as propaganda value, inclusion of the question also had a valid legal purpose in that it began the public debate about what could potentially be a highly controversial question and – even more alarming to the War Cabinet – one that could have completely unpredictable consequences for the propaganda war.

The wartime authorities clearly felt the question to be of sufficient importance to give their own analysis and their own answer, under the heading: 'What would you do with the war criminals?' First, the authors of this section (written anonymously and hence likely to have originated in

Whitehall, if not Downing Street) set out fairly the nature of the problem.

What about the subordinate official?
The BBC recently broadcast a dramatic sketch about the German station master at a small railway station in Poland. It was his duty to dispatch the hundreds of trains into which each night hundreds of Jews were herded so tightly that they died for lack of air. The man was represented as being perfectly aware of what he was doing but as thinking only of keeping his job and of his family and his comfort. Should he be tried and punished as a murderer? Not an easy question to answer.

He was only obeying orders?
If he refused to obey orders, he risked being sent to a concentration camp and tortured. Should not those who drew up the orders be punished, rather than a subordinate, a mere cog in the wheel of German officialdom?

On the other hand we can feel pretty sure that it would be very hard to find anyone on our side who would knowingly carry out such an order, whatever might be coming to him if he disobeyed.

What about the generals?
But whether or not we think the subordinates should be punished in such a case, most people would agree that the 'higher-ups' should not escape. Let us see where this carries us.

It takes us to the German High Command. But they will have a ready defence. They are waging war and war nowadays is 'total war'. There is no place in it for humanitarian sentiment, for tender feelings towards individuals. They would turn round on us and bring up the bombing of German cities. Do we regard the Head of Bomber Command as a war criminal?

There is a retort to be made to the Generals; for we cannot allow them to get away so easily with their excuses.

Does 'total war' justify brutality?

It is quite true, as they plead, that this war is quite different from any previous war in its relation to the civil population. It is quite true that wars are no longer waged by soldiers alone but with the aid of all the workers and all the resources of the combatant countries. It is also true that these new conditions of war have driven a cart and horse through the rules drawn up in the older days for the proper conduct of war.

But this does not alter the fact that such rules exist and ought to be observed as far as military needs permit – first in the letter, then in the spirit. We ourselves have been most scrupulous in this respect.

The answer

The answer to the generals is that 'total war' does *not* excuse deliberate brutality. If the rules do not fit the new conditions, it is their duty, as it is ours also, not to sink to a bestial level but to maintain a sense of decency and to apply it to present circumstances. It is only in this way that new and more up-to-date rules can ever be drawn up.[1]

The first thing to be said about this view is that it is pre-eminently the voice of British common sense and reason. This is no cry for bloody vengeance but a calm and measured assessment that prefers the long view to any short-term ideas of exacting revenge. It is difficult, if not impossible, for a reasonable person to disagree with anything written here.

But there is a secondary purpose in these words. For the War Cabinet was already aware that, once the war was won, it might prove extremely difficult to bring anyone – even Hitler himself – to justice with complete certainty of a successful prosecution. Even worse, there was a slight but real prospect that some of those brought to trial might actually get off.

Take the station master in Poland referred to earlier, for instance. *BWP* asks 'should he be tried and punished as a murderer?', as though this were the easy option open to any post-war prosecutor. In fact, the burden of proof required to establish 'beyond reasonable doubt' that the station master acted 'with malice aforethought' in a conspiracy to murder required an extremely high standard of proof by the legal standards of the day, just as now. (Indeed, the crime of 'conspiracy' to commit murder did not even exist in Germany or France in 1939–45, but was an artefact of Anglo-American law.)

In a normal, peacetime court of law, a prosecutor bringing a charge of murder would expect to have to produce extensive forensic evidence, such as matching traces of blood or saliva, fingerprints, handwriting, fibres, hairs, footprints, tyre tracks, ballistics, telephone records, and similar physical evidence. Eyewitness evidence of identification would also be produced, but less weight would be given to this evidence than physical evidence because people can be mistaken, or misled, or have their own hidden agenda, while physical evidence cannot be wrong in this way.

It's clear that – unless there are some extraordinary circumstances – it is unlikely that a prosecutor will be able to produce any such physical evidence against the German station master and similar subordinates after the passage of so much time. He would have to be convicted on eyewitness evidence alone, and juries do not like sending people to the gallows on eyewitness evidence alone. Even a tribunal panel of judges must have unequivocal evidence presented to them before they can feel that a guilty verdict is a safe one in such a serious capital case, or they, too, will fail to convict.

There was also the matter of the rhetorical question asked in *BWP* about the Head of Bomber Command (Sir Arthur Harris). Do we regard Harris as a war criminal? The question was posed in wartime to show how preposterous such an idea was from the British standpoint. But already, in 1945, the question was taking on a different complexion. In the nine months of the Blitz against London in 1940, the Luftwaffe killed just over 20,000 people, mainly civilians. In the last years of the war, the British and American air forces killed around 1 million civilians in German cities. How exactly was an Allied prosecutor to deal with the potentially awkward Nazi defence that the actions of British commanders were no different from those of German commanders – both were following the dictates of their political masters? And if the generals were culpable, what about Churchill, Attlee and the War Cabinet? Were they murderers? What was the legal difference?

In 1945, the question of bringing the guilty men to justice ceased to be an intricate debating question and became a live issue. With Hitler dead and Germany in ruins, the British government decided that it had at last an opportunity for a reckoning on the international stage with its fiercest rival. England and Germany had vied with each other in a damaging and merciless propaganda war for 30 years. Now Germany was defeated and its leaders in chains – a perfect opportunity for a trial before the international community that would once and for all pin the guilt of the previous decades of blood on German hands. Regardless of legal difficulties or tricky questions of ethics, the decision was taken at the highest level in Britain, France, Russia and America that this was an opportunity not to be passed up.

The Palace of Justice in the ancient town of Nuremberg was readied for use as the court room. This choice of venue was, from the outset, a clear sign that the motivation for the trials was primarily their PR value, since Nuremberg had been chosen by the Nazis as the setting for their annual national rallies attended by tens of thousands and watched by hundreds of thousands more on cinema newsreels.

The architects of those rallies, Hitler and Goebbels, had already escaped the hangman by means of cyanide, but some 21 other prominent German leaders were appre- hended and brought to Nuremberg to stand trial before the whole world for the conduct of the war and the deaths of some 50 million. Among them were Hermann Goering, Rudolf Hess and Albert Speer, together with senior army, navy and SS generals.

An international panel of four judges (one from each Allied nation) was selected, and the court officials and administrative apparatus set up. An international meeting was convened in London to draw up the indictments, and almost at once hit trouble. The Allies had captured hun- dreds of tons of Nazi documents and carried them away for analysis. But it would take decades for it all to be carefully sifted by language and historical experts. (It was not until the early 1980s, for example, that the first Nazi papers were identified that provided solid documentary confirmation of the gas chambers at Auschwitz – the lack of which had prompted some Holocaust-deniers to doubt the existence of the extermination chambers.) But the Nuremberg trial was to be held right away, without delay, in the last months of 1945. There was no time for detailed analysis of so much material. Equally there was no realistic prospect of finding fingerprint evidence, or footprints, or ballistics evidence that would in any way link high-up politicians like Goering or Hess to mass exterminations.

If Goering, Hess, Speer and the others were tried according to established legal practices, current internationally in 1945, there was a possibility – however remote – that they might get off. But it was inconceivable that a monster like Goering should walk free simply because there wasn't enough evidence to convict him of a specific crime – this or that murder, this or that military atrocity. Anyone who followed the trial of Slobodan Milosevic at the International Court of Justice in the Hague will be aware that the kind of objections raised above are not merely technical but very real.

The choice of defendants was to some extent arbitrary from a legal standpoint, since it depended not on how much evidence had been collected against each individual but on how well known he was, and hence his PR value in representing the various branches of the Nazi state and war machine. In addition to the big political fish like Goering, Hess and Speer, there was Karl Doenitz, commander of the navy, Alfred Jodl, Chief of Army Operations, Ernst Kaltenbrunner, senior surviving Gestapo and SS chief, Wilhelm Keitel, Chief of Staff of the High Command of the Armed Forces, and Admiral Erich Raeder. Hitler's deputy,

Martin Bormann, was missing presumed dead, but was tried in his absence, just in case.

But present or absent, politician or soldier, prime mover or puppet, it made little difference to the outcome of the trial because the indictments were rigged from the outset. Realising the difficulty of obtaining conventional murder convictions, the prosecutors instead created four new major crimes. They were: conspiracy to wage aggressive war, waging aggressive war, or 'crimes against peace', war crimes, and crimes against humanity.[2]

All of these were novel charges, brought for the first time, with the intention of making sure senior Nazis could not escape on a technicality. In the event, all of them had serious legal defects which might well have caused them to be thrown out of a conventional European court by the standards of the time, but which were permitted and maintained by the Allied tribunal in the interests of achieving a kind of over-arching justice for the millions who had suffered and died under Nazism.

Secondly, the prosecutors also indicted six Nazi organisations, including the Nazi Party, the SS and the Gestapo. This was an even greater departure from established judicial practice because it meant that if an organisation was found guilty of being illegal, and a defendant was proved to have been a member of that organisation, then he was guilty by association, rather than by virtue of his direct actions.

In a rather similar way, the new crimes were framed such that a defendant could be defined as guilty, rather than proved guilty by facts. For example, if it were decided by the court that invading Poland was the crime of 'waging aggressive war', and if it were proved that a defendant was party to this act, then that defendant was guilty. But the court had in fact prescribed in advance that the Second

World War was an 'aggressive war', so it must follow that the defendants were automatically guilty before they even entered the courtroom.

The British prosecutor, Sir Hartley Shawcross, was quite candid about the aims of the prosecutions in his opening address.

> Human memory is very short. Apologists for defeated nations are sometimes able to play upon the sympathy and magnanimity of their Victors, so that the true facts, never authoritatively recorded, become obscured and forgotten. One has only to recall the circumstances following upon the last World War to see the dangers to which, in the absence of any authoritative judicial pronouncement a tolerant or a credulous people is exposed. With the passage of time the former tend to discount, perhaps because of their very horror, the stories of aggression and atrocity that may be handed down; and the latter, the credulous, misled by perhaps fanatical and perhaps dishonest propagandists, come to believe that it was not they but their opponents who were guilty of that which they would themselves condemn. And so we believe that this Tribunal, acting, as we know it will act notwithstanding its appointment by the victorious powers, with complete and judicial objectivity, will provide a contemporary touchstone and an authoritative and impartial record to which future historians may turn for truth, and future politicians for warning. From this record shall future generations know not only what our generation suffered, but also that our suffering was the result of crimes, crimes against the laws of peoples which the peoples of the world upheld and will continue in the future to uphold by international cooperation, not

based merely on military alliances, but grounded, and firmly grounded, in the rule of law.[3]

Shawcross went on to claim that

It is, as I shall show, the view of the British Government that in these matters, this Tribunal will be applying to individuals, not the law of the victor, but the accepted principles of international usage in a way which will, if anything can, promote and fortify the rule of international law and safeguard the future peace and security of this war-stricken world.[4]

Yet when he opens his case against the defendants, the uniquely inescapable nature of these charges is at once apparent.

[I]t is my task, on behalf of the British Government and of the other states associated in this Prosecution, to present the case on Count Two of the Indictment and to show how these defendants, in conspiracy with each other, and with persons not now before this Tribunal, planned and waged a war of aggression in breach of the treaty obligations by which, under international law, Germany, as other states, has thought to make such wars impossible.

The task falls into two parts. The first is to demonstrate the nature and the basis of the Crime against Peace, which is constituted under the Charter of this Tribunal, by waging wars of aggression and in violation of treaties; and the second is to establish beyond all possibility of doubt that such wars were waged by these defendants.

As to the first, it would no doubt be sufficient just to say this. It is not incumbent upon the Prosecution to prove that wars of aggression and wars in violation of international treaties are, or ought to be, international crimes. The Charter of this Tribunal has prescribed that they are crimes and that the Charter is the statute and the law of this Court. Yet, though that is the clear and mandatory law governing the jurisdiction of this Tribunal, we feel that we should not be discharging our task in the abiding interest of international justice and morality unless we showed to the Tribunal, and indeed to the world, the position of this provision of the Charter against the general perspective of international law. For, just as in the experience of our country, some old English statutes were merely declaratory of the common law, so today this Charter merely declares and creates a jurisdiction in respect of what was already the law of nations.[5]

As the trial progressed, it became apparent that it was by no means as simple as Shawcross had suggested to brand all Hitler's conquests as 'waging aggressive war', that is, as wars fought 'in violation of international treaties, agreements, and assurances'.

It was alleged, for example, that Germany had violated international agreements such as the Kellogg-Briand Pact of 1928 in which a dozen major nations had agreed to renounce war as an instrument of international policy. But this pact did not define what would constitute an 'aggressive war', and in any case, Russia, one of the four prosecuting powers, had also broken the Kellogg-Briand Pact when it invaded Finland and Poland.

There were many more such awkward facts to be swept under the carpet. One prime allegation of Germany waging an illegal and aggressive war was its invasion of Norway in 1940. The problem was that it had been Britain who had first violated Norwegian neutrality. The Royal Navy unilaterally carried out an offensive mining operation in the waters around Norway and later brushed aside the neutral Norwegian navy in order to attack and board the German supply vessel *Altmark* which had sought refuge in Norwegian neutral waters but was believed to have British prisoners on board. Soon after, Churchill commanded that a British occupying force be landed on Norwegian soil without consultation with the Norwegian government.

Conspiracy to wage aggressive war was the charge brought by the United States prosecutor. The aim of the charge was to bring home to the Nazis crimes that were committed before the beginning of the Second World War in September 1939, such as the invasion of Poland, which would otherwise fall outside the other charges, all of which were concerned with the war itself. The thinking behind the idea was sound, but it hit a number of problems from the outset. The first was that, although 'conspiracy' was a crime in both Britain and America, it was unknown to French, Russian and German courts.

Defining the offences of 'war crimes' and 'crimes against humanity' was rather more straightforward for the French and Russian prosecutors who brought them. But there still remained the problem of a scarcity of physical, scientific evidence linking individual defendants with individual murders. In some rare cases, documentary evidence was found; for instance, an order signed by Field Marshal Wilhelm Keitel ordered that 50 Soviet soldiers be shot for every German soldier killed by partisans. Finding such specific incriminating evidence against even someone like Goering was much more difficult.

However, at the end of the trial, whatever legal difficulties they faced, the judges had no trouble finding the big fish guilty as charged.

Goering, Jodl, Kaltenbrunner and Keitel were all sentenced to hang, along with Hans Frank, Governor-general of occupied Poland, Interior Minister Wilhelm Frick, Alfred Rosenberg, Minister of the Occupied Eastern Territories, Fritz Sauckel, labour leader, Arthur Seyss-Inquart, Commissar of the Netherlands, Julius Streicher, rabidly anti-Jewish editor of the newspaper *Der Stürmer*, and Foreign Minister Joachim von Ribbentrop. Goering took cyanide in his cell hours before he was due to be hanged.

A few, including propaganda director Hans Fritzsche, Economics Minister Hjalmar Schacht, and former Chancellor Franz von Papen, were acquitted and freed. The rest received long jail terms from ten years to – in most cases – life imprisonment.

Some readers may be wondering what exactly I am getting at with this rehearsal of the facts of Nuremberg: am I claiming that the defendants at Nuremberg were the victims of a kangaroo court? That is certainly not the case. Those on trial had brought about the most destructive war in history, killing millions, for reasons of national gain. The mass murderers who hanged deserved the maximum penalty. If anything, some of the defendants were lucky to get off with just a jail sentence.

But it seems to me that the victorious Allies wanted, needed and deserved a show trial – not simply to punish the individuals in the dock who were finished anyway, but to put Germany and Nazism on trial. For that they needed symbolic or representative defendants. The Allies were perfectly entitled to put Nazi leaders in the dock and send most of them to the gallows. In doing this they were following the wishes of the civilised world. I have not the slightest doubt about the guilt of the Nazis as mass murderers and will never lose a moment's sleep over the treatment they received. But, in the light of everything that has gone before in this book, I am uneasy both as to the legal propriety of the Nuremberg proceedings and as to the real reason for them. I think it is clear that at the very least they were flawed in matters of legal principle. I also believe that, seen in the context of the long history of Anglo-German propaganda wars, Nuremberg represents the final and decisive clash of PR stories.

The Allies achieved in 1945 what neither side had been able to achieve in the previous 30 years of on-off, hot-and-cold, love-hate exchanges – they had got the complete, undivided attention of the whole world and they had the entire resources of their PR and propaganda machines intact and running at full throttle, while – paradoxically – the defendants had nothing to fall back on except the legalities of their position.

The United States in particular was careful not to repeat the mistake it had made in 1919 when it had disbanded its propaganda bureau as being, in peacetime, an unconstitutional interference with democratic liberties. On the contrary, Allied generals now started openly talking about 'winning the peace' just as they had won the war. What they meant by this phrase was winning the propaganda war, and in this new kind of battle, Nuremberg was worth ten divisions of heavy armour.

What I think the facts of Nuremberg show is that the trial wasn't about justice but about something else, whatever the Allied prosecutors may have claimed to the contrary.

The penalty exacted from the accused was paid partly with their lives, but it was paid also in the coinage of which myths are made. The guilty men were turned unwittingly into actors in what might perhaps be considered to be an early prototype of 'reality TV', so that German war guilt, and the brutal militaristic nature of the German people, could be established – unambiguously, finally, decisively, conclusively – and placed, as Hartley Shawcross openly stated, on the historical record. And with the establishment of German guilt, the innocence of the British and Americans was equally conclusively established and written into the history books, to be accepted by future generations for all time. This was not just the equitable reckoning up of accounts: it was also the presentation by the victors of a bill to be paid; an exercise in reputation management and the 'engineering of consent' that Edward Bernays, the inventor of PR, would have recognised immediately.

21

Natural Selection

B y the time the accused at Nuremberg heard their death sentences pronounced, most of the British intellectuals who despised mass culture and had wanted to declare war on the masses were themselves history. Their ideas on eugenics, sterilisation and the rest died in the ruins of Nazism and, once the Allies had released films of Auschwitz and the other death camps, there were few people so foolish or so insensitive as even to refer to their ideas again.

Public revulsion and disgust at the revelations of Nazi genocide which emerged at the Nuremberg trials put paid to the kind of public writing and lobbying that members of the Eugenics Society had made their stock-in-trade for the previous three decades. Even the most rabidly racist and elitist members realised that the game was up, at least for the foreseeable future, and that any further pronouncements such as that of the Bishop of Birmingham about the 'elimination' of 'the unfit, the defective and the degenerate' were no longer acceptable in public.

However, though no longer able to speak out publicly on the subject, most members of the Eugenics Society remained unchanged in their views and, in private, many continued to urge such measures. Dr Carlos Blacker, a Secretary of the society, told a meeting of fellow members in 1951 that Nazi experiments using live people to develop an economical method of mass sterilisation did not work but that it was in order to continue such experiments.

As they had been compelled by events to cease their attempts at lobbying for laws on compulsory sterilisation of those they considered 'unfit', members of the society turned instead to lobbying for subtly different legislation of areas of life that would ultimately have similar results. There were three main areas where lobbying was continued and even intensified in post-war decades. The first was in birth control, which was aimed mainly at working-class women. The second was in supporting euthanasia, aimed at eliminating costly elderly patients from the National Health Service, and the third was in changing the law on abortion, again aimed at mainly working-class young women who became pregnant.

Sir Julian Huxley, Britain's best-known biologist as well as president of the Eugenics Society, also became a committee member of the Euthanasia Society and, too, argued passionately for the development of an oral contraceptive – the birth pill.

As noted earlier, in *Essays of a Humanist*, published in 1964, Huxley wrote:

But our best hope, I think, must lie in the perfection of new, simple and acceptable methods of birth control, whether by an oral contraceptive or perhaps preferably by immunological methods involving injections. Compulsory or semi-compulsory vaccination, inoculation and isolation are used in respect of many public health risks: I see no reason why similar measures should not be used in respect of this grave problem, grave both for society and for the unfortunate people whose increase has been actually encouraged by our social system.

These ideas may be consonant with the times in which they were expressed, but even with the benefit of hindsight the very least one can say about such views is that they give a whole new meaning to the word 'humanist'. In the event, Huxley's compulsory methods were not needed because the availability of cheap oral contraceptive pills, which he and his fellow eugenicists promoted, has meant that they are today almost universally used to prevent unplanned conception.

But despite the success of the chemical control branch of their strategy, the eugenicists continued to press for legalised euthanasia and also for the legalisation of abortion.

While the idea of euthanasia has been slow to become accepted, the campaign for abortion has exceeded the wildest dreams of the eugenicists. Just how successful it has been can be judged from the fact that since its introduction in 1970, according to government statistics, some 6 million abortions have been carried out in the United Kingdom – a number that was only a remote dream to eugenicists of the 1930s, whether British or German.

But by 1945, those who had yearned for a natural aris-tocracy, composed of people like themselves, not only found their aims confounded by Nazi war crimes, they also found they were caught in a personal paradox that they were never able to resolve. They saw themselves as exem-plars of the new man, the meritocrat who would succeed in life and be recognised by society by virtue of his talents and intellect rather than merely birth, or anything as mean as mere democratic election. The paradox arose because the individuals who expounded this view – whether still alive like Wells, Shaw and Eliot, or dead like Lawrence and Woolf – were themselves largely ineffectual at much else other than their writing. Far from being the kind of intrepid men of action their novels envisaged, writers like Shaw and Wells (notable for his squeaky voice and portly frame) tended to be hopeless at dealing with others and, in many cases, dependent on the women around them rather than being audacious supermen.

Even the toughest-talking of them, D.H. Lawrence, with his wish to personally shepherd the lame of body and mind into his Crystal Palace-sized gas chamber, ended up as a prototype hippie, espousing new-age visions of a return to nature.

In a similar way, even the original arch-apostle of the superman, Nietzsche, had turned out to have feet of clay. Though a brilliant youthful prodigy, Nietzsche had a nervous breakdown and became a sickly invalid, nursed and looked after by his sister. From this undignified position of weakness and dependence he spent the remainder of his life railing futilely against weakness and dependence; in society, in mankind, in women. Throughout this he continued to see himself, in fantasy, as a natural aristocrat and leader who was above common men.

Nietzsche was quite incapable of putting into action any of his own ideas or theories, let alone aspiring to superman status, by reason of his personal shortcomings. He famously wrote, in the voice of Zarathustra: 'If you visit a woman, don't forget your whip.'[1] But, as Bertrand Russell observed, 'nine women out of ten would get the whip away from him, and he knew it, so he kept away from women'.[2]

Poor old Nietzsche. He is the figure most frequently identified as the godfather of Nazism, with its programme of racial purity designed to breed a nation of supermen, yet he scarcely merits such a title. As Alan Taylor points out, Nietzsche distrusted nationalism, hated socialism, disliked mass movements, and detested the workers. An organisation named the National Socialist German Workers' Party would have repelled him with every syllable of its title, every stitch of its uniform dress, every knee-jerk salute of mass obedience.[3] Taylor also points out that, contrary to the received wisdom, Nietzsche's writings contain no anti-Semitism. Indeed, Nietzsche specifically warns against erecting a philosophy on the false foundations of resentment (*ressentiment*), and he specifically refers to anti-Semitism as the kind of resentment to be avoided by the superior man.[4] Nietzsche saw himself as the self-created, self-actualising individual who goes his own way and cares nothing for mediocrity, yet the reality of his life was the very opposite. As John Carey observes: 'We should see Nietzsche, I would suggest, as one of the earliest products of mass culture. That is to say, mass culture generated Nietzsche in opposition to itself, as its antagonist. The immense popularity of his ideas among early 20th century intellectuals suggests the panic that the idea of the masses aroused.'[5]

If writers were impotent, at least scientists like Galton and Huxley could form societies, hold meetings and speak out on the need for eugenics policies. On occasion, some might even go further and deny medical treatment to babies they considered defective, but even these actions were ultimately unable to influence government legislation or significantly alter national perceptions or policy – it was liberal democracy, humanitarian values and the welfare state that ultimately won out.

In the end, neither intellectuals who wrote about eugenics, nor scientists who attempted to practise it, could gain any support for their beliefs. Those who perceived themselves to be superior and believed they merited special attention could not make their fellow citizens see how superior they were, nor could they persuade society to agree to pay for them out of the public purse. But even more curious than this personal paradox was the unexpected outcome of the 'Admass' society that they loathed so much.

For when the advent of mass culture really did make it possible for men to succeed on merit and personal qualities alone, rather than birth, what they got was not at all what they were hoping for. Rather than natural aristocrats or intellectuals like themselves, they got Hitler and Stalin and Mussolini; working-class or lower-middle-class men of little education, with no social connections, who were entirely self-made on the strength of their intelligence and will alone but who were monsters who didn't appreciate intellectual authors at all, let alone wish to elevate them to the pantheon of the great and the good. They also got men like Goering, famously alleged to have remarked: 'When I hear the word culture, I reach for my revolver.'

Did Hitler agree with the intellectuals' view on the masses and on eugenics? Was he influenced philosophically by Nietzsche and other thinkers, like Houston Stewart Chamberlain? Was Hitler's personal aim to create a new society modelled along eugenic lines?

Hitler is one of the most closely recorded people in history. Even his early life as a common soldier and as a dosser in Vienna are quite well documented because of the bureaucratic nature of Austrian and German society at the time. From the first moment that he rose to prominence in German politics in the 1920s and came to power in 1933, there is scarcely a day of his life that we do not know about in minute detail from his personal physicians, his secretaries, his aides, the generals and politicians who worked with him on a daily basis. We even know what he ate for breakfast. But despite this mountain of detail, it remains a common observation among his biographers that we don't really know Hitler the man at all. It isn't merely the roots of his philosophical or political beliefs that are difficult to discern; it is the even more fundamental question of what Hitler himself wanted – what exactly he was after.

Hitler's Foreign Minister, Ribbentrop, wrote in 1945:

[I]f I am asked today whether I knew [Hitler] well – how he thought as a politician and statesman, what kind of man he was – then I'm bound to confess that I know only very little about him; really, nothing at all. The fact is that although I went through so much together with him, in all the years of working with him I never came closer to him than on the first day we met, either personally or otherwise.[6]

One of his last Chiefs of Staff, General Zeitler, wrote:

I witnessed Hitler in every conceivable circumstance – in times of fortune and misfortune, of victory and defeat, in good cheer and in angry outburst, during speeches and conferences, surrounded by thousands, by a mere handful, or quite alone, speaking on the telephone, sitting in his bunker, in his car, in his plane; in brief on every conceivable occasion. Even so, I can't claim to have seen into his soul or perceived what he was after.[7]

In the final chapter of his masterly fable *Animal Farm*, George Orwell conjures a scene that I believe depicts better than any other his uncanny insight into the psychological roots of political behaviour. The animals discover that the pigs, who have taken over the running of the farm, have learned to walk on their hind legs and have begun to ape the tyrannical farmer whom they expelled:

> After that it did not seem strange when next day the pigs who were supervising the work of the farm all carried whips in their trotters. It did not seem strange to learn that the pigs had bought themselves a wireless set, were arranging to install a telephone, and had taken out subscriptions to *John Bull*, *TitBits*, and the *Daily Mirror*. It did not seem strange when Napoleon was seen strolling in the farmhouse garden with a pipe in his mouth – no, not even when the pigs took Mr Jones's clothes out of the wardrobes and put them on, Napoleon himself appearing in a black coat, ratcatcher breeches, and leather leggings, while his favourite sow appeared in the watered silk dress which Mrs Jones had been used to wear on Sundays.[8]

Finally, when a deputation of neighbouring farmers turns up to inspect Animal Farm, the animals creep up to the farmhouse to peer through the windows and eavesdrop on their meeting:

> They tiptoed up to the house, and such animals as were tall enough peered in at the dining-room window. There, round the long table, sat half a dozen farmers and half a dozen of the more eminent pigs, Napoleon himself occupying the seat of honour at the head of the table. The pigs appeared completely at ease in their chairs. The company had been enjoying a game of cards but had broken off for the moment, evidently in order to drink a toast. A large jug was circulating, and the mugs

were being refilled with beer. No one noticed the wondering faces of the animals that gazed in at the window.[9]

One of the neighbouring farmers, Mr Pilkington, raises his
glass and proposes a toast to Animal Farm.

There was enthusiastic cheering and stamping of feet.
Napoleon was so gratified that he left his place and came
round the table to clink his mug against Mr Pilkington's
before emptying it.[10]

Although the immediate target of his satire is clearly the
corrupt apparatchiks of Soviet communism, Orwell was
here commenting on the nature of all totalitarian governments, of both left and right, and the revolutions that bring
them into being. Wherever there is an honest Jacobin revolt
against tyranny, there is a Robespierre waiting in the wings
to make an entrance, and behind him is a Napoleon waiting to crown himself king. This same stealthy hijacking of
the revolution was the process that enabled Lenin to come
to power and Stalin to seize absolute power after him, and
it was the same process that enabled Hitler and the Nazis to
seize power from the Weimar Republic.

I believe that to find the philosophical roots that underlie political revolutions, whether of the left or right, one
need look no further than the pathological desire for personal power, whatever the public utterances and protesta-
tions of the revolutionaries to the contrary. In one sense, the
statement that tyrants are motivated by purely personal
desires is neither novel nor profound. Yet, banal though this
observation may be, it is a truism that often escapes notice
when one seeks to analyse the political motives that underlie historical events. To ask, 'Was Hitler influenced by the
philosophy of Nietzsche or Hegel?' is like asking, 'Were the

pigs of Animal Farm influenced more by Aristotle or by Plato?'

Hitler's conscious intellectual processes may well have been influenced by the ideas of Nietzsche. But Hitler's actions and his political policies were motivated by his desire to live in the farmer's house, dress in the farmer's clothes, and toast the future with the farmer's beer – or whatever his personal equivalent goal may have been. The same is true of Stalin, Lenin, Robespierre and Napoleon, regardless of what they may have written in their memoirs or confided to their contemporaries.

The scientists and intellectuals who despised the masses, and who sought special status for themselves, expected the superman of the future to be the monocle-wearing sportsman who won the battle of Waterloo on the playing fields of Eton, with a eugenically-engineered high IQ for good measure. What they got was a failed watercolour painter with a head for figures and the ability to charm the birds out of the trees, who started the most destructive war in history because he considered himself a man of destiny, and who wanted an empire like the Englishmen he so much admired.

Even with all we know about Hitler, we come closest to knowing the real man, I believe, with the image of him flicking eagerly through the pages of *The Tatler*, eyes alight with pleasure, pointing to the pictures of the English aristocrats relaxing at home and remarking: 'Those are valuable specimens – those are the ones I am going to make peace with.'

22

Lucky Winners

The century-long love-hate affair between Germany and Britain culminated in a final ironic twist of fate at Nuremberg. For the British nation that defeated Nazi Germany and put its leaders on trial in 1945 bore the opposite political complexion to the one that went to war against them in 1939. Before the war, Britain was fully committed to maintaining its world domination through the traditional imperial means of military conquest and gunboat diplomacy. The country and its armed services were run and administered mainly by men from English public schools, and the views of its ruling class on race and eugenics issues were little different from those of the Nazis, the Americans, the Swedes and many others. A significant proportion of Britain's intellectuals, a fair few of its aristocrats – and even some of its politicians – thought that Hitler was our natural ally against Bolshevism and that a partnership with the Nazis would offer the best guarantee that Britain would keep its empire.

The picture in 1945 was very different, and Britain was extremely fortunate to find itself on the winning side.

A socialist government was swept into office by a land-slide victory on a ticket promising dramatic social reform. While many of the new ruling class continued to come from public school and Oxbridge, a fair leavening were grammar-school boys from red-brick universities, and there was a significant sprinkling of women MPs. Many provincial accents were heard at Westminster for the first time, including those of the authentic working class. Some of the new boys were ex-servicemen who had been exposed to the reality of a world war and its effects on ordinary people. And there was also a backlog of reforms that had been put to one side by the conflict and were now brought into action. The full ghastly reality of 'eugenic' racial policies had been revealed at Auschwitz and Buchenwald.

All of this meant that the tenor and tone of the government of 1945 was considerably more liberal and more inclined to measures that would bring positive social benefits to a war-weary population than that of the pre-war government. At the same time it was far less inclined to any kind of extremist measure. Above all, there was little sign of any ivory-tower intellectualising and a strong emphasis on the sensible, the practical and the down-to-earth, such as nationalisation of the mines and the railways and the foundation of a National Health Service. Perhaps it was no coincidence that H.G. Wells died in 1946, having published his final book, *Mind at the End of its Tether*.[1] At any rate it would have been all but impossible in 1946 to find any respected British intellectual to speak on a eugenic platform or to sign his or her name to the kind of books that were commonplace before the war.

Even when the Tories were returned in 1951 and Winston Churchill came back into office, there was still a distinctly new look to the government, with its front-bench seats now occupied by educational reformers like Rab Butler and brilliant young men with military experience who had opposed appeasement, like Macmillan and Eden.

Of course, none of these developments happened by accident or took place in a vacuum – they were the result of a long, costly and painful learning process, both at the personal and national level, over six long years. But the fact remains that many of those who ruled Britain were extremely lucky to have found themselves on the winning side in 1945.

Those who had been most vocal in support of Hitler and the Nazis, men like Oswald Mosley and the Duke of Windsor, were allowed to slip quietly out of the public eye, apart from a few last-ditch attempts at retrospectively massaging the historical record by means of personal memoirs. Many who remained in government and civil service, and who had leaned rather too heavily to the right before the war, now felt it was time to let bygones be bygones and face up to the brave new post-war leftist world with a smile. More simply, they were tacitly permitted to forget quietly all the pre-war skeletons in their own cupboard, their pro-Nazi sympathies, their anti-Semitism or racism, in the interests of national unity and reconciliation.

After a few years had passed, by the 1950s, it became possible for some of the strongest pre-war Nazi supporters to re-invent themselves as misunderstood patriots. Sir Oswald Mosley discovered that he had not been anti-Jewish after all, merely against anyone who he believed was dragging his country into an unnecessary war. If Jews came in this category, he was against Jews; if Scotsmen, then he was against Scotsmen; if Eskimos, then he was anti-Eskimo.[2] Mosley and his wife Diana took up residence in France close to the Windsors, with whom they remained on friendly terms and whom they saw frequently as they lived out their lives in empty and impotent exile.

The older generation of appeasers such as Halifax and Sir Samuel Hoare faded away in national memory as well-meaning but bumbling in an endearingly and typically English way. Some younger MPs, such as Rab Butler, reinvented themselves as liberal-minded but traditional politicians of the new post-war era.

But if the British were lucky to find themselves on the winning side, then – although the leading Nazis tried and convicted at Nuremberg richly deserved their fate – there is no denying that some Germans were extraordinarily unlucky to find themselves on the losing side. For they were caught in a situation in which, for purely historical reasons, they were bound to be depicted as monsters of depravity whatever they may or may not personally have done.

Hitler's Foreign Minister Ribbentrop is a case in point. His actual influence over Nazi Germany's conduct of the Second World War was close to, if not actually, zero. His usefulness consisted solely in the fact that he had lived and worked in England, spoke good English, was fascinated by the English aristocracy and longed to be accepted into upper-class circles as an equal. His snobbish social climbing made him appear useful to Hitler during the 1930s, since he was able to cultivate so many upper-class English acquaintances. Yet he went to the gallows just like Ernst Kaltenbrunner, head of the SS, who actually was a real-life monster responsible for murdering millions. It's difficult to resist the conclusion that Ribbentrop's real crime was that his name was well known from the newspaper headlines in Britain and the US.

Similarly, take the case of General Alfred Jodl, a career army officer who became Head of Operations of the armed forces high command. Jodl was convicted at Nuremberg and sentenced to hang. The principal French judge at the trials, Henri Donnedieu de Vabres, protested strongly against Jodl's conviction, on the grounds that it was a miscarriage of justice for a professional soldier to be convicted when he held no allegiance to Nazism. His protest was ignored, ostensibly because the other judges believed Jodl to be one of the leaders responsible for the war. In reality the Frenchman's plea went unheard because Jodl was one of the most senior army officers to be caught and was thus a handy figurehead representing collective German military war guilt. Eight years later, in 1953, Jodl was posthumously exonerated by a German de-Nazification court, which cited Judge Donnedieu's statements and found Jodl not guilty of crimes under international law.

From a military standpoint, the Second World War was often closely balanced. There were several occasions on which the Axis and Allies came close to a negotiated peace. Had America not entered the war on the Allied side, it is possible that the outcome could have been either stalemate or even an Axis victory. Had fate rolled the dice the other way and British politicians and soldiers had stood in the dock before Nazi prosecutors in 1945, what would have been the outcome? Who would have been the British Ribbentrop, or Jodl, sent perhaps unjustly to the hangman? And who the British Kaltenbrunner?

Of course, there is no comparison between Britain's defence of its own empire and Nazi Germany's campaigns of genocide in its death camps. Yet the uncomfortable facts remain that it would not have been difficult for a Nazi prosecutor to construct a powerful case against Britain: the nation that invented the concentration camp in which tens of thousands died, the nation that ruled a quarter of the world by military force, the nation that had founded an empire on the slave trade and on the slaughter of men, women and children who opposed it, and the nation that had killed 1 million German civilian men, women and children in area bombing raids.

The authors of *British Way and Purpose*, writing in 1941, had been very sure that no British person would have allowed himself to become the pawn of a Nazi tyranny. As noted earlier, speaking of a hypothetical German station master who crams Jews onto trains at the behest of the SS, knowing some will not survive, the authors of *BWP* wrote:

> If he refused to obey orders, he risked being sent to a concentration camp and tortured. Should not those who drew up the orders be punished, rather than a subordinate, a mere cog in the wheel of German officialdom?
>
> On the other hand we can feel pretty sure that it would be very hard to find anyone on our side who would knowingly carry out such an order, whatever might be coming to him if he disobeyed.[3]

This confident statement, held sincerely about the British way of life, remained an article of faith in England's view of itself until the 1960s when a psychologist at Yale University, Stanley Milgram, performed a famous experiment that exploded the myth of the honourable, independent-minded individual who rejects coercive authority.

Milgram conceived the experiment because, in 1960, Adolf Eichmann was tried in Israel and found guilty of playing a key role in the murder of millions of Jews and others in the concentration camps. The trial gained world-wide publicity, and Eichmann's defence – that he was just a soldier obeying orders – became the subject of heated debate. Milgram said he devised his experiment the following year to answer the question: 'Could it be that Eichmann and his million accomplices in the Holocaust were just following orders? Could we call them all accomplices?'

Milgram published his findings in 1963 in the *Journal of Abnormal and Social Psychology*, in an article entitled 'Behavioral Study of Obedience'. Most people are familiar at least in outline with the experiment.[4]

Milgram advertised in newspapers for people to participate in 'a study of memory' in exchange for $450. He got responses from a cross-section of American people – students, teachers, housewives, businessmen and so on – with a range of educational backgrounds, from drop-outs to people with doctorates. The volunteers were put together in pairs, one of them randomly chosen to be the 'Teacher' and the other the 'Learner'. In reality, members of the public who applied were always assigned the 'Teacher' role, while the 'Learner' was always arranged to be one of Milgram's students and was secretly in on the experiment.

Under the direction of an 'Experimenter' (a man in white coat and glasses with a clipboard and pen), the 'Teacher' reads pairs of words from a list to the 'Learner', who is strapped into a chair in the next room with electrodes attached to his body. If the Learner gets a word wrong, the Teacher is instructed by the Experimenter to turn a dial to administer an electric shock in order to improve his memory. In reality, there are no electric shocks and the dangerous-looking apparatus is just a dummy. Milgram's students merely act up to the 'shocks' by writhing in their chair and yelping in pain.

At 135 volts on the dummy dial, the student in the next room begins to make agonised noises, pleads with the experimenter and bangs on the walls. At 300 volts on the dial, the student starts to complain about his heart condition.

Most subjects begin to express doubts about continuing at this stage or before, but the Experimenter insists that the trial must be completed or it will be valueless. Every time the subject objects to continuing, the Experimenter gives him a verbal prod to continue. If the subject still wants to stop after four successive verbal prods, the experiment is halted. Otherwise the experiment is continued until the subject is 'administering' shocks to the student at the lethal level of 450 volts.

Before he began his experiments, Milgram asked his fellow psychologists what they thought the results would be. They unanimously believed that only a few sadists would go all the way to administering 450 volts. In fact, Milgram found that around 65 per cent of experimental participants administered the final, apparently lethal, shocks at 450 volts. Moreover, no participant stopped before the 300-volt level.

Milgram's experiments have been repeated under different circumstances and with different selections of subjects (all women for instance), and the results have been confirmed. Something like two-thirds of us, under the right circumstances, are willing to go along with something that we know to be injurious to others, if we are instructed by authority to do so.

In 1965, Milgram summed up his experiment this way:

With numbing regularity good people were seen to knuckle under the demands of authority and perform actions that were callous and severe. Men who are in everyday life responsible and decent were seduced by the trappings of authority, by the control of their perceptions, and by the uncritical acceptance of the experimenter's definition of the situation, into performing harsh acts. ... A substantial proportion of people do what they are told to do, irrespective of the content of the act and without limitations of conscience, so long as they perceive that the command comes from a legitimate authority.

'The social psychology of this century', wrote Milgram in 1974, 'reveals a major lesson: often it is not so much the kind of person a man is as the kind of situation in which he finds himself that determines how he will act.'[5]

When reading conclusions such as Milgram's, there is a strong temptation to see them as applying only to those with an open desire to don the black uniform and jackboots of perverted authority. The real tragedy is, if anything, even worse. It is that, under the right circumstances, almost all of us are willing to acquiesce in playing such a role.

23

This Happy Breed

Throughout the long German love affair with England, despite its many ups and downs, there was one constant theme from the German perspective – that the English, especially its ruling classes, are admirable because they are a cold, cruel and ruthless people. As noted earlier, in *Mein Kampf*, Hitler said that

> [As the] Englishman had succeeded, we too were bound to succeed, and our definitely greater honesty, the absence in us of that specifically English 'perfidy', was regarded as a very special plus.[1]

A little later in his book, he added:

> England, in particular, should have been recognised as the striking refutation of this theory [peaceful expansion through trade] for no people has ever with greater brutality better prepared its economic conquests with the sword, and later ruthlessly defended them than the English nation.[2]

To an English mind, this perception seems as though the world has been turned upside down. Perfidy? Brutality?

Ruthlessness? Can Adolf Hitler, one of the bloodiest mass murderers in history, really be talking about us? What's going on?

In 1943, Noël Coward wrote a patriotic play called *This Happy Breed* which charted the life of an ordinary British family, the Gibbonses, living in Clapham between the wars from 1919 to 1939. Frank Gibbons is a decent, ordinary lower-middle-class chap who has done his bit from 1914 to 1918 and now longs for a quiet life with his wife Ethel and their two children, Queenie and Reg. The play was a hit with war-weary Londoners when it was produced at the Haymarket Theatre and the following year was filmed by David Lean. Though very dated, the film still has the power to move today, in a nostalgic way.

In the final scene of Act 1, Frank Gibbons gives his son Reg some fatherly advice. Reg has been mixing with friends who have become enamoured of Marxist ideals and who want to campaign for a vaguely 'better world', but are too young to know how to set about it other than protesting in the streets.

We know the date of this scene with some precision as May 1926, because Coward depicted it as coinciding with the General Strike. In the scene, Reg has joined in the street demonstrations supporting the strike under the impression that he is changing the world. He has been brought home after being knocked down in the street, and Frank offers his son the following advice:

It's this, son. I belong to a generation of men, most of which aren't here any more, and we all did the same thing for the same reason, no matter what we thought about politics. Now all that's over and we're all going on as best we can as though nothing had happened. But as a matter of fact several things did happen and one of them was the country suddenly got tired, it's tired now. But the old girl's got stamina and don't you make any mistake about it and it's up to us ordinary people to keep things steady. That's your job, my son, and just you remember it ...[3]

At the end of the final act, set in June 1939, with storm clouds gathering, Frank again offers some advice, this time to his baby grandson in his pram.

Well Frankie, boy, I wonder what you're going to turn out like! You're not going to get any wrong ideas, see? That is, not if I have anything to do with it. ... There's not much to worry about really, so long as you remember one or two things always. The first is that life isn't all jam for anybody, and you've got to have trouble of some kind or another whoever you are. But if you don't let it get you down, however bad it is, you won't go far wrong. ... Another thing you'd better get into that little bullet head of yours is that you belong to something that nobody can't ever break, however much they try. And they try all right – they're trying now. Not only people in other countries who want to do us in because they're sick of us ruling the roost – and you can't blame them at that! But people here, in England. People who have let 'emselves get soft and afraid. People who go on a lot about peace and goodwill and the ideals they believe in, but somehow don't seem to believe in 'em enough to think they're worth fighting for. ... The trouble with the world is, Frankie, that there are too many ideals and too little horse sense. We're human beings we are – all of us – and that's what people are liable to forget. Human

beings don't like peace and goodwill and everybody loving everybody else. However much they may think they
do, they don't really because they're not made like that.
Human beings love eating and drinking and loving and
hating. They also like showing off, grabbing all they can,
fighting for their rights and bossing anybody who'll give
them half a chance. You belong to a race that's been
bossy for years and the reason it's held on as long as it
has is that nine times out of ten it's behaved decently and
treated people right. Just lately, I'll admit, we've been
giving at the knees a bit and letting people down who
trusted us and allowing noisy little men to bully us with
a lot of guns and bombs and aeroplanes. But don't worry
– that won't last – the people themselves, the ordinary
people like you and me, know something better than all
the fussy old politicians put together – we know what we
belong to, where we come from, and where we're going.
We may not know it with our brains, but we know it with
our roots. And we know another thing too, and it's this.
We 'aven't lived and died and struggled all these hundreds of years to get decency and justice and freedom
for ourselves without being prepared to fight fifty wars
if need be – to keep 'em.[4]

Looked at in one way – perhaps with a jaundiced eye – this
speech comes straight from the same government press
office that produced *British Way and Purpose*, suitably
translated into demotic for the benefit of working-class cinema audiences, and cries out to be deconstructed in a thoroughly postmodern fashion. Coward's words ring true, yet
he was scarcely a spokesman for the common man. Rather,
he was a social-climbing snob who jettisoned his own working-class background at the first opportunity and affected

the cringe-making accent and manners that he mistakenly supposed to be those of the upper classes (silk dressing gown, cigarette holder, 'dear boy'). Despite this – or perhaps because of it – his writing was seen as 'typically English' and hence desirable wartime propaganda by some in government who acted as his patron in making several films that contributed to raising morale.

It served a useful national purpose for the man on the Clapham omnibus to identify with Frank Gibbons in the dark days of 1943. Very obviously, Frank Gibbons, as Everyman, is speaking not just to a wayward and misguided son but to the whole world, including inhabitants of the empire and to Adolf Hitler and the Nazis.

Yet, even if Coward is an imperfect representative of ordinary British people, I still see in his rose-tinted romantic drama something that goes beyond self-interest and class and careerism and jingoistic flag-waving. Coward came from a home very much like the Gibbons home. His remarkable ear for authentic dialogue was not merely a matter of accurate recording, but of an instinctive feel for and recollection of his own thoughts and feelings as a young boy. When he wrote the advice that Frank Gibbon gives to his son and grandson, I believe it was Coward, the English patriot, speaking from the heart words that he felt deeply on behalf of every Frank Gibbons up and down the country who saw themselves as moderate men who had done their duty when the need arose and had now gone back to modest family life. Men who wanted no truck with Nazism or Marxism or any other kind of 'ism', but simply wanted to be left alone to get on with living their lives as they saw fit. That the Frank Gibbons who thrust a bayonet into the guts of a German soldier on the Western Front was a temporary, made-up creature called into life by the mythic power of his nation's desperate hour of need; while the real Frank Gibbons was the gentle man who was scolded like a child by his wife for getting slightly tipsy at the regimental reunion each year, and who travelled every day uncomplainingly on the 8.30 to London Bridge and the office where he balanced columns of figures in a neat copperplate hand.

I believe that one reason for Coward's great success is that he tapped this vein of self-belief that we, the British, hold about ourselves. We see ourselves as Frank Gibbons does, as decent, reasonable, easy-going, democratic people who only want to live and let live, unlike the Nazis or Bolsheviks (the 'noisy little men with guns and bombs and aeroplanes') who are always trying to take over the world and enslave people.

Yet the disturbing truth is that at the time Frank Gibbons was supposed to be delivering his speech, Britain's empire was at its greatest extent and British men, just like Frank Gibbons – decent, honest, hardworking men who had served their country and wanted nothing but a quiet life – were keeping a quarter of the world's population in subjugation by means of the threat of violent military reprisals against anyone who questioned or rebelled against that rule. It was we, the British, who were the noisy little men with guns and bombs and aeroplanes. Even more disturbing is the fact that countless hundreds of thousands of foreign people had, over a period of two hundred years or more, been slaughtered by decent, moderate British soldiers like Frank Gibbons, only because they attempted to challenge Britain's right to rule over them. During the three or four decades that followed, tens of thousands more foreign people would be killed by ordinary British soldiers, following orders from their superiors, in Israel, Kenya,

Malaya, Aden, India, Pakistan, Suez, Afghanistan, Iraq, and many other places around the world. Until as recently as the Suez crisis of 1956 (and perhaps even later) the killing of these men, women and children was justified because they were dark-skinned, and hence regarded as inferior – referred to openly as 'wogs' – and also because it was considered necessary for Britain, as the world's policeman, to knock a few native heads together now and then to keep order.

Gibbons tells his grandson that the reason Britain has held on to its empire so long is that 'nine times out of ten it's behaved decently and treated people right'. By an ironic coincidence, at just the time that Coward set his play – the years immediately following the First War – ordinary, decent Britishers were committing one of the greatest atrocities in the history of British rule in India.

In April 1919, the Punjab was the scene of many peaceful demonstrations against British rule. Mahatma Gandhi was arrested as he tried to travel there to speak, on the orders of the governor of the Punjab, Sir Michael O'Dwyer. In the holy city of Amritsar two other leaders were also arrested, and their followers tried to march to the bungalow of the local commissioner, Miles Irving, to demand their release, but were fired on by British troops, resulting in several deaths and woundings. An enraged mob rioted through Amritsar's old city, burning British banks, murdering several Englishmen, and attacking two Englishwomen.

General Reginald Dyer was sent with troops from Jullundur to restore order, and, though no further disturbances occurred in Amritsar, Dyer marched 50 armed soldiers into the Jallianwallah Bagh (a small park surrounded by high walls) that afternoon and ordered them to open fire – without warning – on a protest meeting attended by some

10,000 unarmed men, women and children. Dyer kept his troops firing for about ten minutes into the terror-stricken crowd, who were unable to escape since soldiers blocked the only exit. Between 300 and 400 civilians were killed and some 1,200 wounded. They were left without medical attention by Dyer, who hastily removed his troops to the camp. Sir Michael O'Dwyer fully approved of and supported the Jallianwallah Bagh massacre, and on 15 April 1919 issued a martial law decree for the entire Punjab.

Questions were asked about the massacre in Parliament, and Dyer was relieved of his command. But he returned to England as a hero to many British admirers, who presented him with a jewelled sword inscribed 'Saviour of the Punjab'.[5]

Amritsar may have been, mercifully, a rare episode in British colonial history. Sadly, though, it was very far from unique. On dozens of similar occasions – some as far away as South Africa or India, some as near as Ireland – civilian men, women and children were shot down by British imperial forces, usually with a rational explanation about 'maintaining the rule of law' or 'protecting society from terrorists' or 'restoring order'.

The men who trained their guns on the women and children at Amritsar were not depraved, sadistic monsters, nor were they candidates for Hitler's SS death squads. They were ordinary, decent British soldiers who had been trained to obey orders, who believed that those set in authority over them knew the right thing to do, and who honestly believed they were acting in the best interests of the community they served.

I feel glad that Coward wrote *This Happy Breed* in 1943, and glad that it acted as an inspiration to people who were suffering the hardships and dangers of wartime Britain, including my own parents. I'm glad, too, that Coward celebrated all that could be best in ordinary British people like myself. I'm glad because his play – even if badly dated – reminds me of my own national heritage, and of the sacrifices that so many ordinary British men and women have made so that I can enjoy the freedoms that I take for granted. But I also feel ashamed at the way in which neither Coward nor 'Frank Gibbons', nor anyone involved in creating the image of the moderate Britisher, seemed to notice that the way we actually treated our fellow inhabitants of the world was as bad as anything the Kaiser or Hitler had in mind for us.

Frank Gibbons was right about one thing: British people don't dress up in fancy uniforms and click their heels, nor do they subserviently raise their arms in salute to leader figures or get excited about rows of tanks and aircraft. But though the British style may be very different from many other nations, Britain's history is no different from any other – proof, if proof were needed, that the British are as human as everyone else on the planet, and that, given its fifteen minutes of fame on the world stage, Britain was both as good, and as bad, as everyone else that fate has granted a roll at the dice of history.

A Postmodern Postscript

In his *Origins of the Second World War*, A.J.P. Taylor observed that 'In principle and doctrine, Hitler was no more wicked and unscrupulous than many a contemporary statesman'.

Taylor was referring primarily to Hitler's foreign policy, not his domestic policies of genocide, which cannot be compared to any other European leader of the period and were monstrous without parallel. But even with this distinction, it's still hard to believe that Hitler can be compared to any other contemporary statesman.

For anyone, like me, brought up to believe in the moderate, shy and retiring nature of the British people, it's almost impossible to take seriously the idea that Prime Minister Stanley Baldwin, the epitome of quiet, moderate, middle-class 1930s Englishness, could be described as in any way equivalent to Adolf Hitler, one of the greatest mass murderers in history.

Yet the facts are that during Baldwin's tenure of office as Prime Minister, three times from 1923 to 1937, he was responsible for keeping one quarter of the world's population in subjugation to the will of the British government, by means of the threat of violence and death to anyone who rebelled against or resisted British rule, and the threat of imprisonment to anyone who even spoke out against that rule – threats that were often tragically carried out.

What I have tried to show in this book is that the similarity of German and British foreign policy pointed to by Taylor and some other historians is no coincidence, but springs from the similarity of the political and philosophical roots of those policies.

The philosophy that underpinned the attitudes and beliefs of the leaders of the Nazi Party seems to a British mind to have been characteristically Germanic in origin – involving extremist ideas on race, on national identity, on a destiny to rule other people, and on imperial aspirations. Yet, hard as it is to accept, these underlying philosophies were not of Germanic origin but rather were the product of English writers and intellectuals of the 19th century.

The Luftwaffe bombs that spread death and destruction from the skies over London in 1940 were a direct result of the thinking of Charles Darwin, Thomas Huxley, Francis Galton, Houston Stewart Chamberlain and Halton Mackinder, half a century or more earlier.

A central assertion of this book is that the received British view of Germany and the Germans as bloodthirsty, reckless militarists in foreign policy is a convenient story – a story that deserves to be deconstructed in the best postmodernist manner. But if the accepted view of the Germans is just a story, then what is this book, if not just another story? And where exactly am I coming from in the telling of it?

I was born in London halfway through the Second World War in 1943. I'm told that a German bomb wrecked the house in which I lay in my cradle, so I suppose I may claim to have suffered the effects of the world war at first hand. But it was not the bruises caused by German bombs that stayed with me in childhood and afterwards, it was the effects of British propaganda.

My fellow countrymen, burdened with the near impossible task of beating the Nazis, acted from what they conceived to be the best of motives in raising public morale, demoralising the enemy, and furthering our war aims through deception. As well as saving me from the Nazis, saving my life and my liberty, they also blighted my childhood, my youth, my growing up and a part of my adult life by teaching me to believe a set of what are at best urban myths and at worst outright lies about Britain, its empire, its royal family, its government, its people and its way of life.

Many who read this may well be thinking: What right do I have – I who had life and liberty handed to me on a plate by the courage and self-sacrifice of the millions of ordinary men and women who fought against Nazism – what right do I have to criticise the decisions taken by the government of the day to cope with impossibly difficult circumstances? Shouldn't I just be grateful and keep my unwanted opinions to myself? I was tempted by this line of reasoning for some years, but with the passing of time I have become convinced that the ordinary people who sacrificed their lives would have been horrified at the actions taken in their name, in secret, by a narrow section of the governing class. I now believe that they would have been even more horrified at the consequences of those secret decisions, even if they were taken from the best of motives.

Of course, you will say, the Germans believed they were the master race and really wanted to enslave the world, whereas we British have no desire to rule the world. We just want to be left alone. The curious paradox is that this sentiment is perfectly genuine and is shared by almost every

British man and woman. Yet the reality is that – in living memory – Britain enslaved a quarter of the world's population, at the point of a gun.

But, you will say, that was then and this is now – Britain no longer has imperial aspirations. Our human rights record is second to none. Yet only four years ago a British government ordered the killing of tens of thousands of innocent Iraqi men, women and children, in the national interest, and based on a case that was a tissue of lies, intended to deceive the British public.

Today, in Pakistan, in Afghanistan, in Iraq, suicide bombers who feel as angry as I do, but who are not ethnically British, are training to manufacture bombs and are video-taping their last words for their friends and families. Lies, even lies told with the best of intentions, can have fatal consequences – and they breed a war of lies.

The lies that led four young Asian British men to blow themselves to pieces in London in 2005, killing 59 of their fellow citizens at the same time, were the children and grandchildren of lies fathered by a British government, beleaguered and at war, who found an easily available but highly addictive palliative for public questioning and unrest – the official lie.

But such lies did not arise in a vacuum. The English governing classes of the 19th and early 20th centuries not only proved themselves to be expert at running a global mercantile empire with ruthless efficiency; they also proved adept at convincing the world that they were the best people to run such an empire, and that their chief motive in running it was the altruism of enlightened self-interest. The reality, as George Orwell observed, was that the British Empire was 'very largely a racket'.

The Victorian and Edwardian English ruling class who ran this racket fooled the world into thinking that they were altruistic benefactors of mankind. They fooled the citizens of the empire into accepting the same belief, and even fooled their greatest rivals, the Germans, into believing it. Worst of all, they duped the great mass of ordinary British people into not only believing the imperial idea, but supporting it with their minds, their hearts and, tragically, even their blood.

References

Chapter 1. Cutting the Cord

1. British National Archives, Propaganda 1914–1918. See online archives page under heading 'Signals Intelligence':
http://www.catalogue.nationalarchives.gov.uk/RdLeaflet.asp?sLeafletID=32
2. See Chapter 2 for detailed references.
3. See Chapters 7 and 8 for detailed references.
4. See Chapter 9 for detailed references.
5. See Chapter 7 for detailed references.
6. See Chapter 8 for detailed references.
7. See Chapter 8 for detailed references.
8. See Chapter 8 for detailed references.
9. See Chapter 3 for detailed references.
10. See Chapter 3 for detailed references.
11. See Chapter 3 for detailed references.
12. See Chapter 4 for detailed references.
13. See Chapters 6 and 17 for detailed references.
14. See Chapter 9 for detailed references.
15. See Chapter 12 for detailed references.
16. See Chapter 20 for detailed references.

Chapter 2. A Marriage of Minds

1. Paul A. Papayoanou, 1996.
2. History of Siemens: http://www.sigtel.com/tel_hist_siemens.html
3. History of Reuters: http://about.reuters.com/aboutus/history/
4. History of Rothschilds: http://www2.rothschild.com/history/
5. History of Voigtlander: http://www.teagleoptometry.com/history.htm
6. Exhibition of 1851:
http://www.vam.ac.uk/collections/prints_books/great_exhibition/
7. 1851 chess championship: http://batgirl.atspace.com/Staunton.html
8. Wilhelm: http://college.hmco.com/history/readerscomp/ships/html/
sh_045600_hohenzollern.htm
9. Foxhunting, see: http://www.nationmaster.com/encyclopedia/Fox-hunting
10. Thomas Cook, see: http://www.spartacus.schoolnet.co.uk/BUcook.htm

11. Edgar Sanderson, 1910.
12. Berlin history, see: http://bdaugherty.tripod.com/
13. Ibid.
14. Edgar Sanderson, 1910.
15. G.P. Gooch and Harold Temperley, 1927, 119, pp. 102–04.
16. http://encarta.msn.com/sidebar_1741503243/
Interview_with_Prince_Otto_von_Bismarck.html
17. *Great Britain and the European crisis, correspondence and statements in Parliament, 1914.*

Chapter 3. War of Words
1. Jonathan Epstein, 1999.
2. Ibid.
3. George Creel, 1922.
4. Jonathan Epstein, 1999.
5. Sanders and Taylor, 1982.
6. Ibid.
7. Ibid.
8. James Bryce, 1915.
9. H.G. Wells, 1914.
10. John Buchan, 1915.
11. Ibid.
12. Stanley Unwin, 1960.
13. Philip Gibbs, 1923.
14. Sanders and Taylor, 1982.
15. Lord Beaverbrook, 1956.
16. Erich von Ludendorff, 1919.
17. Thomas Fleming, 2003.
18. Ibid.
19. George Creel, 1920.

Chapter 4. Atrocious Behaviour
1. A.J.P. Taylor, 1985.
2. *Great Britain and the European crisis, 1914.*
3. A.J.P. Taylor, 1985.
4. Thomas Pakenham, 1982.
5. Jonathan Epstein, 1999.
6. Ibid.

7. A.J.P. Taylor, 1985.
8. B.C. Yates, 1940.
9. James Bryce, 1915.
10. Ibid.
11. Ibid.
12. Ibid..
13. *The Times*, 27 August 1914.
14. *The Times*, 15 January 1915.
15. Phyllis Campbell, 1915.
16. Margaret Cole, 1949.
17. See http://www.spartacus.schoolnet.co.uk/FWWatrocities.htm
18. Robert Graves, 1961.
19. German 'White Book', 1915, cited in Epstein, 1999.
20. *Ohm Kruger*, 1941, film directed by Hans Steinhoff.
21. Arthur Ponsonby, 1928.
22. Ibid.
23. Ibid.

Chapter 5. The Sorcerer's Apprentice

1. Jonathan Epstein, 1999.
2. Ibid.
3. http://www.firstworldwar.com/source/usnavy_creel.htm
4. Randolph Bourne, 1917.
5. Larry Tye, 1998.
6. Ibid.
7. News item in *New York World*, 1919.
8. Edward Bernays, 1928.
9. Ibid.
10. Edward Bernays, 1965.

Chapter 6. Engineering of Consent

1. Edward Bernays, 1965.
2. Edward Bernays, 1928.
3. Ibid.
4. Ibid.
5. Ibid.

Chapter 7. The Master Race

1. Charles Darwin, 1901; Charles Darwin, 1902.
2. Thomas Huxley, 1910.
3. Charles Darwin, 1902.
4. Ibid.
5. Richard Milton, 1997.
6. Ernst Haeckel, 1876.
7. J. Assmuth, 1918.
8. Larry Adelman, genetics website:
http://www.newsreel.org/guides/race/whatdiff.htm
9. Francis Galton, 1889.
10. Ibid.
11. Jakob Graf, 1936.
12. Arthur de Gobineau, 1855.
13. T.P. Taswell-Langmead, 1919.
14. Houston Stewart Chamberlain, 1889.
15. See http://www.hschamberlain.net/index.html
16. Ibid.
17. Ibid.
18. Ibid.
19. http://www.hschamberlain.net/index.html
20. Ibid.
21. Adolf Hitler, 1925.
22. Geoffrey Field, 1981.

Chapter 8. Man and Superman

1. See http://geogate.geographie.uni-marburg.de/vgt/english/brd/module/
m1/u5.htm
2. Ibid.
3. W.T. Stead, 1885.
4. J.B. Priestley, 1955.
5. John Carey, 1992.
6. Friedrich Nietzsche, 1967 edn.
7. Gustave Flaubert, 1981 edn.
8. H.G. Wells, 1967 edn.
9. G.B. Shaw, 1883.
10. Friedrich Nietzsche, 1967 edn.
11. D.H. Lawrence, 1971 edn.

12. John Carey, 1992.
13. D.H. Lawrence, 1971(A) edn.
14. James T. Boulton, 1979.
15. G.B. Shaw, 1986 edn.
16. Ezra Pound, 1986.
17. W.B. Yeats, 1938.
18. Friedrich Nietzsche, 1973.
19. Francis Galton, 1905.
20. See http://www.altonweb.com/cs/downsyndrome/ index.htm?page=booth.html
21. Ibid.
22. Ibid.
23. E.W. Barnes, 1933.
24. E.W. Barnes, 1949.
25. Richard Berry, 1930.
26. William Beveridge, 1942.
27. William Beveridge, 1906.
28. Leonard Darwin, 1925.
29. Julian Huxley, 1966.
30. H.G. Wells, 1901.
31. Ibid.
32. H.G. Wells, 1905.
33. Ibid.
34. See Eugenics Watch website: http://www.eugenics-watch.com/ briteugen/index.html
35. Ibid.
36. Charles Webster, 1997.
37. Ibid.
38. Ibid.

Chapter 9. More English than the English

1. Barbara Tuchman, 1981.
2. See http://www.teagleoptometry.com/history.htm
3. John Seeley, 1887.
4. G.K. Chesterton, 1917.
5. Clive Ponting, 1990.

Chapter 10. Influential Friends

1. Joe Hicks, 1999.
2. Winston Churchill, 1935.
3. Edward Grey, 1925.
4. Chris Jones, 2003.
5. Andrew Walker, 2003.
6. Ibid.
7. See http://www.spartacus.schoolnet.co.uk/
8. See http://www.spartacus.schoolnet.co.uk/
9. Martin Allen, 2003.

Chapter 11. Perfidious Albion

1. Adolf Hitler, 1925.
2. Ibid.
3. Ibid.
4. Ibid.
5. Ibid.
6. Ibid.
7. Ibid.
8. David Irving, 1977.
9. Adolf Hitler, 1925.

Chapter 12. The Playing Fields of Eton

1. Martin Allen, 2003.
2. Ibid.
3. Ibid.
4. Ibid.
5. Ibid.
6. Ibid.
7. Ibid.
8. Ibid.
9. Ibid.
10. Ibid.
11. David Irving, 1977.
12. Martin Allen, 2003.
13. Alan Wykes, 1972.
14. See http://www.historylearningsite.co.uk/hitler_youth.htm
15. Adolf Hitler, 1935.

16. Baden Powell, 1941 edn.
17. See http://www.spartacus.schoolnet.co.uk/GERschacht.htm
18. Michael Bloch, 2003.
19. Peter Conradi, 2004.

Chapter 13. Mass Observations

1. See http://www.gallup.com/content/default.aspx?ci=1357
2. http://www.lse.ac.uk/resources/LSEHistory/bowley.htm
3. Robert Cecil, 1935.
4. See http://www.gallup.com/content/default.aspx?ci=1357
5. Tom Harrison and Charles Madge, 1982.
6. Ibid.
7. Ibid.
8. Ibid.
9. Ibid.
10. Ibid.

Chapter 14. Finest Hour

1. Clive Ponting, 1999.
2. David Irving, 1977.
3. Clive Ponting, 1999.
4. Martin Allen, 2003.
5. Clive Ponting, 1996.
6. Ibid.
7. Ibid.
8. Henry 'Chips' Channon, 1996.
9. Clive Ponting, 1999.
10. Winston Churchill, 1949.
11. Clive Ponting, 1999.
12. Ibid.
13. Ibid.
14. Ibid.
15. David Irving, 1977.
16. Martin Allen, 2003.

Chapter 15. The British Way

1. Tom Harrison and Charles Madge, 1982.

2. See http://www.oxford-union.org/
mod.php?mod=userpage&menu=11&page_id=4
3. *The British Way and Purpose*, 1943 edn.
4. See http://www.cecc.gov/pages/roundtables/121004/Feickert.php
5. *The British Way and Purpose*, 1943 edn.
6. Ibid.
7. Ibid.
8. Ibid.
9. John Seeley, 1887.
10. *The British Way and Purpose*, 1943 edn.
11. John Bright, House of Commons, 31 March 1854.

Chapter 16. Black Games

1. *The Man Who Shot Liberty Valance* (1962 film).
2. C.P. Scott, 1921, 'A Hundred Years', essay in the *Manchester Guardian*.
3. Sefton Delmer, 1961.
4. Ibid.
5. Ibid.
6. Sefton Delmer, 1962.
7. Ibid.
8. Ibid.

Chapter 17. The Pied Piper

1. Larry Tye, 1996.
2. Joseph Goebbels, 1934A.
3. Joseph Goebbels, 1944.
4. Ibid.
5. Joseph Goebbels, 1934.
6. G. Stark, 1935.
7. Joseph Goebbels, 1939.
8. Ibid.
9. Joseph Goebbels, 1928.

Chapter 18. Business as Usual

1. Personal communication.
2. Siemens website: http://web.ukonline.co.uk/freshwater/histsibr.htm
3. Oregon state archive website: http://arcweb.sos.state.or.us/exhibits/
war/ww1/american.html

4. Charles Higham, 1983.

5. Ibid.

6. Ibid.

7. Ibid.

8. Ibid.

9. Ibid.

10. Ibid.

11. Ibid.

12. Ibid.

13. Ibid.

14. See http://www.globalethics.org/newsline/members/ issue.tmpl?articleid=07080214010778

15. Ibid.

Chapter 19. Class Distinction

1. Clive Ponting, 1990.

2. Randolph Churchill, 1967.

3. John Lukacs, 2002.

4. Winston Churchill, 1942 edn.

5. Andrew Roberts, 2004.

6. Ibid.

7. Ibid.

8. Ibid.

9. Ibid.

Chapter 20. Judgement at Nuremberg

1. *The British Way and Purpose,* 1943 edn.

2. Yale Law School website: http://www.yale.edu/lawweb/avalon/imt/imt.htm

3. Ibid.

4. Ibid.

5. Ibid.

Chapter 21. Natural Selection

1. Friedrich Nietzsche, 1961 edn.

2. Bertrand Russell, 2000 edn.

3. Alan Taylor, 1996.

4. Ibid.

5. John Carey, 1992.

6. David Irving, 1977.
7. Ibid.
8. George Orwell, 1986 edn.
9. Ibid.
10. Ibid.

Chapter 22. Lucky Winners

1. H.G. Wells, 1946.
2. Oswald Mosley, 1968.
3. *The British Way and Purpose*, 1943 edn.
4. Stanley Milgram, 1963.
5. Stanley Milgram, 1974.

Chapter 23. This Happy Breed

1. Adolf Hitler, 1925.
2. Ibid.
3. Noël Coward, 1943.
4. Ibid.
5. Amritsar website: http://www.amritsar.com/Jallian%20Wala%20Bagh.shtml

Bibliography

Adelman, Larry, 'Race and Gene Studies: What Difference Makes a Difference?'. Online article: http://www.newsreel.org/guides/race/whatdiff.htm

Allen, Martin, 2003, *The Hitler/Hess Deception: British Intelligence's Best-Kept Secret of the Second World War*, HarperCollins, London

Allen, R.C., 1998, 'Agricultural Output and Productivity in Europe, 1300–1800', UBC Economics Department discussion paper, 98–14. Available online at: www.econ.ubc.ca/dp9814.pdf

Assmuth, J., 1918, *Haeckel's Frauds and Forgeries*, London

Baden-Powell, Robert, 1941 edn, *Scouting for Boys*, C. Arthur Pearson, London

Barnes, E.W., Bishop of Birmingham, 1933, 'Men do not Gather Grapes of Thorns', address in Liverpool Cathedral. Quoted at: http://www.eugenics-watch.com/briteugen/eug_babh.html

Barnes, E.W., 1949, quoted in *The Times*. Quoted at: http://www.eugenics-watch.com/briteugen/eug_babh.html

Beaverbrook, Lord, 1956, *Men and Power 1917–1918*, Hutchinson, London

Bernays, Edward, 1923, *Crystallizing Public Opinion*, Boni & Liveright, New York

Bernays, Edward, 1928, *Propaganda*, Horace Liveright, New York

Bernays, Edward, 1955, *The Engineering of Consent*, University of Oklahoma Press

Bernays, Edward, 1965, *Biography of an Idea*, Simon and Schuster, New York

Berry, Richard, 1930, 'The Mental Defective: a Problem in Social Inefficiency', in *Eugenics Review*, Vol. 22, p. 155. See: http://www.eugenics-watch.com/briteugen/eug_babh.html

Beveridge, William, 1906, *The Problem of the Unemployed.* Available online at: http://www.eugenics-watch.com/ briteugen/eug_babh.html

Beveridge, William, 1942, 'Eugenic Aspects of Children's Allowances', Galton Lecture in 1942–43, *Eugenics Review,* Vol. 34, p. 117. See http://www.eugenics-watch.com/briteugen/eug_babh.html

Bloch, Michael, 2003, *Ribbentrop,* Abacus, London

Boulton, James T., 1979, *The Letters of D.H. Lawrence, Vol. 1, 1901–1913,* Cambridge University Press

Bourne, Randolph, 1917, *The War and the Intellectuals,* article in *Seven Arts* magazine

Bryce, James, 1915, *Report on Alleged German Outrages in Belgium,* 12 May 1915. Available online at: http://www.firstworldwar.com/source/brycereport.htm

Bytwerk, Randall L., 2004, *Bending Spines: The Propagandas of Nazi Germany and the German Democratic Republic,* Michigan State University Press

Campbell, Phyllis, 1915, *Back to the Front,* quoted in *Women's Writing on the First World War,* 2002, edited by Agnès Cardinal, Dorothy Goldman and Judith Hattaway, Oxford University Press

Carey, John, 1992, *The Intellectuals and the Masses: Pride and Prejudice Among the Literary Intelligentsia, 1800–1939,* Faber and Faber, London

[Cecil, Robert], 1935, National Declaration Committee (Great Britain), Adelaide Lord Stickney Dame Livingstone, Marjorie Scott Johnston, Walter Ashley, and Robert Gascoyne-Cecil Cecil of Chelwood, Viscount, *The Peace Ballot: The Official History,* Victor Gollancz, London.

Chamberlain, Houston Stewart, 1899, *Die Grundlagen des neunzehnten Jahrhunderts* (The Foundations of the 19th Century). Text in English available online at: http://www.hschamberlain.net/grundlagen/division0_index.html

Channon, Henry 'Chips', 1996, *Chips: Diaries of Henry Channon,* Orion, London

Chesterton, G.K., 1917, *Utopia of Usurers and other essays*, Boni & Liveright, New York. Available online at: http://www.nalanda.nitc.ac.in/resources/english/ etext-project/chesterton/uusry10/chapter8.html

Churchill, Randolph, 1967, *Winston S. Churchill:Volume II: 1901–1914:Young Statesman*, Heinemann, London

Churchill, W.S., 1935, 'Hitler and His Choice', in *The Strand Magazine*, November 1935

Churchill, W.S., 1942 edn, *Great Contemporaries*, Macmillan, London

Churchill, W.S., 1949–50, *History of the Second World War*, Cassell, London

Cole, Margaret, 1949, *Growing Up into Revolution*, Longmans Green, London

Collins, Esmond, *Did World War One and British Government Propaganda Affect the Culture of Publishing During the War?* Online article: http://www.greatwar.nl/students/papers/ collins/propaganda.html

Conan Doyle, Arthur, 1902, *The Great Boer War*. Available online at http://www.classic-literature.co.uk/scottish-authors/ arthur-conan-doyle/the-great-boer-war/ebook-page-02.asp

Conradi, Peter, 2004, *Hitler's Piano Player:The Rise and Fall of Ernst Hanfstaengl, Confidant of Hitler, Ally of FDR*, Carroll & Graf, New York

Coward, Noël, 1943, *This Happy Breed*, William Heinemann, London

Creasy, Sir Edward, 1861, *Fifteen Decisive Battles of the Western World*, Richard Bentley, London

Creel, George, 1920, *How We Advertised America*, Harper, New York

Creel, George, 1922, 'The Battle in the Air Lanes', article in *Popular Radio*, September 1922, pp. 3–10.

Creel, George, 1944, *War Criminals and Punishment*, Robert M. McBride, New York

Creel, George, 1947, *Rebel at Large*, G.P. Putnam's, New York

Creel, George, 1920, *The War, the World and Wilson*, Harper & Brothers, New York

Darwin, Charles, 1901 edn, *The Descent of Man*, John Murray, London

Darwin, Charles, 1902 edn, *On the Origin of Species*, John Murray, London

Darwin, Leonard, 1925, 'Race Deterioration and Practical Politics', *Eugenics Review*, 1925–26. See http://www.eugenics-watch.com/briteugen/eug_d.html

de Gobineau, Arthur, 1853–55, *An Essay on the Inequality of the Human Races*, Heinemann, London

Deighton, Len, 1977, *Fighter: the True Story of the Battle of Britain*, Jonathan Cape, London

Delmer, Sefton, 1961, *Trail Sinister*, Martin Secker & Warburg, London

Delmer, Sefton, 1962, *Black Boomerang: The story of his secret 'Black Radio' operation in World War 2 – and how it has boomeranged today*, Secker & Warburg, London

Drake, M.J., I.W. Mills and D. Cranston, 1999, 'On the Chequered History of Vasectomy', *British Journal of Urology*, London

Epstein, Jonathan A, 2000, 'German and English Propaganda in World War I', a paper given to New York Military Affairs Symposium on 1 December 2000 at the Columbia University New York Graduate Center. Online at: http://libraryautomation.com/nymas/propagandapaper.html

Eugenics Watch website – records of members of the British Eugenics Society – at: http://www.eugenics-watch.com/briteugen/index.html

Ferguson, Niall, 2004, *Empire; How Britain Made the Modern World*, Penguin, London

Field, Geoffrey G., 1981, *Evangelist of Race: The Germanic Vision of Houston Stewart Chamberlain*, Columbia University Press, New York

Fisher, Ronald, 1930, *The Genetical Theory of Natural Selection*, Oxford University Press

Flaubert, Gustave, 1981, *Correspondance*, Flammarion, Paris, quoted by John Carey in *The Intellectuals and the Masses*, 1992, Faber and Faber, London

Fleming, Thomas, 2003, *The Illusion of Victory: America in World War I*, Basic Books, New York

Galton, Francis, 1889, *Natural Inheritance*, Macmillan, London

Galton, Francis, 1905, 'Eugenics, its Scope, Definition and Aims', paper read at the inaugural meeting of the Sociology Society, London School of Economics, 1903. Available online at: http://www.mugu.com/browse/galton/search/essays/pages/galton-1905-socpapers-eugenics-definition-scope-aims_9.htm

Gibbs, Philip, 1923, *Adventures in Journalism*, Heinemann, London

Goebbels, Joseph, 1934, *Erkenntnis und Propaganda, Signale der neuen Zeit. 25 ausgewählte Reden von Dr Joseph Goebbels*, pp. 28–52, Zentralverlag der NSDAP, Munich, translated by Randall Bytwerk. See http://www.calvin.edu/academic/cas/gpa/goeb54.htm

Goebbels, Joseph, 1934A, *Der Kongress zur Nürnberg*, Zentralverlag der NSDAP, pp. 130–41, Frz. Eher Nachf., Munich, translated by Randall Bytwerk. See: http://www.calvin.edu/academic/cas/gpa/index.htm

Goebbels, Joseph, 1938, *Der Rundfunk als achte Großmacht, Signale der neuen Zeit. 25 ausgewählte Reden von Dr Joseph Goebbels*, pp. 197–207, Zentralverlag der NSDAP, Munich, translated by Randall Bytwerk. See: http://www.calvin.edu/academic/cas/gpa/index.htm

Goebbels, Joseph, 1939, *Die abgehackten Kinderhände, Die Zeit ohne Beispiel*, pp. 181–87, Zentralverlag der NSDAP, Munich 1941, translated by Randall Bytwerk. See: http://www.calvin.edu/academic/cas/gpa/goeb27.htm

Goebbels, Joseph, 1944, *Nun, Volk steh auf, und Sturm brich los! Rede im Berliner Sportpalast, Der steile Aufstieg*, pp. 167–204, Zentralverlag der NSDAP, Munich, translated by Randall Bytwerk. See: http://www.calvin.edu/academic/cas/gpa/goeb36.htm

Gooch G. P., and Temperley, Harold, eds, 1926, *British Documents on the Origins of the War, 1898–1914. Vol. XI: The*

Outbreak of War: Foreign Office Documents June 28th–August 4th, 1914, His Majesty's Stationery Office, London

Gooch G.P., and Temperley, Harold, eds, 1927, *Letter No 338 from Sir F. Lascelles to the Marquess of Salisbury regarding Anglo-German Relations*, pp. 102–04, His Majesty's Stationery Office, London

Graf, Jakob, 1936, *Heredity and Racial Biology for Students*, London

Graves, Robert, 1961, *Goodbye to All That*, Penguin, London

Haeckel, Ernst, 1866, *The General Morphology of Organisms*, London

Haeckel, Ernst, 1876, *The History of Creation*, London

Haeckel, Ernst, 1889, *The Last Link*, London

Harrison, Tom and Madge, Charles, 1986, *Britain by Mass-Observation*, Cresset Library reprint, Century Hutchinson, London

Hicks, Joe and Allen, Grahame, 1999, *A Century of Change: Trends in UK Statistics Since 1900*, House of Commons Library, London

Higham, Charles, 1983, *Trading With The Enemy: An Exposé of the Nazi-American Money Plot 1933–1949*, Delacorte Press, New York

Hitler, Adolf, 1925, *Mein Kampf*. Text available online at: http://www.hitler.org/writings/Mein_Kampf/

Hitler, Adolf, 1935, speech at the Reichsparteitag, translated by Randall Bytwerk. See: http://www.calvin.edu/academic/cas/gpa/index.htm

Huxley, Thomas, 1910, *Lectures and Lay Sermons*, London, J.M. Dent

Huxley, Julian, 1966, *Essays of a Humanist*, Penguin, London

Huxley, Julian, 1935 (as presenter), *Enough to Eat?*, documentary film made by Gas Board

Irving, David, 1977, *Hitler's War*, Hodder & Stoughton, London

Jones, Chris, BBC News 2003, profile of Wallis Simpson. Online at: http://news.bbc.co.uk/1/hi/uk/2699035.stm

Lawrence, D.H., 1971 edn, *Kangaroo*, Penguin, London

Lawrence, D.H. 1971(A) edn, *Fantasia of the Unconscious and Psychoanalysis and the Unconscious*, Penguin, London

Lloyd George, David, 1936, article in the *Daily Express*, 17 September 1936

Ludendorff, Erich von, 1919, *My War Memories 1914–1918*, Hutchinson, London

Lukacs, John, 2002, *Churchill:Visionary. Statesman. Historian*, Yale University Press

Milgram, Stanley, 1963, 'Behavioral Study of Obedience', in *Journal of Abnormal and Social Psychology*, Vol. 67, pp. 371–78

Milgram, Stanley, 1974, *Obedience to Authority*, Harper & Row, New York

Milton, Richard, 1996, *Alternative Science*, Park Street Press, Vermont

Milton, Richard, 1997, *Shattering the Myths of Darwinism*, Park Street Press, Vermont

Milton, Richard, 2001, *Bad Company: Behind the Corporate Mask*, House of Stratus, London

Mosley, Oswald, 1968 edn, *My Life*, Thomas Nelson, London

Munsterberg, Dr, 1914, article in *Norddeutsche Allgemeine Zeitung*, 24 November 1914

Nietzsche, Friedrich, 1973, *Twilight of the Idols/The Anti-Christ*, Penguin, London

Nietzsche, Friedrich, 1967 edn, *The Will to Power*, Vintage, New York

Nietzsche, Friedrich (trans. R.J. Hollingdale), 1961 edn, *Thus Spake Zarathustra: A Book for Everyone and No One*, Penguin, London

Orwell, George, 1986 edn, *Animal Farm*, Penguin, London

Pakenham, Thomas, 1982, *The Boer War*, MacDonald, London

Papayoanou, Paul A., 1996, 'Interdependence, Institutions, and the Balance of Power: Britain, Germany, and World War I', *International Security*, Vol. 20, no. 4, Spring 1996

Paxman, Jeremy, 1999, *The English: A Portrait of a People*, Penguin, London

Ponsonby, Arthur, 1928, *Falsehood in War-time*, George Allen & Unwin, London

Ponting, Clive, 1990, *1940: Myth and Reality*, Hamish Hamilton, London

Pound, Ezra, 1986, *The Cantos*, Faber and Faber, London

Priestley, J.B., 1955, *Journey down a Rainbow*, Heinemann-Cresset, London

Regan, Geoffrey, 2000, *Great Military Blunders*, Channel 4 Television, London

Roberts, Andrew, 2004, *Hitler and Churchill; Secrets of Leadership*, Phoenix, Weidenfeld & Nicolson, London

Russell, Bertrand, 2000 edn, *History of Western Philosophy*, Routledge, London

Sanderson, Edgar, 1910, *King Edward VII, His Life and Work*, Gresham Publishing, London

Sanders, M.L., and Taylor, Philip M, 1982, *British Propaganda During the First World War, 1914–1918*, Palgrave Macmillan, London

Seeley, J.R., 1887, *The Expansion of England: Two Courses of Lectures*, Macmillan, London

Shaw, George Bernard, 1883, *The Perfect Wagnerite: A Commentary on the Niblung's Ring*. Online at: http://www.marxists.org/reference/archive/shaw/works/wagner.htm

Shaw, George Bernard, 1986 edn, Preface to *On the Rocks*, Penguin, London

Simkin, John, Spartacus website at: http://www.spartacus.schoolnet.co.uk/

Stark, G., 1930, *Moderne politische Propaganda*, Verlag Frz. Eher Nachf., Munich, translated by Randall Bytwerk. See http://www.calvin.edu/academic/cas/gpa/index.htm

Stead W.T., 1885, 'The Maiden Tribute of Modern Babylon', in *Pall Mall Gazette*, 4 July 1885

Taswell-Langmead, T.P., 1919, *English Constitutional History: From the Teutonic Conquest to the Present Time*, Stevens and Haynes, London

Taylor, Alan, 1996, 'Nietzsche the Nazi?', The University of
  Texas at Arlington:
  http://www.uta.edu/english/apt/fritz/anietzschenazi.html
Taylor, A.J.P., 1985 edn, *The First World War, an Illustrated
  History*, Penguin, London
Tobias, Fritz, 1959, *Der Reichstagsbrand 1933*, Der Spiegel,
  Hamburg
Tuchman, Barbara, 1981, *The Zimmerman Telegram*, Papermac,
  Macmillan, London
Tye, Larry, 1998, *The Father of Spin*, Henry Holt, New York
Unwin, Stanley, 1960, *The Truth about a Publisher*, Allen &
  Unwin, London
Walker, Andrew, BBC News 2003, profile of Edward VIII.
  Online at: http://news.bbc.co.uk/1/hi/uk/2701965.stm
Webster, Charles (NHS historian), 'Eugenic Sterilisation:
  Europe's Shame', in *Healthmatters*, Issue 31, Autumn 1997.
  Available online at:
  http://www.healthmatters.org.uk/issue31/eugenicshame
Wells, H.G., 1967 edn, *Kipps: the Story of a Simple Soul*, Collins,
  London
Wells, H.G., 1901, *Anticipations of the Reaction of Mechanical
  and Scientific Progress Upon Human Life and Thought*,
  Chapman and Hall, London
Wells, H.G., 1905, comments made at Sociology Society
  meeting on Francis Galton's paper 'Eugenics, its scope,
  definition and aims'. Available online at: http://www.mugu.com/
  browse/galton/search/essays/pages/galton-1905-socpapers-
  eugenics-definition-scope-aims_9.htm
Wells, H.G., 1914, *The War That Will End War*, Frank & Cecil
  Palmer, London
Wells, H.G., 1928, *The Open Conspiracy: Blue Prints for a World
  Revolution*, Victor Gollancz, London
Wykes, Alan, 1972, *Himmler*, Pan/Ballantine, London
Yates, B.C., Superintendent, Kennesaw Mountain National
  Battlefield Park, 1940, 'The Role of Artillery in the Atlanta
  Campaign', *The Regional Review*
Yeats, W.B., 1938, *On the Boiler*, Cuala Press, Dublin

Other Sources

Great Britain and the European Crisis, Correspondence and Statements in Parliament, 1914, His Majesty's Stationery Office, London

The British Way and Purpose, 1944, consolidated edition of *BWP* booklets 1–18, prepared by The Directorate of Army Education

Amritsar massacre website: http://www.amritsar.com/Jallian%20Wala%20Bagh.shtml

Oregon State Archives, available online at: http://arcweb.sos.state.or.us/exhibits/war/ww1/american.html

For reporting on German atrocities, see: http://www.spartacus.schoolnet.co.uk/FWWatrocities.htm

For history of Berlin, see Brian Daugherty's website at: http://bdaugherty.tripod.com/

Boer War: http://www.anglo-boer.co.za/concentration.html

British National Archives, Propaganda 1914–1918, see under heading 'Signals Intelligence' at: http://www.catalogue.nationalarchives.gov.uk/RdLeaflet.asp?sLeafletID=32

Article in *The Times* on German atrocities, 27 August 1914

German population statistics: http://geogate.geographie.uni-marburg.de/vgt/english/brd/module/m1/u5.htm

History of Siemens Brothers: http://web.ukonline.co.uk/freshwater/histsibr.htm

The Nuremberg trials, Yale Law School website: http://www.yale.edu/lawweb/avalon/imt/imt.htm

Special Acknowledgements

The many sources consulted in the preparation of this book are listed in the Bibliography. However, I particularly wish to acknowledge a number of books, articles and websites that have been especially important to me in understanding the exceptionally complex period of the two world wars and in peeling away the layers of myth that have accumulated around them.

Professor John Carey's book *The Intellectuals and the Masses*, first published in 1992, was a revelation in several ways. First, Carey explains through detailed historical analysis the impact that industrialisation and rapid population growth had on modern nations in terms of the creation of mass culture. Second, he illustrates the way in which many individuals among the privileged classes of those nations resented what they regarded as 'the masses' who had dispossessed them of their privileged positions and lifestyle. And third, he shows how this resentment manifested itself in the writing and thinking of many of the 20th century's most celebrated writers as fascist ideas, indistinguishable from those of the Nazis.

In December 1999, Jonathan Epstein presented a paper to the New York Military Affairs Symposium at Columbia University, entitled 'German and English Propaganda in World War I'. His paper is the most detailed account I have found of British and German propaganda aimed at Americans during the First World War which, as he notes in his introduction, has been labelled 'the first press agents' war'. Drawing on many declassified American sources, Epstein's paper provides a fascinating insight into what it

349

was like to be on the receiving end of British and German propaganda.

Clive Ponting's 1990 book *1940: Myth and Reality* is a daring deconstruction of one of Britain's most cherished national myths. While paying tribute to the courage of those who faced up to the Nazis in 1940, Ponting brings forward a mass of detail to show that Britain's finest hour also called for significant amounts of spin by the government of the day.

Martin Allen's *The Hitler/Hess Deception: British Intelligence's Best-Kept Secret of the Second World War* is of great interest to students of the Second World War because Allen brings forward persuasive evidence to show that Rudolf Hess's flight to Scotland may have resulted from a deception plan by British intelligence. However, Allen's book is also fascinating because, among other things, it provides strong evidence of the extent to which top Nazis, including Hitler himself and his closest associates, were Anglophiles whose overriding wish was to conclude a strategic alliance with Britain.

Index

Aden 319
AEG (Allgemeine Elektricitäts-
    Gesellschaft) 12
Afghanistan 104, 319, 326
Africa 94–5, 127, 137–9, 143–4, 193,
    218, 235
  North 192, 202
  South 51, 180–2, 320
Albert, Prince 11, 14, 18, 20
Allen, Martin 172–3, 211
Allies, the 34, 44, 47–8, 59, 71, 185,
    245, 262–3, 272, 282, 289–90,
    293
Altmark 288
America, *see* United States of
    America
American Civil War 54
Amor, Marjorie 154
Amritsar 319–20
  see also Punjab, Jallianwallah
    Bagh
Anarchists 149
Anderssen, Adolph 15
Angles, Saxons and Jutes 105
Anglo-German
  alliance 168, 170, 222
  entente 179
  Fellowship 154–5
  non-aggression treaty 210
  peace accord 181
  relations 4, 8, 19–21, 40, 67–8, 75,
    147, 159, 166, 181
  Review 156
Anglophilia 17, 21, 166, 169–71, 174,
    180–5, 188–91
Anglo-Saxon(s) 19, 102, 106, 151,
    243
  see also Angles, Saxons and Jutes
anti-Semitism 107, 109, 151, 156,
    159, 185, 203, 297, 305
Antwerp 65
appeasement 157, 189–90, 203, 239,
    305
Armstrong, Robert 67
Arthur, Dr Leonard 122

Aryans 6, 93, 102–10, 136, 151, 155,
    158, 178, 182, 194
  see also master race, Teutonic,
    Übermensch
Asquith, Herbert 23–5, 38, 273
Astor, Lord 157
Auschwitz 283, 293, 304
  see also death camps
Australia 6, 94–6, 113, 131–3, 182
Austria 14, 17, 39, 48, 137, 148, 150,
    264, 272, 298
Avestan 103
  see also Indo-European, Sanskrit,
    Vedas
Axis, the 263, 307

Baden-Powell, General Robert 145,
    182–3
Bahamas 153
Baldwin, Stanley 153, 178, 190, 198,
    323
Balfour, Arthur 62–3, 123, 273
Balkan Crises (1912–13) 21
Bank for International Settlements
    259, 263–5
Bank of England 263
Bank of France 263
Barnes, E.W. 123
Barrington-Ward, Robert 157
Bavaria 11, 156, 173–5
Bayreuth 107, 110–11
BBC 243, 273, 278
Beatty-Kingston, William 21
Beaverbrook, Lord 39, 212
Bedford, Duke of 157
Beer Hall Putsch (1923) 187
Beethoven, Ludwig van 13, 113
Belgians
  atrocities against 65
  neutrality 44, 48–53
  refugees 57–61
Belloc, Hilaire 30
Bennett, Arnold 7, 27, 30
Benz, Karl 12
Berghof 156, 166, 212, 274

351

Berlin 18–21, 24, 30, 33, 42–3, 58,
    62, 68, 74, 97, 138, 140, 152,
    166, 171, 178–9, 182, 188,
    191, 202, 209, 217, 221–2,
    240–2, 248, 251, 254, 257,
    261, 265, 275
  capital of Europe 138
  Chancellery 274
  cricket club 16
  golf club 16
Berliner, Emil 12
Bernays, Edward 7–8, 75–89, 195,
    248–54, 291
Berry, Dr Richard 124
Bethmann-Hollweg, Theo von 21–3,
    49–50
Beveridge, William 124
Bismarck, Otto von 21, 110, 137, 272
Black and Tans 271
Blacker, Dr Carlos 129, 294
Blackshirts 155
  see also British Union of Fascists
Blair, Tony 237
Blitzkrieg 214
Boer War 51, 64, 142
Bohle, Ernst 171, 180–1
Bolsheviks 318
Bolshevism 149, 243, 303
Bon, Gustave le 87–8
Bone, Muirhead 37
Bormann, Martin 284
Bouhler, Phillipp 178
Bourne, Randolph 74
Bowley, A.L. 195–6
Boy Scout Movement 145
Brahms 13
British Empire 8, 12, 106, 127, 136–47,
    158, 162, 165, 177, 189, 193,
    211, 216–18, 221, 233–6, 269,
    302–08, 317–19, 325
British Intelligence 7, 46, 153, 212,
    242, 247
  see also MI5
British Legion 156
British Union of Fascists 154–55,
    203, 226
  see also Blackshirts
British War Propaganda Bureau 26,
    42, 47, 55, 68
British Way and Purpose (BWP) 227,
    230–6, 277, 280–1, 308, 316
British Way of Life 223–5, 228–9, 308

Broadway 74–6
Brooke, General Alan 276
Bryce Committee 55
Bryce, James 7
Bryce Report 56–7, 61–3, 66
Bryce, Viscount 30, 55
Buccleuch, Duke of 157
Buchan, John 7, 27–8, 31–3, 37–9, 56
Buchenwald 304
  see also concentration camps
    (German)
Bullitt, William 214
Butler, Rab 189, 214–17, 305–06
BWP, see British Way and Purpose

Calder, Angus 197
Cambridge Foreign Science Students'
    Committee 175
Cambridge 123, 149, 175, 186
Campbell, Alistair 252
Campbell, Phyllis 57
Canada 140, 182, 185, 274
Carey, John 115–17, 297
Carnegie, Lord 154
Caruso, Enrico 76–7
Catholic(s) 184
  Centre Party 23
  Society 57
  see also Roman Catholic Church
Cavell, Edith 38
Cecil, Robert 196
Central Powers 39, 45
Chamberlain, Houston Stewart 93,
    107–11, 298, 324
Chamberlain, Joseph 175, 273
Chamberlain, Neville 159, 175–8,
    189–90, 203, 210–18
Channon, Henry 'Chips' 215
Cheney, Dick 267
Chesterton, G.K. 7, 27, 30, 141
China 148, 175–7, 199
Church, Major Archibald 129
Churchill, John see Marlborough, first
    Duke of
Churchill, Lord Randolph 270
Churchill, Sir Winston 4, 169, 178,
    181, 189–90, 194, 209,
    212–13, 243, 246, 281
  Germany, peace with 190, 214–22
  Hitler, comparison with 270–1
  Hitler, opinion of 149–50, 272–6,
    282

Norwegian neutrality 288
Prime Minister 190, 213, 304
Citibank 266
Cobb, Irving 59
Cole, Margaret 58
Committee on Public Information
(CPI) 72–7, 83
communism 150–4, 176, 301
communists 116, 135, 156, 215,
240–1, 253, 271
Communist Party 240
British 203
concentration camps
British 51, 64, 307
German 153, 185, 278, 308
see also Buchenwald, Dachau
Congress, US 41, 72, 76–7, 255
Continental Times 24
Cook, Thomas 17
Coolidge, Calvin 8, 79, 88
Coupland, Sir Reginald 234
Coward, Noël 314–21
CPI, see Committee on Public
Information
Cranborne, Viscount 179
Creel, George 24–5, 72–3, 77
crimes against humanity 185, 284,
288
see also war crimes
Cripps, Stafford 252
Cruikshank, R.G. 201
Czechoslovakia 264
crisis (1938) 157, 200–01

Dachau 185
see also concentration camps
(German)
Dahlerus, Birger 182, 216
Daily Chronicle 29, 39
Daily Express 39, 212
Daily Mail 38, 51, 157
Daily Mirror 213, 300
Daily Telegraph 157
Daimler, Otto 12
Daladier 214
Dalton, Hugh 242–3
Dammers, General 156
Darlington, C.D. 129
Darwin, Charles 5, 19, 93–102, 111,
118–30, 324
see also Darwinism, evolution,
Origin of Species

Darwin, Major Leonard 121, 125
Darwinism 5–6, 96, 127, 130
see also Darwin, evolution, Origin
of Species
Dawson, Geoffrey 157
D-Day 245
death camps 293, 307
see also Auschwitz
Delius 15
Delmer, Sefton 241–6
Denmark 137, 217
Dent, J.M. 33
Department B5b 154
see also MI5
Department of Information 38
Der große Krieg im Bildern (The Great
War in Pictures) 24
Der Stürmer 185, 289
Diaghilev, Serge 75
Diesel, Rudolf 13
Dinant 48, 52–3
Doenitz, Admiral Karl 171, 188, 283
Domvile, Admiral Sir Barry 154, 158,
193
Donald, Robert 39
Doyle, Arthur Conan 7, 27, 30–3
Dresden 214, 223
bombing of 237
Dunkirk 214, 223
Dyer, General Reginald 319–20

Eden, Anthony 159, 178–82, 203,
210, 214, 252, 305
Edward VII 15, 17, 19–20, 169, 182
Edward VIII 152–3, 187, 305
abdication of 153, 198
as Prince of Wales 152
Egypt 142, 177, 203
Eichmann, Adolf 308–9
Elgar, Edward 15, 230
Eliot, T.S. 296
Emden 3
Empire Day 141–3
Erzberger, Matthias 23
Espionage Act (1917) 72
Eton 149, 171, 191–3, 302
eugenics 5–6, 19, 93, 101, 120–33,
158, 293, 297–8, 303
First International Congress
(1912) 123
Eugenics Society 121–32, 151, 293–4
euthanasia 294–5

Euthanasia Society 125, 294
evolution, theory of 5, 19, 94–102
    see also Darwin, Darwinism,
        Origin of Species

Far East 137–9, 143, 259
fascism 118, 148, 203, 226
FBI 153
Ferdinand, Archduke Franz 21
Field, Geoffrey 111
Finland 287
First World War 4, 8, 36, 45–7, 59,
    64, 67–8, 82–5, 109, 113–115,
    129, 136, 142, 148–50, 156,
    181, 184–8, 192, 212–13, 225,
    239, 244–6, 263, 319
Fisher, Sir Ronald 129–30
Flaubert, Gustave 116
Fleet Street 196–99
Fleming, Thomas 41–2
Focke-Wulf 265–6
Ford, Ford Madox 27
Ford, Henry 262
Ford, John 239
Foreign Office 23, 62, 141, 180–1,
    242
Foreign Services Office 23
Forster, E.M. 118
fox hunting 16–17
France 3, 14–17, 20, 34–7, 47–50,
    57, 61, 71–4, 105, 118, 137,
    153, 167, 263, 280–2, 305
    Belgian neutrality 48, 52–3
    fall of (1940) 214–23
    German invasion (1914) 47–54,
        65
    German war reparations 44–5
    Hitler's views on 168–9, 187, 222
    imperialism of 137
Franco-Prussian War 50, 137
Frank, Hans 289
Frank, Walter 111
Frankfurt 12
Franks 104
Frederick William IV 20
Freud, Sigmund 7, 75, 87
Freudian psychology 79, 87, 230
Frick, Wilhelm 289
Fritzsche, Hans 289
Froebel, Friedrich 13
Führer, see Hitler, Adolf

Gallipoli 30, 156
Gallup, Dr George 195–6
Galsworthy, John 27, 30
Galton, Francis 5, 93, 99–102, 111,
    121, 297, 324
Gandhi 319
Gedye, Eric 157
General Electric 79
General Strike 314
genocide, see Holocaust
George V 20, 152, 186
German Empire 109, 151
German Foreign Office 23
German High Command 51, 68,
    278, 283
German Information Bureau 6, 23,
    26, 68
Gestapo 188, 243, 264–6, 283–4
Gibbs, Philip 34–5
Gilbert and Sullivan 15
Gilmour, T.L. 39
Gobineau, Joseph Arthur de 105–08
Goebbels, Joseph 64, 82, 111, 155,
    179, 230, 282
    Hanfstaengl, relations with 187
    personal life 248, 258
    portrayal in British press 253
    propaganda pioneer 8, 82–8,
        242–58
    Reichstag fire 241–2
    truthfulness of 89, 253–7
Goering, Hermann 5, 138, 155, 171,
    179–82, 216, 241–3, 274,
    282–3, 289, 298
Goethe 113
Gollancz, Victor 157
Goschen, Sir Edward 21, 49
Goths 104
Government of National Unity 203
Graf, Jakob 104
Grand Fleet, British 3, 13, 42
Graves, Robert 59
Great Exhibition (1851) 14–15
Guernica 237

Haeckel, Ernst 5, 96–8, 121
Halifax, Lord 159, 178–9, 189–90,
    214–20, 306
Hamilton, Sir Ian 156–8
Handel, G.F. 13
Hanfstaengl, Dr Ernst 'Putzi' 171,
    187–8

Hardy, Thomas 7, 27
Harris, Sir Arthur 281
Harrison, Tom 197–201
Harrow 149, 193
Haushofer, Albrecht 172–4, 177–81
Haushofer, Karl 171–6
'Haw Haw, Lord', see Joyce, William
Hefferich, Emil 264
Henderson, Nevile 182
Hess, Rudolf 5, 111, 138, 153, 156, 167, 171–81, 194, 211–12, 282–3
Hesse, Grand Duke Ernst Ludwig of 18
Heydrich, Reinhard 171, 179, 188
Higham, Charles 262–5
Hill 60 36
Himmler, Heinrich 5, 93, 111, 138, 155, 158, 179, 182–3, 188, 264
Hintze, Paul von 136–8
Hitler, Adolf 5, 8, 82, 88–9, 147–51, 156, 167, 172, 176–9, 181, 188, 221, 258
    Anglophilia 8, 138, 145, 158, 163–71, 182–8, 191–4, 302, 313
    anti-Semitism 185
    Britain, peace with 220–2, 302–03
    British establishment's regard for 152–9, 187, 205, 213, 305
    British peace overtures to 189–90, 210–12, 217–19
    Churchill, dislike of 275–5
    death of 257, 281
    eugenics, views on 298–302
    Mein Kampf 111, 161–3, 176–7
    Messiah figure 110, 245
    Mitfords, meeting with 155
    Mosley, opinion of 155
    plot to kill 185
    policies 93, 145, 159, 167, 172, 179, 184–5, 219, 223, 323
    Reichstag fire, role in 240–2
Hitler, Alois 188
Hitler Jugend 183–4
Hoare, Sir Samuel 159, 189–90, 306
Hoare-Laval Pact 190
Hodson, Mrs Cora 130
Holland 24, 62, 223, 264
Holocaust 253, 293, 307, 309, 323
    deniers 283

Huxley, Sir Julian 125, 294
Huxley, Thomas 93–6, 100–02, 121, 125–7, 295–7, 324

IBM 262–3
Illustrierter Kriegs-Kurier (Illustrated War-Courier) 24
Imperial College London 36, 127
Imperial War Museum 36
India 63–4, 103–04, 143–4, 175–7, 192–3, 234–5, 319, 329–30
Indo-European 103–04
    see also Avestan, Sanskrit, Vedas
International Court of Justice 283
International Health Exhibition (1884) 100
International Peace Campaign 196
Iraq 237, 319, 326
Ireland 182, 193, 271, 320
Irving, David 167
Irving, Miles 319
Israel 308, 318
Italy 17, 44, 65, 118, 137, 148, 157, 167–8, 190, 210, 214, 217, 259, 263

Jallianwallah Bagh 319–20
    see also Amritsar, Punjab
Japan 148, 175–7, 221, 259
Jena University 96–7
Jennings, Blanche 117
Jennings, Humphrey 196–7
Jews 83–4, 103, 108–09, 111, 162, 176, 184–5, 243, 262, 278, 289, 305, 308
    see also anti-Semitism, Holocaust
Jodl, Alfred 171, 188, 283, 289, 306–07
John Bull 300
Journal of Abnormal and Social Psychology 309
Joyce, William ('Lord Haw Haw') 242
Jutes see Angles, Saxons and Jutes

Kaiser see Wilhelm II
Kaltenbrunner, Ernst 283, 289, 306–07
Keitel, Field Marshal Wilhelm 283, 288–9
Kellogg-Briand Pact (1928) 287
Kenya 217, 318

Kindergarten system 13
King, Cecil 213
Kipling, Rudyard 7, 27, 30, 144, 191, 230
Kitchener, General Lord 41, 51
Knight, Maxwell 106, 154
Kölnische Zeitung (Cologne Daily News) 65
Korea 175
Kriegs-Chronik (War Chronicle) 24

Labour Party 131–2, 203
    see also New Labour
Landon, Alfred 196
Landsberg Fortress 161, 176
Lascelles, Sir Frank 20
Laval, Pierre 190
Lawn Tennis 16
Lawrence, D.H. 6, 117–18, 296
Le Matin 65
League of Nations 45, 77
Lenin 301–02
Lindemann, Karl 264–5
Link, The 155
    see also Anglo-German Fellowship
Lloyd George, David 7, 25–6, 30, 38–9, 55, 212–13, 222, 271
Lokal Anzeiger (Local Journal) 62
London
    Blitz 281, 324
    East End 141, 145
    German embassy in 152, 186
    Ribbentrop in 186–7
    School of Economics 120
    slums 233
    suicide bombing of 326
Los Angeles Times 41
Louvain 48, 52–3
Lubbe, Marinus van de 240–2
Ludendorff, General Erich von 40, 110
Luftwaffe 222, 281, 324
Lusitania 38
Luther 113

Machiavelli, Niccolò 80
Mackinder, Halton 173–5, 324
Macmillan, Harold 28, 82, 305
Macready, General Nevil 271
Madge, Charles 196–201
Madison Avenue agency 7, 78, 81, 84
    see also Bernays, Edward

Mair, G.H. 29
Malaya 319
Mallet, Victor 221–2
Malthus 118
Manchester Guardian 34, 240
Mandelson, Peter 252
Marlborough, John Churchill, first Duke of 270
Marxism 116, 149, 226–8, 314, 317
Masefield, John 7, 27, 30
Mass-Observation 196–204, 225–8, 250
master race 8, 105–08, 135, 151, 158, 276, 325
    see also Aryan, Teutonic, Übermensch
Masterman, Charles 26–43, 55, 61–3, 73, 256
McKittrick, Thomas Harrington 259, 263
Medical Research Council 123
Mein Kampf, see Hitler, Adolf
Mendelssohn 13
MI5 154
    see also British Intelligence
Milgram, Stanley 308–11
Miller, Joan 154
Milosevic, Slobodan 283
Mitford, Deborah 155
Mitford, Diana 155
Mitford, Jessica 155
Mitford, Nancy 155
Mitford, Pamela 155
Mitford, Unity 155–8
Moltke, General von 49
Montague, C.E. 34
Montgomery, General 192
Montrose, Duke of 157
Moore, Jo 252
Mosley, Sir Oswald 154–8, 193, 203, 226, 305
Munck, Helen de 154
Munich 156, 171–6, 187, 215, 261
Münsterberg, Dr 52–3
Mussolini 189, 203, 210, 217, 298

Napoleon 53, 191, 302
Nash, Paul 37
National Health Service 124, 131, 294, 304
National Insurance Act 26, 271
National Socialism, *see* Nazism

National Socialist German Workers'
    Party see Nazi Party
National Socialist Party see Nazi
    Party
National Socialist Workers' Party see
    Nazi Party
Naval Intelligence, British 154
Naval Intelligence, US 153
Nazi Party 5, 109, 138, 147, 169,
    171–6, 180–3, 186–8, 221,
    254–5, 284, 297, 324
Nazism 6, 90, 113, 120, 152–3, 172,
    179, 187, 228, 236, 248, 262,
    275, 284, 289, 293, 297, 307,
    317, 325
Nevinson, Charles 37
New Labour 252
    see also Labour Party
New Statesman 196–7
New Zealand 182
Newbolt, Sir Henry 27
Nietzsche 116–20, 296–302
Nijinsky 75–7
Norddeutsche Allgemeine Zeitung 52
Nordic League 154
North Africa, see Africa, North
Northcliffe, Lord 34, 38–40, 51, 246
Norway 131, 217
    neutrality, violation of 288
NSDAP, see Nazi Party
Nuremberg
    rallies 89, 255
    war crimes trial 8, 185, 282–3,
        289–93, 303, 306–07

O'Dwyer, Sir Michael 319–20
Observer 157
Offenbach 13
Ohm Kruger (film) 64
Old Testament 108
Origin of Species 5, 95–6
    see also Darwin, Darwinism,
        evolution
Orpen, William 37
Orwell, George 197, 299, 301
Ostend 53
Owen, Arthur 230
Oxbridge 304
Oxford
    Union debate (1933) 226
    University 129, 149, 175, 234
    University Press 28

Pakistan 104, 319, 326
Pall Mall Gazette 29, 115
Papen, Franz von 289
Paris 24, 57, 65, 77, 214, 249
    Peace Conference 186
Pax Britannica 236
Pearl Harbor 264
Phipps, Sir Eric 179
Picasso 237
Poland
    crisis (1939) 210
    German invasion of 210, 284–8
    Russian invasion of 287
Political Intelligence Department,
    Foreign Office 242–3
Political Warfare Executive 212, 252
Ponsonby, Arthur 64, 67
Ponting, Clive 142, 209–20, 270
Pool, Ernest 76
Popular Radio 24
Portugal 148
Pound, Ezra 118
Priestley, J.B. 115
Procter & Gamble 79
propaganda
    Allied 45–7, 171, 253
    black 30–1, 40, 61, 64, 212,
        242–4, 247–8, 252
        see also Delmer, Sefton
    Bureau 26–7, 38, 42, 47, 55–6,
        61–2, 66–8, 290
        see also Masterman, Charles
    British 8, 25, 33, 39–43, 48, 66,
        230, 253, 256–7, 317, 325
    German/Nazi 3, 38, 42–3, 64,
        71–2, 78–9, 89, 162, 248, 255
    Goebbels' views on 257
    US 24, 71, 76–7
    wars, Anglo-German 3, 7–8, 34,
        38, 67, 81, 147, 261, 277, 282,
        290
Protestant(s) 109, 113, 184
Prussian(s) 14, 17, 20, 50, 107,
    136–7, 244
Public Relations 78
Punjab 319–20
    see also Amritsar, Jallianwallah Bagh

Raeder, Admiral Erich 283
Raemakers, Louis 56–7, 66
RAF 181, 190, 223
    Bomber Command 279, 281

Ramsay, Archibald 154–5, 158–9, 178
Rathenau, Emil 12
Red Army 257
Redesdale, Lord 154–9, 193
Reich Propaganda Office 255
Reichstag 23, 240–2
burning of 240–2
Report on the Alleged German Outrages 30, 55
Reuter, Julius 12
Reuters 25
Ribbentrop, Joachim von 138, 152, 171, 185–7, 216, 220, 289, 299, 306–07
Right Club, the 154
Roberts, Andrew 273
Roberts, Herbert 176
Roberts, Patrick 178
Robertson, John Mackinnon 120
Robespierre 301–02
Rockefeller family 264–5
Roman Catholic Church 108–09, 131–2
Rommel, Erwin 192, 274
Roosevelt, Franklin D. 196, 217
Rosenberg, Alfred 111, 289
Rothenstein, William 37
Rothermere, Lord 157–8
Rothschild, House of 12
Royal Geographic Society 125
Royal Navy 107, 288
Russell, Bertrand 296
Russia 24, 41, 48–9, 104, 137, 148, 154, 162, 168–9, 174–5, 179, 186, 216, 221–2, 227, 254, 273–4, 282, 287–8

Sanskrit, *see also* Avestan, Indo-European, Vedas 103–04
Sauckel, Fritz 289
Saxe-Coburg-Gotha, House of 20
Saxons, *see* Angles, Saxons and Jutes
Schacht, Hjalmar 171, 184–5, 263, 289
Schellenberg, Walter 265
Schlieffen, Count von 49, 54
Plan 54, 219
Schröder, Baron Kurt von 264–5
Schubert 13
Schumann 13
Scott, C.P. 240

Second World War 28, 54, 58, 181, 192, 211, 216, 222, 225, 239, 247, 253, 256, 259, 261–3, 270, 288, 306–07, 323, 324
Sedan 137, 219
Sedition Act (1918) 72
Seeley, Sir John 141, 234
Seyss-Inquart, Arthur 289
Shaw, George Bernard 6, 15, 109, 116–18, 121, 296
Shawcross, Sir Hartley 285–7, 291
Shrapnel, Henry 53
Siemens, William 12
electrical engineering company 260–1, 266
Simon, Sir John 178–9
Simpson, Mrs Wallis, *see* Windsor, Duchess of
socialism 109, 297
Sociological Society 120, 125
Somme, battle of 31, 38
South Africa, *see* Africa, South
South America 24, 177
Special Operations Executive (SOE) 212, 244
Speer, Albert 171, 188, 282–3
SS (Schutzstaffel) 179, 182–3, 186–8, 262, 283–4, 306–08, 320
Stalin 275, 298, 301–02
Stalingrad 254
Standard, the 29
Star, the 200–01
Staunton, Howard 15
Stead, W.T. 115
sterilisation 102, 124–32, 293–4
Stimpson, Henry L. 252
Stopes, Dr Marie 130
Strand Magazine 149
Streicher, Julius 185, 243, 289
Stuart, Ewen 84
Sudetenland 157
Suez 217, 319
suicide bombers 326
Sumner, Welles 217
Sweden 6, 104, 113, 131–3, 182, 221
Switzerland 17, 24, 185, 259, 262

Taswell-Langmead, T.P. 106
Tatler, The 166–7, 190, 302
Taylor, A.J.P. 49, 53, 297, 323–4
Telconia 3

Teutonic 19, 106–07, 151
Knights 42, 106, 162
see also Aryan, master race,
Übermensch
Third Reich 172, 245, 258, 262–4
Thule Society 173
Times, The 38, 51, 57, 62, 65, 124,
156–7, 267
Tirpitz, Admiral von 68
TitBits 300
Tobias, Fritz 242
'Tommy Atkins' 43, 234
Trevelyan, G.M. 27
Trotter, Wilfred 87–8
Truman, Harry S. 275
Tuchman, Barbara 136
Turkey 148, 169

Übermensch 119
see also Aryan, master race,
Teutonic
U-boats 69, 73
UNESCO 125
United States of America
special relationship with Britain 4
bombs German cities 281
enters the First World War 41, 71,
136
Eugenics Society of 131
intelligence service 152–3, 177
neutrality of 68–71
peacemaker (1940) 217, 220
press 3, 23, 27–8, 52–3, 184
propaganda target for Britain and
Germany 34, 41, 68, 71
public opinion 35, 41, 71–2
racism 131
Unwin, Stanley 33

Vabres, Henri Donnedieu de 307
Vandals 104
Vedas 104
see also Avestan, Indo-European,
Sanskrit
Verdun 173
Versailles, Peace Treaty of 44–6,
76–7, 89, 176, 179, 189, 217
Victoria Melita, Princess 18
Victoria, Queen 11, 15, 18–20
Vienna 14, 157, 261, 298
Vietnam War 35
Voigtlander, Johan 13–14

Wagner, Cosima 107
Wagner, Eva 107
Wagner, Richard 13, 107, 276
Wall Street Crash 81
Wall Street Journal 267
War Cabinet 123, 190, 217–22, 237,
252, 277, 280–1
war crimes 47, 64, 185, 284, 288, 295
see also crimes against humanity,
Nuremberg
War Office 35–7
Waterloo, battle of 53, 191, 302
Waugh, Evelyn 118
Webster, Charles 131–3
Wehrmacht 183, 214, 222, 262
Weigand, Karl von 83–4
Weimar Republic 301
Weintraub, Robert 12
Weissauer, Dr Ludwig 221
Welfare State 26, 124, 297
Wells, H.G. 7, 15, 27, 31, 116–18,
121, 127–8, 296, 304
Western Front 3, 11, 30–1, 34–6, 53,
59, 74, 81, 85, 177, 259, 273,
317
Whitehall 38, 68, 142, 154, 171, 178,
181, 188, 198–9, 202–05, 215,
227, 246, 278
Wilhelm I 137
Wilhelm II 15–20, 32, 42–5, 49, 66,
74, 108–09, 321
Wilhelmine Germany 144
Wilson, President Woodrow 45, 71–2,
76–7, 249, 254
Windsor, Duchess of 153, 305
Windsor, Duke of, *see* Edward VIII
Windsor, House of 20
Wodehouse, P.G. 155
Wolfe, General 140
Woolf, Virginia 118

Yeats, W.B. 118
Ypres 36, 173

Zeitler, General 299
Zend Avesta 102
Zentralstelle für Auslandsdienst
(Central Office for Foreign
Services) 23
Ziegfeld, Florenz 76
Zollverein (customs union of
German states) 15